# CHINA UNDER JIANG ZEMIN

# CHINA UNDER JIANG ZEMIN

EDITED BY
HUNG-MAO TIEN
YUN-HAN CHU

LYNNE
RIENNER
PUBLISHERS

BOULDER
LONDON

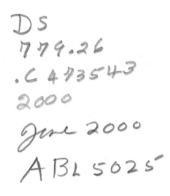

Published in the United States of America in 2000 by
Lynne Rienner Publishers, Inc.
1800 30th Street, Boulder, Colorado 80301
www.rienner.com

and in the United Kingdom by
Lynne Rienner Publishers, Inc.
3 Henrietta Street, Covent Garden, London WC2E 8LU

**Library of Congress Cataloging-in-Publication Data**
China under Jiang Zemin / edited by Hung-mao Tien and Yun-han Chu
   p. cm.
  Includes bibliographical references and index.
  ISBN 1-55587-844-X (hardcover: alk. paper). ISBN 1-55587-927-6 (pbk.: alk. paper).
  1. China—Politics and government—1976–   2. China—Economic policy—1976–
3. China—Social conditions—1976–   4. Chiang, Tze-min, 1926–   I. Tien, Hung-mao.
II. Chu, Yün-han.

DS779.26.C473543   2000
951.05'7—dc21                                99-051381

**British Cataloguing in Publication Data**
A Cataloguing in Publication record for this book
is available from the British Library.

Printed and bound in the United States of America

     The paper used in this publication meets the requirements
∞  of the American National Standard for Permanence of
     Paper for Printed Library Materials Z39.48-1984.

   5  4  3  2  1

# Contents

v

# 1

# China Under Jiang Zemin: An Introduction

## Hung-mao Tien and Yun-han Chu

The historic Fifteenth National Congress of the Chinese Communist Party (CCP), which took place in Beijing in September 1997, marked the end of the Deng Xiaoping reign and the dawn of the Jiang Zemin era. With power consolidated in the party-state, Jiang is positioned to put his own stamp on the reform agenda, which includes a continued push for painful restructuring of state-owned enterprises (SOEs) as well as the government bureaucracy, an emphasis on science and education, a strategy for sustainable economic development, the development of the rule of law, and the further enhancement (or consolidation) of China's international standing. Except for foreign policy, each of Jiang's goals subtly highlights an area that the current party leadership believes Deng neglected.

During the 1990s, China watchers in the West have consistently underestimated Jiang. To the surprise of outsiders, the seemingly unimpressive Jiang emerged as the winner, time and again, after each round of intraparty power struggles. He asserted his control over the People's Liberation Army (PLA) by removing Yang Shangkun and Yang Baibing from the Central Military Commission; he effectively crushed the corrupt and ambitious party bosses through the unusual purges of Chen Xitong and his protégés in their Beijing stronghold; he repacked the party center to his liking by forcing his potential rivals to retire from the Politburo Standing Committee; and he pulled the rug out from under the recalcitrant princeling by shutting down PLA-affiliated enterprises. After the Congress, he was poised to make further crackdowns on the powerful deviants in Guangdong province. The repeated failure of China watchers to predict his rise to the top of the power heap calls for a focused examination of his political skills, power base, ideological orientation, and reform agenda.

With Jiang as their "core," the CCP leaders of the postrevolutionary generation face daunting challenges. Broadly speaking, Jiang is burdened with the difficult task of bolstering the legitimacy of the one-party authoritarian regime against a global current of democratization and sustaining

1

China's economic growth in the midst of the current regional economic crisis. Much like a man repairing a ship in the middle of the ocean, Jiang has a very thin margin of error because he lacks the revolutionary credentials of his predecessors, deriving his power more from formal institutions than personal allegiance among the rank and file. Jiang and his colleagues are confronted with a complex and unprecedented mix of internal and external challenges.

They reign over a rapidly marketized economy without the necessary mechanisms for macroeconomic fine tuning and without effective regulatory and monitoring capacities. They face the glaring contradiction between growing socioeconomic disparity and lingering socialist ideology, with its formidable political implications. They have limited experience in dealing with the economy's vulnerability to external shocks now that the trend of plugging China into a highly integrated global economy seems to have become irreversible. They must anchor China's position in world politics, now that the crystal clarity of the Cold War era has been replaced by the apparent confusion of the so-called new world order. They have pursued the nationalistic ambitions of executing an unprecedented "one country, two systems" formula in Hong Kong and forcing a newly democratized and increasingly assertive Taiwan back into Beijing's one-China cage.

This book concerns the politics of power consolidation and the political economy of market-oriented reform in the Jiang Zemin era. *China Under Jiang Zemin* represents the first major academic effort to analyze the evolution of Jiang's leadership in China and takes as its starting reference point the pivotal Fifteenth National Congress of the CCP, the first convened under the "third generation" of postrevolutionary leaders. This volume comprises chapters written by several of the world's leading China experts. Together, they present a detailed portrait of the political landscape at the opening of the Jiang Zemin era.

In Chapter 2, Richard Baum sets the tone for the book. He focuses directly on Jiang's performance during and around the time of the Fifteenth Party Congress, dissecting Jiang's keynote speech to that body. Baum begins with a discussion of Jiang's most important policy statement, the program for SOE reform. Describing how Jiang devised an ideological justification for reform with the theory of the "primary stage of socialism," Baum states that the speech "served less to break new policy ground than to signal the end of a long and divisive intraparty debate" on the subject.

In the area of political reform, however, Baum finds less to report. Largely parroting existing slogans, the only political initiative in Jiang's speech was a call for a modest enlargement of the scope of local elections. In foreign policy, his only innovation was to endorse the concept of multilateralism. And in the final section of his speech, which dealt with the problem of corruption, Jiang's "stern rhetoric" did not necessarily indicate a significantly invigorated campaign. Baum follows with an analysis of the personnel shifts and appointments during the Congress and concludes that although Jiang has succeeded in consolidating his position at the top and has removed most of his putative rivals, he has not done so without cost to his power position in the form of limitations on his political independence. Finally, although recent years have seen a string of important triumphs for Jiang, from the funeral of Deng Xiaoping to the Congress and the summits with U.S. president Bill Clinton, he remains vulnerable in the event of significant economic dislocation or other disturbance.

In Chapter 3, "Sizing up China's New Leadership," Lowell Dittmer provides a systematic analysis of the personnel changes at the Fifteenth Party Congress. Working from the bottom up, he assesses the changes in the Congress itself, in the Central Committee, and in the Politburo and its Standing Committee. A process of extensive advance consultations, as well as internal elections, produced some notable changes. The Central Committee experienced an unusually high turnover rate: significant shifts include greater numbers of technocrats, provincial representatives, military representatives, and central government officials. In contrast, the Politburo experienced the lowest rate of turnover ever, with almost all the changes due to the newly created principle of mandatory retirement. Also noteworthy was Jiang's failure to pack the Politburo or its Standing Committee with his protégés, which may reflect the results of bargaining at the highest level. The average age in all three leadership organs is slightly higher than before, and most members will be at or near the retirement threshold by the time the next Congress convenes.

Dittmer analyzes Jiang's consolidation of his position since his appointment in 1989 and in particular the protracted tension with Qiao Shi. He concludes that the conventional wisdom regarding the "end of strongman leadership" and the emergence of "collective leadership" is at best only partially true. Although in a less brutal fashion than previously, Jiang clearly has triumphed over Qiao. In addition, his relative lack of stature and charisma compared to Mao Zedong and Deng is largely irrelevant to the current competition among members of the postrevolutionary generation. Furthermore, his lack of policy initiative should not be confused with a failure to consolidate power: Jiang has concentrated almost exclusively on the latter and has achieved his objective rather handily.

In his final section, Dittmer proposes a model for the succession process as experienced not only in Jiang's case but also for those of Hu Yaobang, Zhao Ziyang, and even earlier cases during the Mao era. In each case, the paramount leader, well before his death, appoints a successor who begins an "advanced internship in which the heir apparent is expected to prove his political mettle, while the incumbent observes from behind the scenes and offers advice and correctives." In addition to these two main players, there is also what Dittmer calls a "Greek chorus" consisting of the small group of senior leaders nearest the center of power. In this model, what Jiang has done is simply to complete the internship successfully where others have failed. This demonstrates not increased institutionalization, but rather Jiang's skills at maneuvering in and manipulating the situation, adjusting his stance as often as necessary. It also enables a prediction: when the "triumvirate" (to use David Bachman's term) of Jiang, Li Peng, and Zhu Rongji "retire" in 2002, they will not necessarily lose their influence but instead will designate their own "interns" and work behind the scenes to ensure their success.

In Chapter 4, "Emerging Patterns of Political Conflict in Post-Deng China," David Bachman continues this probe into China's elite politics. Starting from the premise that mass involvement in politics is possible only when the ruling elites are split, he assesses the possibility of such splits in the foreseeable future. Bachman concludes that the current triumvirate is highly likely to remain stable in the near term because Li and Zhu would rather work with Jiang than with each other, enabling Jiang to play them off each other to maintain his position and providing an incentive for all three to occupy mutually accommodating positions. Even more interesting is the opening salvo that Bachman fires in the inevitable scholarly debate over the succession to Jiang himself. When the current terms expire at the Sixteenth Party Congress in 2002, Jiang may well have to step down, along with Li and Zhu and the other members of the third generation. Bachman presents a short list of candidates for the succession and some of the critical factors affecting their chances.

In an even longer-term perspective, Bachman poses the question of the following successions, from the fourth to the fifth and sixth generations. Scarred and tainted by the experience of the Cultural Revolution, the fifth generation may be deemed unfit for high office; however, they may be more receptive to genuine mass politics. The sixth generation is the most modern, technocratic, and industrialized in Chinese history. Bachman asserts that although the succession to Jiang may not create radical change, the rise of these later cohorts cannot help but significantly change the political environment in China.

In the final chapter of Part 1, "The Problematic Quest for Stability," Frederick C. Teiwes analyzes succession, institutionalization, governability, and stability from a historical perspective, after cautioning that our understanding of Chinese elite politics is paradoxically even less clear in some ways than it was in previous periods. Teiwes examines what recent developments reveal about the future position of the CCP in China's polity and suggests that although the party's authority is not likely to face insurmountable challenges in the near term, the medium and long term are much less certain. In something of a counterpoint to Dittmer's analysis,

Teiwes describes the succession to Jiang as a rather smooth arrangement, even remarking on the surprising lack of anti-Jiang maneuvers among the upper elites. He asserts that the fact that arrangements have even begun for the future transition to the "fourth generation" under Hu Jintao represents a certain amount of institutionalization. This institutionalization has two major limitations. First, it is not yet clear exactly how policy is made: for example, Jiang's actual clout in decisionmaking is unknown. As Teiwes puts it, "the notions of 'core' and collective leadership push in different directions." The second limitation is that to the extent it has developed, institutionalization exists almost purely within the elite and not between the state and the society (witness the continued failure to curb corruption).

As for governability, Teiwes argues that the current Chinese state is technically more capable than ever and probably at least as much so as most developing states. Although there are several significant problems, for example, in extracting revenue and managing center-local relations, the regime is likely to be able to "muddle through," at least for the immediate future. The main danger might be the possibility of steadily declining leadership quality à la Brezhnev's Soviet Union, leading to an inability to cope with the more challenging stages of reform.

Despite this mixed outlook, there remains a serious question mark over the regime because of its lack of legitimacy. Teiwes traces the decline of legitimacy since the death of Mao and asserts that even with what he calls "substitute supports" such as nationalism and the popular desire for stability and economic growth, the regime may not be able to withstand a true crisis. He predicts two possible outcomes. First, an acute crisis may precipitate a serious leadership split or even complete regime disintegration, Soviet-style. Such a crisis currently seems unrealistic unless the economic situation worsens dramatically. Second, and more probably, he expects a gradual evolution of the CCP over a very lengthy period into something approaching a competitive party.

In Part 2, the contributors begin to expand the discourse beyond the inner workings of the party by discussing the role of the PLA. In Chapter 6, "The People's Liberation Army and Politics: After the Fifteenth Party Congress," Ellis Joffe describes the fundamental shift in party-army relations that has taken place in the transition to the Jiang Zemin era. Jiang simply does not enjoy the personal stature within the military that Mao and Deng had, which enabled them to impose their will upon the military and subordinate it firmly to the party. At the same time, Jiang needs the PLA more, not so much because of the unlikely event of a coup but because unequivocal military support is necessary to quell potential dissent from rivals within the elite. This crucial PLA support is only granted to Jiang conditionally, based on his satisfactory performance on issues dear to it. Jiang's assiduous use of his control over appointments and promotions and his generosity with the military budget, thus far have been successful in building a solid working relationship with the PLA leadership. The military's new influence gives it greater leverage over policymaking than it has had at any time previously, especially because its influence also extends equally to potential rivals to Jiang, all of whom suffer from the basic deficiencies of the postrevolutionary generation.

In purely military matters, the PLA is more autonomous and free of party controls. In addition, it has increased its influence over other areas, particularly foreign policy, where its self-image as guardian of China's national honor gives it a special role (as during the 1995–1996 Strait crisis). This influence, however, is constrained by the steadily increasing professionalism of the officer corps, due to modernization and the imperatives of preparing for limited but high-tech warfare, which diminishes the party's day-to-day role in military affairs, encourages obedience, and discourages political adventurism. In conclusion, Joffe sees the PLA of the future as being both "in and out" of politics, playing a key role in intraelite struggles but, at the same time, less likely to intervene on the ground in mass actions. It will use its power primarily to secure its own goals of force modernization and national security.

Next, Michael Swaine provides a clear statement of the background, current status, and future prospects for PLA-party relations and assesses its implications within the context of regional security and the domestic political environment. He builds his argument from a lucid analysis of the changes in China's strategic position since the economic opening in the 1980s and the resulting shifts in its threat perceptions and military doctrines. Swaine details the goals of the modernization program for each service of the PLA and the progress each has made during the 1990s. Next, he discusses the obstacles the program still faces, especially in terms of indigenous technology development and organizational deficiencies. Swaine makes projections of the capabilities this modernization will provide China over the coming years, given both current progress and the extant difficulties. He predicts that these new, expanded capabilities, especially in the key area of power projection, are likely to have significant effects on the region by simultaneously increasing the costs and risks of U.S. deployments in the western Pacific and by creating a decline in confidence among other regional states, leading either to arms races or to more pro-China policies. Taking the example of Taiwan, Swaine cautions that it is not China's absolute capabilities that are crucial, but its relative capacities.

Finally, Swaine analyzes the shifting role of the PLA in China's domestic politics. He finds that with modernization, the PLA is becoming more professional and therefore less likely to intervene directly in politics. At the same time, however, the issue of the PLA's commercial ventures is a serious one, with its attendant problems of corruption. Barring a protracted leadership struggle, the PLA's role is likely to consist of increasing influence (although by no means complete decisionmaking power) over policies with strong national security implications, such as those toward Taiwan.

In Chapter 8, "The Challenge of Economic Reform and Social Stability," Nicholas R. Lardy provides a trenchant analysis of the problems facing China in this crucial area. Based on the clear evidence of financial data, Lardy demonstrates that the economic difficulties facing the current government, particularly regarding SOEs and the banking system, are indeed dire. He assesses the results thus far and the prospects for the most important element of reform, the program for reorganizing SOEs first laid out at the Third Plenum of the Fourteenth Party Congress and reaffirmed by the full Fifteenth Party Congress with the strong endorsement of Jiang Zemin. The financial performance of the state-owned sector is truly alarming: at least half of all SOEs were insolvent at the end of 1994, and this figure has risen at a brisk pace since then. These enterprises have been kept afloat by ever-increasing bank loans, such that these firms are already much more highly leveraged even than Korean *chaebol*. The loans present a threat to the banking system as a whole, especially under the economic slowdown that has emerged since early 1998. This looming banking crisis may have already started: Lardy calculates that three of the largest state banks are themselves already insolvent.

The reform package, especially its emphasis on restructuring SOEs into other types of firms, certainly is needed, but Lardy points out several important shortcomings in its implementation so far. Since the inception of reform in 1993, very few SOEs have accomplished reorganization. Most of these have opted for either state ownership of shares or control by the current management, neither of which is likely to improve performance as the role of external shareholders is minimal. Furthermore, even reorganized firms continue to be obligated to provide social and other services to their employees, reducing any impact on labor mobility. Lardy points to newly elected Premier Zhu Rongji's announcement of a new strict timetable for financial reform as the most recent positive sign. He concludes, however, that if the leadership hesitates at all, for example by balking at the inevitable political costs of rising and unevenly distributed unemployment, a major banking crisis may be unavoidable, with its attendant risks of inflation and currency instability.

Michel Bonnin's chapter, "Perspectives on Social Stability," provides a more detailed analysis of the problem of labor discontent in China today. Bonnin describes the different categories of "joblessness" that comprise what he calls "the third wave of unemployment": the registered unemployed, laid-off workers, and "workers in difficulty." In total, Bonnin estimates that there are at least 30 million such workers in China's urban areas at the end of the century. So far, official efforts to address the needs of these workers have been unsatisfactory, due to a lack of funds and poor co-ordination among the relevant departments. In addition, the problem exists in the context of similarly large numbers of surplus workers in the state sector; if the promises of genuine SOE reform are to be carried out, these workers will have to be laid off. In addition, migrants from the country-side, who cannot be absorbed or forced back to the rural economy, total perhaps 70 million already and do not include another 130 million or so surplus laborers idling in rural areas.

In this context, Bonnin assesses the prospect of large-scale unrest. Al-though he finds that there has indeed been a surge in labor unrest and rural disturbance and that workers as a whole have become more alienated from the party (ironically, more "class-conscious"), he finds it probable that the government will be able to maintain control in the near term. The prime factor in his assessment is the fragmented nature of the discontented sec-tors and the relative unity of the government, which is actively engaged in preventing any broader mobilization from occurring. He predicts that a leadership split, due, for example, to more serious economic collapse, would be necessary to shift the balance. Even then, competing factions may well decide to refrain from drawing on wider social forces out of a general fear of instability.

In Chapter 10, "The People's Republic of China's Quest for Great Power Status," Stuart Harris provides a useful overview of the current state of Chinese foreign policy. He begins by noting that the Fifteenth National Congress was significant for foreign policy largely in its reinforcement of the direction that has developed in recent years. The consolidation of Jiang's position at the Congress paved the way directly for the enhance-ment of his leadership in this area, epitomized by the two successful Jiang-Clinton summits. Despite this development, however, Harris points out that Chinese foreign policy is becoming less and less a personal arena, but one driven increasingly by the interests of the state as a whole.

Determining those interests and China's means for pursuing them is far from simple. According to Harris, China has many of the attributes of a great power (e.g., permanent membership on the UN Security Council, a nuclear arsenal, a large and growing economy) but nonetheless is dissatis-fied by its inability to compete directly with the most powerful nations, particularly the United States, on many issues. It has been restrained by economic backwardness, military weakness (especially in terms of power projection), the need to conserve political capital for the Taiwan issue, and the simple fact that as a latecomer to the international system, it has not had a chance to shape the institutions of that system.

Nonetheless, Harris believes the "China threat" is overblown, at least in the near term. A process of cognitive learning is under way, through which China's policymakers are coming to grips with the workings of the international system, learning how to "play the game," and realizing how China benefits accordingly. Harris shows how this learning already has taken root with respect to international economic relations, where the elites gradually abandoned many of their old assumptions about the global economic order and have learned to work within it. He also asserts that a similar process is under way in security affairs, as evidenced by China's increasing willingness to participate in multilateral institutions. For example, China understands that its involvement in the Association of Southeast Asian Nations (ASEAN) Regional Forum serves its interests by helping to constrain the United States and Japan. Indeed, the explicit acceptance of multilateralism was the only significant foreign policy development of the Fifteenth Party Congress. Thus, Harris predicts that China is likely to pursue a generally cautious foreign policy, one that poses few direct challenges to the regional or global orders, in the near term. He cautions, however, that the longer term may prove more problematic: not only does history suggest that China will put its increasing power to use, but it may discover, through its learning process, that other "great powers" often feel they have the right to exempt themselves from international norms and act accordingly.

In Chapter 11, Kenneth Lieberthal analyzes the cross-Strait problem from the triangular Beijing-Taipei-Washington perspective. After describing the historical background of the issue and demonstrating its crucial nature for regional stability, he delineates the divergent views of each side. China cannot abandon its demand to "recover" all the territory lost during the period of imperial decline and therefore cannot abide the de jure independence of Taiwan, which it surely would counter with a military response. Taiwan, while still formally adhering to the "one China" principle, has developed its separate identity quite substantially during its democratic transformation and is not politically ready to enter into any kind of permanent union with China at present. The United States merely hopes that major conflict can be avoided and that some agreement can be reached that is acceptable to both sides. In the meantime, it will continue to sell arms to Taiwan, in view of the strong political support for the Taiwanese people in the U.S. Congress and the general public.

To overcome this seemingly inextricable knot, Lieberthal proposes that China and Taiwan come to an interim agreement, with negotiations on a permanent solution postponed for fifty years. The main components of such an agreement would include exchanging pledges not to declare de jure independence (for Taiwan) and not to use force (for China); changing the names of both de facto countries to more neutral, less ideologically charged formulae, perhaps inventing a name for the "greater China" that incorporates both sides of the Strait; and reaching a modus vivendi on the diplomatic activities of Taiwan. Such an agreement should be buttressed by regular high-level consultations and confidence-building measures in the military sphere and in the development of further economic and other exchanges.

Although Lieberthal's proposal is controversial and domestic politics in Taiwan in the near term do not favor a major foreign policy breakthrough, it nonetheless is a bold effort to rethink the terms of the debate. Such creative thinking on all sides ultimately will become necessary if the cross-Strait dilemma is ever to be resolved peacefully.

In a chapter entitled "Making Sense of Beijing's Policy Toward Taiwan," Yun-han Chu next offers an analysis of cross-Strait relations in the new era from a neo-institutional perspective. He suggests that four parametric changes have taken place in Beijing's Taiwan affairs policy apparatus during the transition to the Jiang era. First, the decisionmaking process has become more regularized and formalized. Second, the decisionmaking function of the Taiwan Affairs Leading Small Group (TALSG) has become better delineated and more focused. Third, the more ideological, personalistic, and top-down pattern of decisionmaking that characterized the Maoist era has been replaced by a more pragmatic, bureaucratic, and consensus-oriented pattern typical of the reform era. Fourth, in the absence of a paramount leader, Jiang succeeded in making Taiwan affairs one of his functional domains. Thus, although ultimate decisionmaking power rests with the Politburo, Jiang, as the leader of the TALSG, enjoys effective control over agenda setting in this highly salient policy domain. He is more than just "first among equals" when it comes to Taiwan affairs, and most new policy proposals have come from his personal initiatives.

As a result, under Jiang's leadership, People's Republic of China (PRC) policy toward Taiwan has become more comprehensible and predictable. It has freed itself more or less from the problems of deadlock and lengthy compromise typically associated with diffuse and fragmented authority. At the same time, the TALSG's Taiwan policy has tended increasingly to carry strong elements of pragmatism and realism, owing in part to the growing significance of think tanks in the policy formulation process. Chu notes that the consensus over Taiwan policy has grown out of a common commitment to some higher-level national strategic priorities, most notably the desire to maintain stability to promote economic reform and recovery and the desire to prevent the West from developing an anti-China containment policy. It also is fostered by a shared assessment of the constraints and opportunities present in the international environment generally, United States-PRC-Taiwan triangular relations specifically, and the changing economic and political climate in Taiwan.

In Chapter 13, "Institutionalizing de Facto Federalism in Post-Deng China," Zheng Yongnian poses the important question: why, despite tremendous stress, is the center not only holding but perhaps even increasing in power relative to the provinces? Zheng postulates the evolution of what he terms "de facto federalism" as an institutional arrangement of power sharing forged by a process of reciprocity. He argues that the post-Mao period has been marked by decentralization to the provinces in economic decision-making, a process not of devolution per se but rather of simple withdrawal of the central government. The power of the provinces was increased and extended to include influence over central government decisionmaking through increased clout in the Central Committee and similar organs. This process has been largely without crisis throughout both the Deng and Jiang eras. During the Deng period, crisis was avoided primarily because of the overwhelming legitimacy of the revolutionary generation of leaders. During the Jiang period, however, there has been a more proactive effort to create a more stable institutional framework for center-local relations. A major component of this effort has been the process of selective recentralization, epitomized by the tax reforms of 1994 and the central bank system reorganization announced by Zhu Rongji in 1998. Both actions create new leverage for the center over the provinces, but in well-circumscribed, limited areas.

Politically, de facto federalism has seen a generally rising trend in the number of provincial leaders represented in the Central Committee and a geographic shift from the party heartland in central China to the economically successful coastal provinces. Zheng contends that this de facto federalism, although gradually becoming institutionalized, is not likely to result in a de jure federal state for China in the foreseeable future, since tremendous ideological resistance to the idea of federalism remains. In practical terms, he argues that the center should not consider this a "second best" solution: in fact, the center needs the creative ambiguity implicit in de facto federalism. This pattern is likely to hold in China for some time.

In the concluding chapter, entitled "Globalization, Legitimacy, and Post-Communism in China," Edward Friedman brings together many of the strains that run through this volume to sketch an overall vision of the country's future. He cautions that the legitimacy of China's post-Mao regime is largely Hobbesian, rather than nationalistic or performance-based. The party-state is supported because of the fear of disorder. Unfortunately, based on the experience of post-Communist states around the world, the pain of reform, whether quick or protracted, will be tremendous, much worse than has yet been expected in China. In addition, as with many other countries, global economic forces beyond the control of any one nation will compound the stresses of reform in China, encouraging xenophobic demagogues to scapegoat reformers as agents of foreign influence.

Friedman's analysis does not stop with this dismal prospect, however. He points out a number of ways in which the same mix of forces could produce a far different outcome. One is that the Asian financial crisis has fostered a new image of China as a responsible guardian of regional economic stability, a perception that could form the basis for a positive nationalistic motivation for the reform effort. Another possible outcome is that federalism and devolution, long discredited in China, could emerge as legitimate options if they seemed necessary to deliver prosperity. Finally, democratization, at least at the local levels, may turn out to be the most effective method of managing the inevitable economic dislocation by sharing the pain of reform and building a national consensus. If democratic experiments proved to enhance social stability, they could be readily accepted, even by many of the ruling elite.

In conclusion, as Friedman writes, there are clear danger signals in China that we should watch carefully, but the situation is not without hope. "We should not be surprised, however, that the apparent stalemate of the Fifteenth Party Congress . . . also holds a happier possibility among its contested projects, a possibility of success for those regions whose political identity promises political reform for China and peace and prosperity for the region."

# PART ONE

⊞

# Jiang Zemin's Consolidation
of the New Leadership

# 2

# Jiang Takes Command: The Fifteenth National Party Congress and Beyond

## Richard Baum

After years of anxious apprehension and uncertainty, the succession to Deng Xiaoping finally was completed in 1997. Though not without its tense moments, the transition to the post-Deng era went more smoothly than most observers had believed possible. Assuming the mantle of leadership with grace and dignity, Jiang Zemin gave a compelling, tearful eulogy at the state funeral for his fallen mentor in late February. Four months later, on July 1, he displayed statesmanlike qualities of poise and polish in presiding over the historic Hong Kong handover. In late October, Jiang's public image received yet another boost as a result of his high-profile summit meeting with U.S. president Bill Clinton in Washington, D.C. The most crucial test of Jiang's first year of post-Deng leadership, however, came at the Fifteenth National Congress of the Chinese Communist Party (CCP) in September 1997. Occupying center stage, Jiang displayed unexpected self-confidence as he defined the CCP's agenda and priorities for the transition to the next millennium.

Calm, orderly, and carefully scripted, the Fifteenth Party Congress afforded few moments of high drama or suspense. Closing ranks behind Jiang Zemin's recycled Dengist economic policies, the 2,048 party deputies dutifully approved Jiang's keynote proposal to push China's reform movement to its next—and arguably most controversial—stage: the sale of market shares in more than 100,000 ailing, inefficient state-owned enterprises (SOEs). To help neutralize lingering resistance to the sell-off of state assets and to further bolster his own status as "core" of the party's post-Deng leadership, Jiang wrapped himself tightly in Deng's mantle. Heaping praise upon his late mentor's concept of "building socialism with Chinese characteristics," Jiang elevated "Deng Xiaoping Theory" (*Deng Xiaoping lilun*) to a canonical status previously reserved exclusively for Marxism-Leninism (*Malie zhuyi*) and Mao Zedong Thought (*Mao Zedong sixiang*).[1]

15

Notwithstanding Jiang's extravagant homage to Deng and the carefully crafted facade of party unity and cohesiveness, there were tangible signs of underlying tension. First, during the run-up to the Fifteenth Congress, remnant CCP leftists launched a fresh ideological offensive against Deng's "capitalist" reforms.[2] Next, on the opening day of the Congress, supporters of former CCP general secretary Zhao Ziyang unexpectedly circulated a petition—subsequently confirmed to have been written by Zhao himself—calling on party deputies to "reverse the verdict" on the 1989 Tiananmen "turmoil."[3] Finally, toward the end of the Congress, Politburo Standing Committee member and National People's Congress (NPC) chief Qiao Shi, Jiang Zemin's most persistent critic and putative rival, was dropped suddenly and unceremoniously from the PBSC. Evidently, he was the victim of a preemptive coup launched by Jiang and Premier Li Peng, with an assist from retired party elder Bo Yibo.[4] Though Jiang thus succeeded in staving off challenges from both left and right, available signs pointed to some rough waters ahead for China's newest helmsman.

In addition to glorifying Deng, reaffirming Jiang's "core" leadership, and ratifying a controversial shareholding scheme for SOEs, the Fifteenth Party Congress also selected a new Central Committee (CC). Significantly larger than the Fourteenth CC (193 full members versus 189; 153 alternates versus 130), with a substantial majority of its members elected for the first time, the Fifteenth CC was younger, better educated, and more technocratic than its predecessor. At the apex of the party pyramid, seven new full members were selected to serve on the twenty-two-person Politburo: Li Changchun, Wu Guanzheng, Gen. Chi Haotian, Gen. Zhang Wannian, Luo Gan, Jia Qinglin, and Wen Jiabao; at the same time, two newcomers were seated on the elite seven-person Politburo Standing Committee (PBSC): Wei Jianxing and Li Lanqing, replacing Qiao Shi and the retiring Admiral Liu Huaqing, respectively. Altogether, four members of the Fourteenth Politburo (Qiao Shi, Liu Huaqing, Zou Jiahua, and Gen. Yang Baibing), all of whom were over the age of 70, were dropped from the Fifteenth CC. Returning to a pattern of civilian dominance established in the 1980s, no professional military officers were seated on the new PBSC.

One important event that did *not* occur at the Fifteenth Party Congress was a revival of meaningful political reform, indefinitely postponed since the Tiananmen debacle of 1989. During preparations for the Fifteenth Congress, there had been persistent rumors of renewed political restructuring. Expectations initially were raised at the end of May 1997, when Jiang Zemin delivered a strikingly progressive speech at the Central Party School in Beijing. In his speech, he resuscitated a number of reform slogans first popularized by his two disgraced predecessors, Hu Yaobang and Zhao Ziyang. He also revived one of Deng Xiaoping's more controversial slogans, a 1992 admonition that "the main thing is to defend against the left" (*zhuyao shi fangzhi zuo*).[5] Next, in the summer of 1997, a spate of media commentaries appeared exhorting the Chinese people to "emancipate thinking," "combat leftist obstruction," and overhaul the country's political institutions.[6]

Expectations of a political breakthrough at the Fifteenth Party Congress, however, proved overblown. Even before the opening gavel, a tone of "politics as usual" was established as the Presidium peremptorily rejected Zhao Ziyang's petition for a reversal of verdicts without even bothering to submit it to the assembled delegates for consideration.[7] And when Jiang Zemin delivered his opening address—devoting one entire section nominally to the topic of political reform—he focused on the need to "uphold and improve" established mechanisms of multiparty cooperation and political consultation "under Communist Party leadership."[8] Although Jiang used the word "democracy" no fewer than thirty-two times in his report, he did not propose any true structural reform of the political system. Indeed, Jiang's only fresh initiative was a rather cautious—if potentially significant—proposal to expand the current system of grassroots village elections upward to the township level. And although Jiang alluded briefly to "political disturbances at home and abroad in the late 1980s and early 1990s," he did not directly address the question of the 1989 Tiananmen "turmoil."

## ENTERPRISE REFORM IN THE "PRIMARY STAGE OF SOCIALISM"

Approximately one-half of China's 118,000 industrial SOEs lost money in 1996 (up from about one-third in 1994). SOE indebtedness was at an all-time high and rising steadily. Naturally, enterprise reform topped Jiang Zemin's list of priorities at the Fifteenth National Party Congress.[9] The centerpiece of Jiang's two-and-a-half-hour, 30,000-word keynote speech to the Congress was his call to conduct "bold experimentation" with new forms of economic ownership, organization, and management, including, where appropriate, the selling of shares in state enterprises. To justify such experimentation, Jiang warmly endorsed the controversial theory of the "primary stage of socialism" (PSS), initially popularized by Zhao Ziyang at the Thirteenth Party Congress in 1987 but subsequently shelved after Zhao's 1989 downfall. In essence, the theory of PSS held that China's chronic economic backwardness required a development strategy that accorded the very highest priority to rapid development of society's productive forces. Under such circumstances, the most important criterion of socialist suitability was economic success.[10]

A perfect complement to Deng Xiaoping's famously protean theory of "building socialism with Chinese characteristics," the theory of PSS established a flexible ideological rationale for ending state domination of China's industrial economy. According to Jiang, so long as public ownership remained the "foundation" of the national economy and so long as new economic forms were favorable to the "emancipation and further development of the productive forces," then "any form of ownership . . . can and should be utilized to serve socialism."

Quoting Deng Xiaoping at every turn, Jiang acknowledged that under the theory of PSS, the Chinese economy was sailing into uncharted waters: "There are no precedents for us to learn from. We can only learn from practice, feeling our way as we go." Because of China's backwardness, he averred, "it would take many generations, a dozen or even several dozen . . . to consolidate and develop the socialist system." A "foundation" could be laid by the year 2010, and "basic modernization" would be achieved by the middle of the twenty-first century. In the meantime, he said, "we are destined to make economic development the central task of the entire party . . . and make sure that all other work is subordinated to and serves this task. . . . Development is the absolute principle."

To create additional wiggle room for doctrinal maneuvers, Jiang enlarged the definition of "public ownership" (*gongyouzhi*) to encompass the mushrooming collective and "fixed" collective-private sectors of the economy (privately owned enterprises protected under a "collective" shell). Defending the vigorous growth of these latter sectors as fully compatible with socialism, he suggested that "even if the state-owned sector [*guoyouzhi*] accounts for a smaller proportion of the economy, this will not affect the socialist nature of our country." Addressing the nettlesome question of the nonpublic sector, Jiang noted with approval the recent, steady expansion of "self-employed and private businesses." Calling the nonpublic sector "an important component part of China's socialist market economy," the general secretary argued that this sector should have its "legitimate rights and interests" protected by law.[11]

After thus semantically stretching the skin of the socialist market economy to cover virtually any form (or combination) of enterprise ownership, Jiang proceeded to the main point of the entire discourse on PSS: the conversion, merger, sell-off, and shut-down of chronically debt-ridden SOEs. Treading carefully and employing oblique language wherever possible, Jiang laid out the party's blueprint for the future:

> We shall convert large and medium-sized state-owned enterprises into standard corporations according to the requirements of "clearly established ownership," well defined power and responsibility, [and] separation of enterprise from administration . . . so that they will become corporate entities and competitors adaptable to the market. . . . [In these enterprises] the state will enjoy owner equity according to the amount of capital it has put into the enterprise and bear limited responsibility for the

debts of the enterprise, [which] will operate independently according to law, responsible for their own profits and losses. . . .

We shall also quicken the pace in relaxing control over small state-owned enterprises and invigorating them by way of reorganization, association, merger, leasing, contract operation, joint stock partnership or sell-off. . . .

We should encourage merger of enterprises, standardize bankruptcy procedures, divert laid-off workers, increase efficiency by downsizing staff and encourage reemployment projects so as to form a competitive mechanism selecting the superior and eliminating the inferior.

In his report, Jiang Zemin provided few programmatic details about just how to achieve the desired goal of creating a preponderance of lean, mean, corporate-style shareholding enterprises. He did concede that the transition would not be painless. "With the deepening of enterprise reforms," he acknowledged, "it would be hard to avoid the flow of personnel and layoffs. It will cause temporary difficulties to some of the workers." To soften the shock of transitional dislocation, he pledged that "the party and the government will . . . show concern for laid-off workers, help them with their welfare, organize job training, and open up new avenues of employment. . . . We shall build a social security system, introducing old-age pensions and medical insurance systems . . . and improve the unemployment insurance and social relief systems."

Notwithstanding the ostensible radicalism of Jiang's overall plan for industrial reform and reorganization, few of the specifics in his report were particularly new in conception or design. Some had been proposed initially in the late 1980s, before the Tiananmen crackdown temporarily mooted all discussion of alternative ownership systems; others had been quietly tried out in various Chinese cities and enterprises since the mid-1990s.[12] What was new was the forceful endorsement of the shareholding scheme by the CCP's top leadership. Like Deng Xiaoping's notorious *nanxun* (southern tour) of 1992, Jiang's keynote speech served less to break new policy ground than to signal the end of a long and divisive intraparty debate over the ideological limits of economic reform. Significantly, Jiang repeated Deng's now-famous 1992 exhortation concerning the need to "defend mainly against the left."

Although Jiang's speech did not provide any concrete target figures for SOE conversion, closure, or consolidation, it was widely hinted that approximately 1,000 of China's largest state-owned firms in strategic, or "pillar," industries would be merged to form corporate conglomerates along the lines of South Korea's *chaebols,* with dominant state ownership but autonomous corporate management.[13] The remaining large and medium-sized industrial enterprises, accounting for perhaps 20 percent of the total, were expected to become "mixed" firms, with some equity (but not necessarily a majority of shares) retained by the state. Finally, at the low end of the spectrum, most of China's more than 85,000 smaller industrial SOEs were expected to become "joint stock cooperatives," with equity shares offered to workers, staff, and management.[14] In the mass media, the new shareholding scheme was referred to as "grasping the large, letting go of the small" (*zhuada, fangxiao*).

Observers were generally cautious in their appraisal of the new enterprise reform scheme. Some analysts lauded the party's objectives but expressed concern that in the absence of either a well-defined legal framework of enforceable property rights or accurate inventories of state-owned industrial assets, the process of enterprise conversion would be subject to manipulation and mismanagement by self-regarding local industrial officials.[15] In particular, there were fears that a sudden upsurge of "asset stripping" and "spontaneous privatization" by factory managers and their cronies would result in the type of widespread industrial paralysis that plagued the Russian economy throughout most of the 1990s. Still others worried that a significant increase in factory closures or worker layoffs would add dramatically to the potential for heightened urban unrest and political volatility.[16]

## POLITICAL REFORM OR POLITICS AS USUAL?

In a lengthy section of his speech devoted to "strengthening democracy and the legal system," Jiang Zemin called for the "gradual institutionalization and codification" of rules and procedures governing socialist democracy. The stated objective was to stabilize the political and legal systems so that "institutions and laws will not change with changes in the leadership or changes in the views or focus of attention of any leader." Although Jiang repeatedly referred in his speech to the putative benefits of "people's democracy," "socialist democracy," and "rule by law," his references were mostly standard political boilerplate—ritualized repetitions of conventional Communist Party reform rhetoric.[17]

Reiterating the CCP's long-standing opposition to Western-style democracy, Jiang Zemin spelled out his basic political vision for China's future:

> Under the precondition of adhering to the Four Cardinal Principles, we should continue to press ahead with the reform of the political structure, further extend the scope of socialist democracy and improve the socialist legal system. . . . The essence of socialist democracy is that the people are the masters of the country. All powers of the state belong to the people. China's state system featuring people's democratic dictatorship and its system of government featuring people's congresses are the result of

struggles waged by the people and the choice of history. It is imperative that we should uphold and improve this fundamental political system, instead of copying any western models. This is of decisive importance in upholding leadership by the party and the socialist system and realizing people's democracy.

Further clarifying the boundaries and parameters of acceptable political restructuring, Jiang ruled out the future development in China of two pillars of Western-style democracy: multiparty electoral competition and interest group pluralism. In their stead, he called for perfecting existing mechanisms of "multiparty cooperation and consultation under CCP leadership" and for creating mechanisms that will "help decision-makers to go deep among the people to see their conditions, adequately reflect their will, and pool their wisdom, so that decision-making will be more scientific, democratic and efficient."

Jiang also ruled out a third pillar of Western-style democracy: freedom of the press. "In press and publicity work," said Jiang, "we must adhere to the principle of upholding the party spirit. . . . We should tighten control over the press and publishing, optimizing their structures and improving their quality." Stressing the need for social stability throughout the primary stage of socialism, Jiang warned that the instruments of the people's democratic dictatorship would be employed to "do away with all factors jeopardizing stability, oppose bourgeois liberalization, and guard against infiltration, subversion, and separatist activities carried out by international and domestic hostile forces."

In his one significant concession to the principle of spontaneous grassroots political participation, Jiang promised to enlarge the arena of local elections in China from rural villages upward to urban townships. Calling such elections "a practice of socialist democracy on the most extensive scale," Jiang cautiously elaborated upon the scope and limitations of local political empowerment:

> The grassroots organs of power and self-governing mass organizations in rural and urban areas should establish a sound system of democratic elections and keep the public informed of their political activities and financial affairs so as to enable the people to take a direct part in the discussion and decision-making concerning local public affairs and welfare undertakings, and exercise supervision over the cadres.

In foreign affairs, Jiang's most interesting departure from previous CCP policy was his embrace of "multilateralism" as a device for resolving international disputes. Previously, Chinese leaders had expressed an exclusive preference for bilateral diplomacy.[18] In a section on "peaceful reunification of the motherland," Jiang wielded both carrot and stick, reiterating

China's long-standing policy of preferring a negotiated cross-Strait settlement with Taiwan while at the same time refusing to renounce the use of force. To this now-standard formulation was appended a strong statement reaffirming the futility of Taiwan's recently accelerated search for international recognition: "Taiwan's future hinges on the reunification of the motherland, and splitting is no way out. With full determination, we are capable of finding a final solution to the Taiwan issue." Finally, in a dig aimed at the United States and its allies, Jiang denounced various (unspecified) international attempts to "use human rights and other issues to interfere in [China's] internal affairs." Combined with his strong statement on the Taiwan question and his previously noted warning against infiltration and subversion by "hostile international forces," Jiang's otherwise generally conventional remarks revealed a discernible undertone of nationalist impatience and assertiveness.

## COMBATING CORRUPTION

The final section of Jiang Zemin's keynote speech took up the challenges facing the 58-million-member CCP on the eve of the new century. Here Jiang focused on the growing problem of official corruption, calling the fight against it "a grave political struggle vital to the very existence of the party and the state." Citing the conventional military aphorism that "the easiest way to capture a fortress is from within," he warned that "if corruption cannot be punished effectively, our party will lose the support and confidence of the people." Adding bite to Jiang's warning, the Central Committee, on the eve of the Fifteenth Congress, stripped former Beijing party chief and Politburo member Chen Xitong of his party membership, thereby lifting his immunity from criminal prosecution.[19] By removing Chen's party shield, China's leaders were ostensibly sending a signal that the CCP's conventional triple standard of criminal justice—generally characterized by prompt, harsh judicial punishment for ordinary offenders, "party discipline" for CCP members and cadres, and a wink and a nod for the "princeling" offspring of senior leaders—would no longer protect corrupt officials at the top of the system.

Although Jiang's stern anticorruption rhetoric was generally welcomed, a certain amount of cynicism was unavoidable. For one thing, Jiang hedged his promise that henceforth no one would be above the law. Calling for "the integration of supervision by party members with that by the law," Jiang exhorted party committees to "adhere to the principle that the party should supervise itself." Moreover, similar pledges to clean up corruption within the party and government hierarchy had been issued many times before but had failed to result in any sustained effort to expose and punish high-level perpetrators or their family members. With Chen Xitong's son already serving prison time and Chen's own criminal trial subjected to repeated, unexplained delays, it remained to be seen whether things would be significantly different this time around.[20]

## A CONGRESS OF UNITY?

Although Jiang Zemin's report was officially declared "the party's declaration of a program of action for the new century," it received only lukewarm praise in some official media. For example, the *Beijing Review,* in an unusually muted editorial, noted in passing that the speech had been received with "warm" (as opposed to enthusiastic) applause and that it represented not Jiang's personal thinking but "a crystallization of collective wisdom." In an accompanying full-page commentary on the proceedings of the Fifteenth Congress, Deng Xiaoping's name and theories were reverentially invoked twelve times. Jiang's name, however, was mentioned only twice and only in passing—the second time bracketed by a telling modifier: "The CCP collective leadership of the third generation, headed by General Secretary Jiang Zemin."[21] Further indicative of the lack of high-pitched, spontaneous enthusiasm for Jiang's solo performance was a report that senior staff members of the Chinese Academy of Social Sciences had been instructed to compose 3,000-word essays praising Jiang's speech, with rewards of up to $350 for those essays deemed suitable for publication.[22]

Perhaps the clearest indication that Jiang's political authority and personal appeal were limited was the surprising stalemate that emerged on the eve of the Fifteenth Congress over the question of proposed personnel changes at the highest levels of the party and government. Throughout the spring and summer of 1997, persistent rumors pointed to a nagging dispute between Jiang and NPC Standing Committee (SC) chairman Qiao Shi.[23] At issue, among other things, was Qiao's political future.

With Li Peng due to retire from the premiership when his second five-year term expired in the spring of 1998, Li was said to covet Qiao's NPC post. Though he reportedly enjoyed Jiang's support, Li could not budge Qiao, who was eligible for a second five-year term as NPC chief. The rivalry soon spilled over onto two important collateral issues. One was a proposal, backed by Jiang, to enlarge the PBSC from seven to nine members, thereby giving Jiang an opportunity to pack that body with his supporters. The second was a debate over the desirability of continued—or possibly even augmented—military representation on the PBSC.[24] Although reliable accounts of the political infighting that took place in the summer of 1997 are hard to come by, there was one sure-fire sign of persistent intraelite conflict. Negotiations and horse-trading over top-level

personnel changes, which should have been completed at the annual summer seaside leadership conference at Beidaihe in August, were still going
hot and heavy right up to the very end of the Party Congress in September.
And when the dust finally settled on the last day of the Congress, Jiang
Zemin found his political independence and preeminence subjected to a
series of new limitations and constraints.

Jiang's attempt to gain support for his scheme to enlarge the Standing
Committee and pack it with additional supporters reportedly hinged on
four interconnected stratagems. He needed to placate Li Peng by securing
Qiao Shi's resignation from his NPC post. He needed to pressure 81-year-
old Admiral Liu Huaqing—the oldest and most devoted Dengist of the existing SC members—to retire. He needed to replace General Liu with one
of Jiang's two carefully cultivated military allies, either Defense Minister
Chi Haotian or Central Military Commission (CMC) vice chairman Gen.
Zhang Wannian. And finally, he needed to add to the PBSC two personal
cronies, fellow Shanghainese deputy premier Wu Bangguo and CCP propaganda chief Ding Guangen. Endorsed by Li Peng but opposed by Qiao
Shi and Liu Huaqing, Jiang's scheme reportedly hit a wall when he failed
to gain the support of three ostensibly uncommitted members of the
PBSC—Li Ruihuan, Zhu Rongji, and Hu Jintao.[25]

Unable to break the ensuing deadlock, Jiang Zemin altered his tactics.
According to one widely circulated account, halfway through the Fifteenth
Congress he convened an "enlarged" meeting of the Politburo, attended by
a handful of retired party elders, including Yang Shangkun, Wan Li, and
Bo Yibo.[26] Jiang reportedly opened the session by noting that Congress
deputies had strongly emphasized the need for rejuvenation of party leadership, though they had failed to agree on a mandatory retirement age for
'veteran comrades.'"[27] With three members of the PBSC already over the
age of seventy (octogenarian Liu Huaqing, 73-year-old Qiao Shi, and Jiang
himself, aged 71), as well as two other Politburo members (Yang Baibing,
77, and Zou Jiahua, 71), Jiang launched a surprise initiative. "I respect the
deputies' wish for rejuvenation," he reportedly stated. "I myself am ready
to retire."

At this point, as if on cue, 89-year-old veteran comrade Bo Yibo is
said to have come to Jiang's rescue, arguing that the party should strive for
unity as well as rejuvenation. Noting that Jiang was due to meet with President Bill Clinton during an important state visit to the United States in
October 1997, Bo reportedly urged the general secretary to "remain in office, since you are the core of the third generation leadership, and the authority of this leadership corps is not yet totally secure." Bo then proposed
that all *other* CCP leaders over the age of 70—specifically excluding
Jiang—should resign to set a positive example for the Party Congress.
Caught off guard, Qiao and the other septuagenarians reportedly had little
choice but to offer their resignations.[28]

Whatever the veracity of this account, Bo Yibo's "surprise attack" did not result in a clear-cut, unambiguous victory for Jiang Zemin. For one thing, in exchange for this permission to continue in office past the age of 70, Jiang was reportedly forced by his comrades to agree to retire from any and all leadership posts in 2002–2003. For another, although Jiang managed to secure the retirement of long-time critics Qiao Shi and Liu Huaqing, he was forced to drop his plan to enlarge the PBSC. Moreover, none of Jiang's four preferred choices for SC membership—Wu Bangguo (56), Chi Haotian (68), Zhang Wannian (69), and Ding Guangen (68)—were promoted to that body.[29] Instead, Qiao's position on the PBSC was filled by his own protégé, acting Beijing party chief and Central Discipline Inspection Committee (CDIC) head Wei Jianxing (66), and Liu's post was taken by Vice Premier Li Lanqing (65), a foreign trade expert without strong factional ties. Although Jiang's two top military allies—Chi Haotian and Zhang Wannian—were added to the Politburo, neither man was named to the Standing Committee.

Additional Politburo vacancies were filled by State Council general secretary and long-time Li Peng associate Luo Gan (62); Beijing mayor Jia Qinglin (57); Henan Province party secretary Li Changchun (53); Central Party Secretariat member Wen Jiabao (55); and Shandong Province party secretary Wu Guanzheng (59). Only one of Jiang Zemin's Shanghai cronies was added to the Politburo as an alternate member—CCP General Office director Zeng Qinghong (58). The second (and final) alternate slot went to veteran foreign trade negotiator Wu Yi (58), who was also the lone female named to the new Politburo.

The removal of Qiao Shi from the CCP hierarchy cleared the way for Li Peng (69) to assume Qiao's post as NPC Standing Committee chair when the latter stepped down as premier in the spring of 1998. Qiao's ouster also helped facilitate the elevation of the previously fifth-ranked Standing Committee member, Vice Premier Zhu Rongji (69), to third place in the new party hierarchy, ahead of Li Ruihuan (63) and behind only Jiang Zemin and Li Peng. Zhu's accelerated ascent through the ranks reflected his enhanced stature as heir-apparent to Premier Li Peng, a promotion that was subsequently confirmed at the Ninth NPC in February 1998.

According to informed sources, in the months preceding the Fifteenth Congress Jiang Zemin gradually came to accept Zhu as an acceptable replacement for Li Peng, after initially expressing a preference for Zhu's fellow vice premier, Wu Bangguo. Zhu is generally regarded as a tough-minded, no-nonsense administrator who is not afraid of offending free-spending local officials by taking unpopular positions in support of enhanced central economic authority (he was once dubiously dubbed "China's Gorbachev" by the Western media before the collapse of the Union of Soviet Socialist Republics [USSR]). Indeed, Zhu received much of the credit for engineering an impressive "soft landing" for China's severely overheated, inflation-ridden economy during the past four years.[30]

## THE FIFTEENTH CENTRAL COMMITTEE

Compared with the Fourteenth Central Committee,[31] the new CC elected by the Fifteenth Party Congress was substantially larger (346 full and alternate members, compared to 319), and less experienced (63 percent of the members and alternates were first-timers[32]). The new CC also was slightly younger (average age 55.9, compared to 56.3), significantly better educated (72 percent college-trained, compared to 61 percent[33]), and considerably more technocratic (56 percent received postsecondary training in engineering, science, finance, or management, compared to 40 percent). Among the 193 full members, the youngest was 43 and the oldest 76. Only 4.1 percent were women (down from 5.3 percent in the previous CC).

Indicative of a growing trend toward the fusion of party and governmental authority at the center, state councilors and ministers of state registered the largest net increase in CC seats, up from thirty-four in the Fourteenth CC (18 percent) to fifty-one in the Fifteenth (26 percent). Provincial representation also increased significantly, from forty-nine seats (26 percent) to sixty-one (32 percent), with the party first secretaries and the governors or mayors of all but one of China's thirty-one provincial administrative units securing full membership on the new CC.[34] Military representation remained roughly constant, with forty-two People's Liberation Army (PLA) commanders, commissars, and their deputies securing full membership on the Fifteenth CC (22 percent).

Reflecting China's shifting center of economic gravity, a small group of top bankers joined the CC, including central bank governor Dai Xianglong and Bank of China head Wang Xuebing. Also added were five members of China's newest industrial elite, the corporate CEOs. One other noteworthy addition was a group of younger foreign policy specialists led by Deputy Foreign Minister Tang Jiaxuan, who was subsequently named to succeed his boss, Foreign Minister Qian Qichen, when the latter announced his retirement at the first session of the Ninth NPC.[35]

At its initial plenary session, held immediately following the close of the Party Congress on September 19, 1997, the Fifteenth Central Committee formally ratified the selection of the new Politburo, as well as the Central Party Secretariat, the Standing Committee of the CDIC, and the CMC. Jiang Zemin ostensibly strengthened his grip on the Central Party Secretariat with the addition of three supporters to that body—Zhang Wannian, Zeng Qinghong, and Luo Gan—to go along with holdovers Hu Jintao, Wei Jianxing, Ding Guangen, Wen Jiabao, and Jiang himself. Reportedly, Jiang was none too pleased with the choice of Wei Jianxing—a protégé of Qiao Shi—to continue heading the CDIC Standing Committee, the body charged with overseeing implementation of the party's anticorruption campaign.[36] By maintaining his CDIC and Secretariat posts while gaining a seat on the PBSC, Wei Jianxing became the only party leader other than Jiang Zemin himself to hold a seat on all three of the party's top civilian command centers.

## THE PARTY CONTROLS THE GUN

Although the Chinese military failed to secure a slot on the new PBSC, the addition of two professional soldiers to the Politburo (Zhang Wannian and Chi Haotian), as well as forty other military figures named to the Central Committee, helped lessen the putative sting of the PLA's exclusion from the pinnacle of political power. Despite appearances to the contrary, the absence of a professional soldier on the PBSC did not represent a defeat for the PLA, which continued to exercise effective veto power over important domains of strategic policy.[37] Out of political necessity, Jiang Zemin has been a good friend to the Chinese army. During his tenure as chairman of the CMC, he has repeatedly supported increased defense spending; promoted the modernization and professionalization of the armed forces; permitted the PLA to engage in freewheeling, for-profit commercial enterprise; and personally pinned promotions on dozens of "his" generals. With a proven friend like Jiang at the top, the PLA arguably did not need one of its own top brass serving on the PBSC to safeguard its corporate interests. Indeed, a more "normalized" civil-military relationship may now be emerging in China, marked on the one hand by routine civilian deference to military requirements and preferences and on the other by military avoidance of day-to-day political involvement.[38]

Whatever the origin of the new, cozier civil-military relationship, Jiang Zemin's one significant military policy initiative at the Fifteenth Party Congress appears to have enjoyed top-level PLA support. Announcing a plan to cut 500,000 troops from the 3-million-strong Chinese army over the next several years, Jiang indicated that the leaner, meaner PLA would emphasize quality over quantity, modernization over manpower, and professionalism over politics. Reportedly, the generals were pleased.[39]

In the immediate aftermath of the Fifteenth Party Congress, it remained unclear just how the decisions of the Congress would affect power relations *within* the PLA. Judging from the composition of the new CMC, Jiang Zemin appeared likely to enjoy even closer relations with the military high command. The retirement of two senior military holdovers from the Deng Xiaoping era, CMC executive vice chairmen Liu Huaqing and Gen. Zhang Zhen (83), seemed to ensure that pro-Jiang loyalists Zhang Wannian and Chi Haotian, both of whom secured reappointment as vice chairmen, enjoyed firm control over the Central Military Commission.[40] There was no turnover at all among ordinary members of the CMC, as the three incumbent heads of PLA staff departments (Gens. Fu Quanyou, Yu Yongbo, and Wang Ke) and one deputy head (Gen. Wang Ruilin) all retained their CMC appointments.

## CONCLUSION: THE ROAD AHEAD

Although Jiang Zemin emerged from the Fifteenth Party Congress with his basic policy agenda intact and his personal prestige only slightly diminished, his biggest challenge lies ahead. With the fallout from Asia's devastating financial crisis mounting steadily, Chinese leaders were hard-pressed to hold the line against a potentially destabilizing currency devaluation. At the same time, as the "Asian flu" cut into China's regional exports and as urban unemployment surged upward past the 11 million mark, the Chinese government was forced to place a temporary hold on Jiang's ambitious program of SOE restructuring, with its twin cornerstones of shareholding and "conglomerization."[41]

As a result of such economic problems and uncertainties, the Chinese government at mid-year revised downward its gross domestic product (GDP) growth rate estimates for 1998. This, in turn, fueled fears of possible future political instability in the Middle Kingdom.[42] Thus, notwithstanding Jiang Zemin's recent string of personal and political triumphs—from his eloquent eulogy at Deng's funeral to his two impressive summit meetings with President Bill Clinton—it may nonetheless be somewhat premature to celebrate Jiang's success in effecting the transition from designated heir to unchallenged leader. Much of the heavy lifting, it seems, remains to be done.

## NOTES

1. Formalizing the glorification of Deng's theories, the Fifteenth Party Congress revised the CCP Constitution to stipulate that "the Communist Party of China takes Marxism-Leninism, Mao Zedong Thought, and Deng Xiaoping Theory as its guide to action." See *Beijing Review,* October 13–19, 1997, 18.

2. The attack took the form of a series of "10,000 word manifestos" (*wanzishu*) published in the CCP's in-house propaganda organs under the guiding hand of the retired conservative propagandist, Deng Liqun. See *South China Morning Post,* February 23, 1997, 1; and Reuters (Beijing), July 30, 1997.

3. *The Economist,* September 20, 1997, 39–40; *Asian Wall Street Journal,* September 23, 1997.

4. *Wall Street Journal,* September 18, 1997; *South China Morning Post,* September 20, 1997.

5. An abridged text of Jiang's May 29 speech, which contained many of the ideas and proposals later incorporated into his keynote speech at the Fifteenth Party Congress, appears in *Beijing Review*, August 25–31, 1997, 10–13.

6. For analysis of key political developments in the run-up to the Fifteenth Congress, see *Far Eastern Economic Review,* July 31, 1997, 14–15; *Asian Wall Street Journal,* September 10 and 11, 1997, 8; *The Economist,* September 20, 1997, 39–40; and *Asiaweek,* September 26, 1997, 54.

7. Zhao's appeal, which was published in the Hong Kong *Apple Daily,* was brushed off as insignificant by Chinese minister of justice Xiao Yang on these grounds: "The party and government have already handled correctly the incident and unrest that occurred in the spring and summer of 1989, thus ensuring the long-term stability of China." After this incident, Zhao, who had been under some form of house arrest since 1989, was reportedly reprimanded and placed under stricter supervision.

8. The text of Jiang's report to the Fifteenth Congress, somewhat awkwardly entitled "Hold High the Great Banner of Deng Xiaoping Theory for an All-Round Advancement of the Cause of Building Socialism with Chinese Characteristics into the 21st Century," appears in *Beijing Review,* October 6–12, 1997, 10–33.

9. According to the State Statistical Bureau, from 1994 to 1996 "triangular debt" among state enterprises shot up from 600 billion yuan to 1 trillion yuan. Despite the fact that SOEs accounted for less than 40 percent of the country's gross industrial output value, bank loans to ailing state enterprises accounted for fully 90 percent of all enterprise loans granted in 1996. See *The Economist,* September 13, 1997, 23–25; also World Bank, *China's Management of Enterprise Assets.*

10. Reputedly coined by liberal Marxist theoretician Su Shaozhi, the term "primary stage of socialism" (*shehuizhuyide chuji jieduan*) first appeared in the text of the CCP's June 1981 "Resolution on Certain Questions in the History of Our Party since the Founding of the People's Republic of China." Zhao Ziyang later appropriated the term, with Deng Xiaoping's approval. On the origins of the theory, see Schram, "China After the 13th Congress," 177–197; and Baum, *Burying Mao,* 218ff.

11. Throughout his speech, Jiang avoided using derivatives of the controversial "p" word ("to privatize"), preferring instead to employ such euphemisms as "to cultivate a diversity of investors."

12. Under a "Company Law" enacted in 1993, for example, the corporate conversion of large and medium-sized SOEs was well under way in Shanghai and other cities.

13. See *Far Eastern Economic Review,* October 9, 1997; *Business Week,* September 29, 1997, 118.

14. See, for example, *Asian Wall Street Journal,* September 23, 1997; *Asiaweek,* September 26, 1997; and *Time* (International), September 15, 1997.

15. A recent World Bank report on the management of China's state assets notes that many enterprises initially corporatized under the 1993 Company Law were being run as private fiefdoms by management at the expense of state banks. See note 9, above; also *Asian Wall Street Journal,* September 23, 1997.

16. Such concerns were additionally fueled by memories of the "snowball effect" of Deng Xiaoping's 1992 *nanxun,* when the paramount leader's fervent exhortations to accelerate the pace of market reform precipitated a manic investment and construction binge throughout the country, marked by runaway bank lending, rampant speculation, economic overheating, and inflationary price increases, among other things. Fears of a similar galvanic response being triggered by Jiang's keynote speech were widely expressed by observers in the aftermath of the Fifteenth Congress.

17. Note, for example, the following, taken from just one section of Jiang's speech: "It is our party's persistent goal to develop socialist democracy"; "we

[must] develop people's democracy and do things in strict accordance with the law"; "we must resolutely correct such erroneous acts as suppressing democracy"; "ruling the country by law is the basic strategy employed by the party."

18. One immediate consequence of China's acceptance of the principle of multilateral diplomacy was a revival of hopes for a peaceful resolution of conflicting sovereignty claims in the Spratly Islands. Prior to the Fifteenth Congress, China had steadfastly refused to negotiate collectively with ASEAN. I am indebted to Stuart Harris for calling this to my attention.

19. Chen had been deeply implicated in a series of financial scandals that rocked the Beijing municipal government in the mid-1990s, culminating in the 1995 suicide of Beijing deputy mayor Wang Baosen. For background on the case of Chen Xitong, see Andrew Wedeman, "Corruption and Politics," 61–94.

20. As an indication of the magnitude of the problem of corruption within the Communist Party, at the Fifteenth Congress it was disclosed that in the five years between 1992 and 1997, more than 725,000 cases of criminal conduct by party members had been investigated. These resulted in the expulsion of 121,000 CCP members, of whom 37,000 were detained for criminal prosecution. The remaining 600,000 or so were subjected to milder forms of organizational discipline.

21. *Beijing Review,* October 6–12, 1997, 4–5. Not all official media were so laconic. On September 19, *Xinhua* quoted Foreign Ministry spokesman Shen Guo-fang to the effect that Jiang's report was of "great significance" due to its "brilliant dialectical exposition" of the current international situation.

22. *Far Eastern Economic Review,* October 2, 1997, 20.

23. See *South China Morning Post,* May 21, 1997, and July 16, 1997. Mutual coolness between Jiang and Qiao reportedly stemmed from the latter's opposition to Jiang's sudden ascent to the post of CCP general secretary in 1989. In his post as head of the National People's Congress since 1993, Qiao had repeatedly stressed the importance of "rule by law" (*fazhi*) while Jiang's supporters generally emphasized "rule by core" (*hexinzhi*). As late as the spring of 1997, in the aftermath of Deng Xiaoping's funeral, Qiao Shi was one of the few top Chinese leaders who did not call for the entire party to rally around the "core" leadership of Jiang Zemin.

24. On these (and other) pre-Congress political maneuverings, see *South China Morning Post,* July 31, 1997; and *Asiaweek,* September 26, 1997, 45.

25. *South China Morning Post,* July 23, 1997, and July 31, 1997.

26. *South China Morning Post,* September 20, 1997.

27. At the Fifteenth Congress it was decided that at least one-half of the newly elected CC members and alternates should be under the age of 55.

28. Apart from the exception made for Jiang Zemin, the only other member of the Fourteenth Central Committee over the age of 70 to be reelected to the Fifteenth CC was former CCP general secretary Hua Guofeng (76).

29. On the eve of the Fifteenth Congress a report circulated in Beijing noting that Ding Guangen had joined a Kuomintang youth group in the 1940s. The timing of the revelation suggests that Ding—a conservative propagandist—was being deliberately smeared by opponents. Although he subsequently managed to retain his seats on both the Politburo and the Central Secretariat, he was not promoted to the Standing Committee.

30. On Zhu Rongji's economic initiatives of the mid-1990s, see Baum, *Burying Mao* (paperback edition, 1996), 382–383. On Zhu's rise to premier-designate, see Lilley, "The Fifteenth Party Congress: A Balancing Act."

31. The following section draws on data presented in *Ming Bao* (Hong Kong), September 19 and 20, 1997; and White and Li, "The Fifteenth Central Committee."

32. The percentage drops to 49 percent if the forty-six alternate members of the Fourteenth CC who were promoted to full membership are subtracted from the list of first-timers.

33. The percentage rises to more than 90 percent if short-term training courses at the Central Party School and other postsecondary in-service training programs are included.

34. The lone exception was Yunnan Province, which secured only one seat.

35. See *Wall Street Journal,* September 18, 1997.

36. Prior to the Fifteenth Congress, it was rumored that Jiang had favored Shanghai party secretary Huang Ju for the CDIC director's post.

37. On the PLA as veto group, see Mulvenon, *Professionalization of the Senior Chinese Officer Corps.*

38. According to Hong Kong sources, Deng Xiaoping personally initiated a proposal to extricate the PLA from top-level political decisionmaking before his death. See *Guangjiaojing* (Wide Angle), October 16, 1997, 12–16.

39. *Far Eastern Economic Review,* October 2, 1997, 21; *The Economist,* September 20, 1997, 40.

40. Reputedly, Generals Zhang and Chi have little liking for one another, thus ostensibly precluding the formation of a cohesive military clique within the Central Party leadership.

41. Even where the shift to shareholding was allowed to proceed, the conversion process was revealed to be riddled with corruption, as factory managers in many places reportedly coerced employees to "invest" their salaries in the purchase of stock shares on pain of being fired for noncompliance.

42. According to some Western economists, if China's 1998 GDP growth rate were to fall below 6 percent (from initial official projections of around 8.5 percent), China would not be able to create enough new jobs to prevent unemployment from reaching critical proportions. As a rule of thumb, each 1 percent of GDP growth creates 1 million new jobs.

# ⊞ 3 ⊞

# Sizing Up China's New Leadership: Division of Labor, Political Background, and Policy Orientation

## *Lowell Dittmer*

The Fifteenth National Congress of the Communist Party of China (CCP), held in September 1997 after unusually painstaking preparation, is of no particular significance in terms of its timing.[1] Unlike some of its predecessors, it was convened in accord with the relatively rigid five-year schedule that reflects the party's post-Mao obsession with institutionalization. But as the first Congress to have been convened under the exclusive jurisdiction of Deng Xiaoping's long-time protégé and "core" member in waiting, Jiang Zemin, it is nonetheless an important watershed, marking the end of an era and the possible advent of the new "Jiang era," with its own distinctive approach and policy agenda. This chapter is concerned specifically with the leadership team introduced to shape that era.

In accord with the formal delegation of authority rather than the informal co-optation of power, I begin my survey at the bottom—that is, with the Party Congress. I follow with an analysis of the Central Committee (CC) and its executive organs, the Politburo and its Standing Committee (PBSC). This analysis of the new leadership cohort will be followed by a more general discussion of the Deng-Jiang transition in what is, after all, only the People's Republic of China's (PRC's) second successful leadership succession.

## THE PARTY CONGRESS

Contrary to widespread speculation that it would convene in October, the Congress took place September 12–18, 1997. The dates of the Fifteenth National Congress were not announced until three days before its commencement. The timing could be considered fortunate because the CCP could report its largest increase in party membership since the Cultural Revolution, despite reports of ideological cynicism (see Table 3.1).

33

**Table 3.1  CCP Membership at the Time of National Congresses**

| CCP Congress | Date | Venue | Delegates | Party Membership |
|---|---|---|---|---|
| First | July–August 1921 | Shanghai | 12 | ca. 50 |
| Second | July 1922 | Shanghai | 12 | 132 |
| Third | June 1923 | Guangzhou | 30 | 432 |
| Fourth | January 1925 | Shanghai | 20 | 950 |
| Fifth | April–May 1927 | Wuhan | 80 | 57,900 |
| Sixth | June–July 1928 | Moscow | 84 | 40,000 |
| Seventh | April–June 1945 | Yenan | 544 | 1.2 million |
| Eighth | September 1956 | Beijing | 1,026 | 11 million |
| Ninth | April 1969 | Beijing | 1,512 | 22 million |
| Tenth | August 1973 | Beijing | 1,249 | 28 million |
| Eleventh | August 1977 | Beijing | 1,510 | 35 million |
| Twelfth | September 1982 | Beijing | 1,575 | 40 million |
| Thirteenth | October 1987 | Beijing | 1,936 | 46 million |
| Fourteenth | October 1992 | Beijing | 1,989 | 51 million |
| Fifteenth | September 1997 | Beijing | 2,048 | 58 million |

Personnel arrangements began in the fall of 1996, with a relative emphasis on extensive consultation. The selected delegates were subjected to intensive training and tests in advance. Nevertheless, shortly before the Congress convened, one delegate committed a serious violation of party discipline and was replaced by an alternate elected from a list of sixty special delegates.[2] The selection process for CC members began even earlier than the search for qualified Congress delegates, in August 1996. Extended consultations thus seem to have become a hallmark of official conduct under Jiang Zemin's "third delegation of leadership."

## THE CENTRAL COMMITTEE

The selection of members of the Fifteenth CC emphasized both local popularity (as measured in the electoral process) and political loyalty (that is, no nomination without the approval of the top leadership). According to reports in official party media, the vetting process traversed eight stages.[3] Beginning in August 1996, all the leading party organs made "democratic recommendations" *(minzhu tuijian)* to the Organization Department of the Party Center. The leadership proposed some 16,000 members in this fashion. Next, the party sent investigation groups *(kaochazu)* to interview more than 12,000 of those proposed to assess their qualifications. The number of potential candidates was sufficiently reduced through this investigatory process that at its Beidaihe conference, the party leadership was able to consider a preliminary list of candidates *(yubei renxuan jianyi mingdan)* for CC membership.

This list of nominees was submitted to the thirty-six CCP delegations for discussion on September 15–16, after which the Presidium of the Party Congress *(zhuxituan)* reviewed the list. On September 16–17, the list of candidates was submitted for consideration to the delegations for a preliminary election process in which the number of candidates exceeded the CC seats available *(cha e yuxuan)*. Based on the results of these preliminary elections *(yuxuan)*, the list was winnowed further by the Party Congress Presidium in a confidential "consultation" *(yunniang)*. Finally, the list was submitted on the last day to the Party Congress for "official election" *(zhengshi xuanju)*, a pro forma process in which the number of candidates corresponds to the CC seats available *(deng e xuanju)*.

The official media did not divulge the distribution of votes in the party nominating process, but since the introduction of the *cha e yuxuan* system there have been "leaks" pointing to a number of failed candidacies, as in previous Congresses. Deng Liqun, a Twelfth CC Politburo member, was unexpectedly dropped from the Politburo because of his failure to be reelected to the CC at the Thirteenth Congress. At the Fourteenth Congress, although Chongqing party secretary Xiao Yang enjoyed Deng's support for Politburo membership, he lost out in the voting for CC membership. During the preliminary elections to the Fifteenth Congress, the casualties of the electoral process fell into two categories: candidates from overrepresented regions (particularly Shanghai) and children of high cadres.

Three Shanghai CC candidates (including two vice mayors and You Guixi, head of Jiang's bodyguard contingent, originally from Shanghai) had to be dropped from full to alternate CC membership due to inadequate votes.[4] Other Shanghai candidates, such as Bai Qifang, a model engineer and old Jiang protégé, and Xu Guangchun, spokesperson for the Congress and former head of the Shanghai branch of Xinhua News Agency, could not obtain even alternate memberships. Although Huang Ju, Xu Kuangdi, and Chen Zhili were all elected to the CC, their vote tallies were relatively low: Huang got only 1,455 of 2,074 votes, the lowest of all candidates elected to the Politburo; Xu and Chen got 1,374 and 1,315 votes, respectively—less than a two-thirds majority. Overall, 5 percent of the candidates were eliminated in the elections, with a particularly severe impact on the "princelings" *(taizi)*, who included Chen Yuan, son of Chen Yun (and highly qualified, as vice chair of the Bank of China), Wang Jun (son of Wang Zhen, president of China International Trust and Investment Company), and Bo Xilai (son of Bo Yibo, mayor of Dalian). Even Deng's son Pufang was relegated to alternate CC membership.

Partly because of the consolidation of a succession leadership and partly because of the uncertainty of the electoral process, the Fifteenth CC had the highest turnover ratio in ten years, boasting 57 percent new full members and 70 percent new alternate members. Of the Fifteenth CC full members, 97.5 percent entered the CC after 1982; of more than 15 alternate members, only five entered before 1977. Before 1982, a large majority were working as engineers. The average age of the Fifteenth CC member fell from 56.3 to 55.9, virtually the same as in the previous two CCs (though markedly lower than in the Tenth through Twelfth CCs). National minority representation (11 percent) also remained constant, whereas female representation (4.1 percent of full members) declined from previous reform-era CCs (which in turn marked a decline from their Cultural Revolution zenith).

Perhaps the most striking feature of the new CC was the rise of the technocrat *(jishu guanliao),* that is, the highly educated engineer or natural scientist who adopted politics as a vocation.[5] The number of full and candidate members with a college degree comprised 318, or 92.4 percent of the total, an increase of nearly 9 percent since the Fourteenth CC. In the Party Congress as a whole, the percentage of deputies with college degrees rose from 70.7 percent in the Fourteenth Congress to 83.5 percent in 1997. The majority of those with college degrees majored in engineering and natural sciences: of the 177 full CC members with college degrees, seventy-eight (44.1 percent) majored in engineering, and twenty (11.3 percent) majored in other fields of science and technology such as geology, agronomy, biology, physics, chemistry, medicine, or economic management.

This pattern was also clear in the Secretariat, (the chief and highest operation unit of the CCP), where six of the seven members were engineers by training, including Wei Jianxing (chair of the Central Discipline Inspection Committee [CDIC]), Ding Guangen (propaganda department chair), and Zeng Qinghong (head of the CC General Office), all of whom replaced political generalists. In the Politburo as well, three-quarters of the members were engineers or senior engineers. Most of them studied at China's top technical universities, such as Qinghua and Jiaotong, followed often (29 percent) by an "internship" in the Soviet bloc.

According to studies of technocratic educational and career background in other systems, increased educational levels tend to lead to a focus on marginal, "technical" adjustments of existing systems rather than radical new departures, a rational and objective approach to problem solving, and a tendency toward political authoritarianism. Yet a technocratic socialization is by no means incompatible with informal political recruitment and patron-client factional networking. It was not coincidental that Jiang himself was an engineer, with two decades' experience working in the First Ministry of Machine Building, where he may have crossed paths with Li Lanqing, Jia Qinglin, or Luo Gan; and a stint as minister of electronics, where he befriended Li Peng, another scion of a revolutionary martyr. The "old school tie" remains a useful *guanxi* (networking) base, with the largest contingent of full CC members hailing from Qinghua University (21 percent) and the second largest from People's University. Personal patron-client links may also be established in the job of personal secretary *(mishu)*; an example is Zeng Qinghong, longtime assistant to Jiang (also a princeling, from a high-ranking CCP cadre family). Because loyalty is based on patron-client ties rather than common educational outlook, there may also be rivalries among technocratic factions. Thus, Hu Jintao is said to have his own political base among fellow Qinghua graduates that is distinct from the Zhu Rongji grouping.

Another large contingent within the CC consists of regionally based elites. Some 31.6 percent of the delegates have regional bases, marking a 20 percent increase from those elected at the Fourteenth CC. All but one of the party secretaries of the thirty-one provincial, autonomous regional, or independent city administrations had full CC seats, the exception being Hainan (where Ruan Chongwu was slated for retirement). Virtually all the governors or mayors also had CC seats, with the exception of those from Guangxi, Hainan, Inner Mongolia, Tibet, and Yunnan. These five provincial executives (Cheng Kejie, Ruan Chongwu, Wu Liji, Gyaincai Norbu, and He Zhiqiang, respectively) all exited the CC at the Fifteenth Congress. And no province has more than two full seats; Jiang's effort to select four Shanghai officials as full CC members was rejected by the deputies in the preliminary election. This factor partially explains why Jiang appointed Chen Zhili, previously a deputy party secretary in Shanghai, to be party secretary of the State Education Commission just a few days before the Fifteenth Congress. As only a member of the Shanghai delegation, she might not have gotten elected to the CC.

Although the full CC seats were distributed quite evenly among provincial leaders, alternate seats were not, and some resented the over-representation of Jiangsu and Shandong natives. There was a growing sense that provincial governments are *entitled* to CC representation and that provincial CC "representatives" might also be expected to represent provincial interests—their positions might be at risk if they did not.[6] To be sure, regional representation does not mean indigenous representation. A majority of the provincial executive leadership is from outside the province: twenty-two of the party secretaries and seventeen of the governors do not serve in the province in which they were born. In only three provinces—Guangdong, Jiangsu, and Jiangxi—are the party secretary and governor both natives. In Guangdong, the center wished to replace indigenous party secretary Xie Fei, the most important politician in his region and a Politburo member, with a non-Cantonese. Guangdong successfully resisted this proposal, but no Cantonese serve in provincial governments outside Guangdong.

It is more difficult to specify the political implications of the localization of CC membership, given that provincial representatives are expected to represent regional interests that are quite diverse and particular. Li Ruihuan is said to cultivate the support of a "local" power base, but it is difficult to see how.[7] Furthermore, it is safer to generalize about negative regional interests than positive ones. The former are likely to be skeptical of new central initiatives, particularly when they threaten local autonomy, as in Zhu Rongji's ambitious reform of the nation's financial and fiscal apparatus in 1994. In this sense, their interests may overlap those of the party's antireform "left" wing. At the same time, however, they are apt to strongly support further decentralization or devolution of power, thereby placing themselves in league with China's radical reformers and marketizers.

Military representation continued to increase, with forty-two full members (21.7 percent) and twenty candidate members (13.2 percent) of the Fifteenth CC, or 22 percent of the total (full plus candidate) CC membership—up from 18 percent of the Fourteenth CC. This continued the trend of increasing military representation that began at the Fourteenth Congress, which reversed the post-1982 trend of declining military representation. At the Twelfth CC, the People's Liberation Army (PLA) enjoyed only 16 percent representation, which sank to 13 percent at the Thirteenth CC. There has been considerable circulation of military elites, however—more than 75 percent of the forty-two military delegates to the Fifteenth CC were newly elected, and only five were promoted from alternate status in the previous CC. As in the case of regionally based civilian politicians, there is a growing sense of entitlement within the military—each of China's seven military districts has at least two full members in the Fifteenth CC. Liu Huaqing and Zhang Zhen, both 80 years of age or older, were replaced in the highest echelon of the CCP by relatively younger generals Chi Haotian (68) and Zhang Wannian (69), neither of whom gained seats on the Standing Committee.[8] The all-time low percentage of military officers on the Fifteenth Politburo (8 percent) was also notable, though the absolute number was unchanged since 1987. Among military elites, a large proportion graduated from the National Defense University or its earlier incarnations, where they usually received technocratic educations.

Among the bloc of delegates representing the central party-state, the party proper has declined in representation during the reform era relative to the central government apparatus (mainly ministers and deputy ministers). In both the Fourteenth and Fifteenth CCs, government-affiliated cadres constituted a relative majority. Representatives of the State Council held seventy of the full CC seats (36.3 percent), up from 26 percent at the Fourteenth CC and 22 percent at the Thirteenth CC. In comparison, there were only thirty-six party representatives (18.6 percent), though this represented a healthy increase from the nadir reached at the Fourteenth CC of 5 percent (versus 9 percent at the Thirteenth CC and 6 percent at the Twelfth CC). At the highest level, half of Fifteenth Politburo members (twelve) held functional positions in the civilian state administration (State Council and National People's Congress [NPC]), a 14 percent increase over the Fourteenth Politburo. In addition, all Politburo members except Zhang Wannian had administrative experience in government, where a majority were bureau directors or ministers. The political implication was that this bloc was Premier Li Peng's natural bureaucratic constituency, perhaps explaining why a politician so widely disliked remained so powerful. Only time will tell whether Li can retain this allegiance as chair of the NPC Standing Committee, but it appears that his NPC responsibilities may distance or detach him from that bloc.

## THE POLITBURO

The Politburo level, in contrast to the CC, experienced the lowest elite turnover in PRC history (despite the retirement of Qiao Shi): 67 percent of the Fourteenth Politburo was reelected to the Fifteenth Politburo. This is less surprising when viewed in the context of the unusually high turnover following Tiananmen, formally registered at the Fourteenth Congress. The death of Hu Yaobang and the fall of Zhao Ziyang and Hu Qili in 1989 left the Politburo with only fifteen members, of whom eight were dropped at the Fourteenth Congress: Song Ping (b. 1917), Yao Yilin (b. 1917), Li Ximing (b. 1926), Qin Jiwei (b. 1914), Wan Li (b. 1916), Wu Xueqian (b. 1921), Yang Rudai (b. 1926), and Yang Shangkun (b. 1907). With the exception of the orthodox Li Ximing and Zhao Ziyang protégé Yang Rudai, the others were retired due to age. This left room for twenty-two new members, or two-thirds of the total: Zhu Rongji (b. 1928), Liu Huaqing (b. 1917), Hu Jintao (b. 1942), Chen Xitong (b. 1942), Jiang Chunyun (b. 1930), Li Lanqing (b. 1932), Qian Qichen (b. 1928), Tan Shaowen (b. 1929), Wei Jianxing (b. 1931), Wu Bangguo (b. 1941), Xie Fei (b. 1932), Yang Baibing (b. 1920), Zou Jiahua (b. 1926), Wang Hanbin (b. 1927), and Wen Jiabao (b. 1942).

To begin at the top, the Fifteenth Politburo Standing Committee retained its seven-member structure, in the following hierarchical order: Jiang Zemin (71), Li Peng (68), Zhu Rongji (68, moving up from fifth place), Li Ruihuan (63), Hu Jintao (54), Wei Jianxing (66), and Li Lanqing (65). The two new members are Wei Jianxing and Li Lanqing, both promoted from the Politburo to replace retiring Qiao Shi and Admiral Liu Huaqing. Wei Jianxing, an engineer and returned Soviet student, has chaired the CDIC for the past five years, where he supervised the investigation and indictment of Chen Xitong. His promotion may signal the determination to give greater priority to the campaign against corruption. Li Lanqing, a Shanghainese economist and former minister of foreign trade (and presumed Jiang protégé) was named vice premier, and Zhu Rongji was named "executive vice premier of the State Council," perhaps signaling an intention to move both Li and Zhu to the positions of premier and executive vice premier when these positions fell vacant at the March 1998 NPC session. Many analysts were surprised by the omissions of Jiang protégés Ding Guan'gen, Wu Bangguo, Huang Ju, and Zhang Wannian, whose ambitions were apparently frustrated by the results of the preliminary elections; Ding's hard cultural line was particularly unpopular.

The PB has twenty-two members, twenty-four if two alternates are included. In addition to the seven PBSC members already mentioned are Ding Guangen (68), Tian Jiyun (68), Li Changchun (53), Li Tieying (61), Wu Bangguo (56), Wu Guanzheng (59), Chi Haotian (68), Zhang Wannian (69), Luo Gan (62), Jiang Chunyun (67), Jia Qinglin (57), Qian Qichen (69), Huang Ju (59), Wen Jiabao (55), and Xie Fei (65). The two alternates are Zeng Qinghong (58) and Wu Yi (58). The seven new Politburo members are Gen. Chi Haotian, Jia Qinglin (party secretary and mayor of Beijing), Li Changchun (party secretary of Henan province shifted to Guangdorg during the second half of 1997), Luo Gan (general secretary of the State Council), Wen Jiabao (former alternate Politburo member and member of the Secretariat), Wu Guanzheng (party secretary of Shandong province), and Gen. Zhang Wannian. There were also two new alternate PB members: Zeng Qinghong (director of the General Office of the CCP) and Wu Yi (minister of foreign trade and the only woman sitting on the Politburo). These replaced retiring members Zou Jiahua, Yang Baibing, Tan Shaowen (deceased), Chen Xitong (purged and indicted), and Wang Hanbin.

Rumors before the Fifteenth Party Congress anticipated emergence of a powerful Jiang clique, but these plans were thrown awry by the problems caused by Qiao Shi, specifically his opposition to Jiang's nomination of Huang Ju as secretary of the CDIC. Consequently, Jiang was obliged to retain such people who usefully opposed Qiao as Li Ruihuan and to make other concessions, such as bringing people from other provinces into the ruling circle. Within the Politburo, five members now have regional bases: Jia Qinglin from Beijing, Huang Ju from Shanghai, Wu Guanzhen from Shandong, Xie Fei from Guangdong, and Li Changchun from Henan. Jiang's attempts to promote Xu Kuangdi (mayor of Shanghai) to the Politburo or to secretary of the State Science Commission were frustrated by the preliminary elections, as were plans to promote Wu Bangguo to the Standing Committee. Because he failed to make the PBSC, Wu had to forfeit his ambition to become first deputy premier in 1998 to Li Lanqing. Still, Jiang enjoys a comfortable majority within the Politburo; those members of that body owing their ascendancy to his support include Ding

Guangen, Zeng Qinghong, Huang Ju, Wu Bangguo, and Jia Qinglin, and those beholden to Li Peng are Luo Gan, Wu Yi, and Jiang Chunyun. Tian Jiyun, Wei Jianxing, and Hu Jintao are political "orphans," so to speak, of Qiao Shi, Zhao Ziyang, and Song Ping, respectively.[9]

In terms of age, the average ages of the PBSC, Politburo, and Secretariat members at the Fifteenth Congress (65.1, 62.9, and 62.9, respectively) are younger than those of the Twelfth Congress, but older (in all three organs) than those of the Thirteenth or the Fourteenth Congresses. In addition, the range of variation within the cohort is narrow: the PBSC average age is about a year older than that of the Politburo, and the PBSC members of 1987 and 1992 were younger than the current members. This may cause problems for political succession in the future because all three leadership organs will be occupied by people 68–70 years old (and on the threshold of retirement, unless the current rule is rescinded) by the next Party Congress.

## SUCCESSION CRISIS

To all appearances, there was no succession "crisis," which may, however, only be a tribute to the skill with which it was handled. In any event, the Fifteenth Congress, specifically the retirement of Qiao Shi, marked its successful resolution. Jiang Zemin, Qiao Shi, Li Peng, Chen Xitong, and Li Ruihuan were all part of a leadership cohort selected during the terminal phase of the Deng regime and were of roughly equivalent age, experience, and status. Deng opted to place Jiang in the position of "core" and did not abandon him as readily as he had Hu Yaobang and Zhao Ziyang, despite explicit misgivings about Jiang's tilt to the left during Deng's tour of the south *(nanxun)* during the run-up to the Fourteenth Congress in 1992. These misgivings, it now seems clear, provided the basis for Qiao's challenge to Jiang during the most politically sensitive phase of Deng's "retirement" and for Zhao Ziyang's post-Deng challenge to Jiang, neither of which were resolved until after Deng's death.[10]

**Table 3.2  Average Ages for PBSC, Politburo, and Secretariat Members**

| Level | Twelfth CC | Thirteenth CC | Fourteenth CC | Fifteenth CC |
|---|---|---|---|---|
| PBSC | 73.8 | 63.6 | 63.4 | 65.1 |
| Politburo | 71.8 | 64.0 | 61.9 | 62.9 |
| Secretariat | 63.7 | 56.2 | 59.3 | 62.9 |

Jiang Zemin's political priority during the early phase of his long "regency" was to avoid the error of his two immediate predecessors in this position, Hu Yaobang and Zhao Ziyang. Both of these men became so closely identified with the "radical reform" grouping that they alienated the powerful "left" wing, then under the leadership of Chen Yun and Deng Liqun, with ultimately fatal political repercussions. Jiang's shift leftward was shrewd in terms of balance-of-power considerations as well because Deng's position had been severely attenuated both by Tiananmen and by his unduly harsh reaction to it. This strategy, however, exposed Jiang to criticism from the right, and in the course of Deng's southern tour his complaints about Jiang's conservatism mobilized a revival of the residual reform bloc, led by Yang Shangkun—who reportedly proposed during a Politburo meeting that Qiao Shi or Tian Jiyun be considered to replace Jiang as general secretary.[11] Jiang subsequently moved rightward to avoid a confrontation with Deng, a compromise that earned Deng's acquiescence at the Fourteenth Congress in the purge of the "Yang family clique." Yet Qiao Shi survived and continued in his public statements to differentiate himself subtly from Jiang. For example, he stressed the "rule of law," while Jiang was emphasizing the role of the party "core" and telling people to "attach importance to politics."[12]

As NPC Standing Committee chair, Qiao continued Peng Zhen's efforts to strengthen this forum—albeit in a far more progressive and substantive direction. He allowed the NPC to send inspection teams to provincial people's congresses to check on the implementation of laws, for example, and discouraged the prevailing practice of allowing retired state and party officials to fill senior NPC positions. Notwithstanding his career in the security apparatus, Qiao also proposed that the party's system of internal spies and personnel files *(dangan)* be disbanded. Meanwhile, Jiang's leftist line was revived at the sixth plenum of the Fourteenth Congress Central Committee (October 7–10, 1996), resolution "Concerning Several Important Issues on Strengthening the Building of Socialist Spiritual Civilization" and announced a special committee to guide in the building of such a civilization with Jiang Zemin as head and Ding Guangen (the CC propaganda department chair and outspoken leftist) as deputy chair. This resulted in a "freeze" on cultural policy since late 1996 that aroused considerable ire in the intellectual and artistic community.

Then, in the spring of 1997, Jiang Zemin suddenly lurched rightward again. In his May 29, 1997, speech to the Central Party School, he presented the first draft of his Fifteenth National Congress Report to the party leadership. In it, he proposed that China should promote the joint-stock system, regroup its state-owned assets, and set up multiprovincial, multi-industrial, multiownership, and multinational conglomerates. Though Jiang omitted any reference to political reform, his speech entailed a significant shift from his previous position on state ownership as a defining criterion of socialism.[13] We may only speculate about Jiang's motives, but the effect was to ingratiate the reform constituency and hence isolate Qiao Shi, who conspicuously failed to attend. Jiang's initiatives, which corresponded substantively to the thinking of China's best-known economist Wu Jinglian, were then ballyhooed in a national publicity campaign.[14]

Conflict between Jiang and Qiao apparently intensified during the Beidaihe meetings (which began in late July and ended August 18, 1997), when they were unable to agree upon high-level personnel changes. The origin of this conflict was Li Peng's wish to assume Qiao's position upon his own forced retirement from the premiership due to a two-term limit. At the seventh (expanded) plenum of the Fourteenth Congress, which took place in Beijing in early September to make final preparations for the Fifteenth Congress, Jiang reported that the PBSC had regrettably been unable to reach consensus on a new "slate," thereby implicitly throwing the onus upon Qiao. Bo Yibo (or, according to some versions, Li Ruihuan) then raised the issue of age limits, leading to a decision that, beginning with the Fifteenth Congress, an age limit of 70 be adopted for the Politburo. Although this decision was established in the wake of the superannuation of Liu Huaqing and Zou Jiahua, it notably excepted only the indispensable "core" of Jiang Zemin (who had just turned 71).

This resolution, expanded to include an age limit of 65 for provincial and ministerial officials, won unanimous acclaim, ostensibly including even Qiao's, even though such limits had hitherto been based upon terms rather than age and applied to government and not party positions.[15] Unexpectedly, Qiao (73) and Liu Huaqing (81) then announced their intention to retire not only from the Politburo but also the Central Committee (CC); their names, along with Zhang Zhen (83) and Zou Jiahua (71), were hence dropped from the recommended short list of candidates given to the delegates. Retiring with Qiao from the Ninth NPC Standing Committee (March 5, 1998) were six NPC vice chairs, giving Li Peng room to install his own team.[16]

In this manner, the postmortem succession crisis was handled far more deftly than the premortem succession crises surrounding Hu Yaobang or Zhao Ziyang, not to mention the crises involving Liu Shaoqi or Lin Biao. Its resolution was so smooth that even spokesmen for the party leadership were apparently left in the dark, as the customary press conference held to introduce the new leadership abruptly canceled a question-answer forum. The elimination of Qiao has clearly redounded to Jiang's political advantage. He quickly moved to consolidate his "core" position with the promotion of new initiatives for economic reform and with a round of international diplomacy to strengthen China's regional and international standing, highlighted by a long-awaited state visit to the United States. In addition, there has been a publicity blitz on Jiang's behalf amounting to at least a minor cult of personality.[17]

Yet resolution of the leadership crisis—though perhaps too short-lived to warrant firm conclusions—has also belied a number of premature inferences about the complexion of China's new leadership:

1. The "end of strongman leadership" thesis has proved only partially true. This was not a "game to win all or to lose all" because Qiao received some concessions to reward him for playing by the rules. For example, Li vetoed Qiao's nomination of reformer Tian Jiyun as Qiao's replacement but allowed him to continue as NPC vice chair and full Politburo member. Moreover, Qiao protégé Wei Jianxing remains chair of the CDIC, overriding Jiang's wish to replace him with Shanghai party secretary Huang Ju. Even so, the process otherwise fits the pattern of a classic power struggle with clear-cut winners and losers.

2. Similarly, predictions of the advent of "collective leadership" following the demise of the charismatic generation of revolutionary veterans seem to have been based on faulty premises. Although even Jiang Zemin would no doubt agree that he lacks the stature of Mao Zedong or Deng, he does not need to compete with men of such stature, who have now faded from the scene. Their charismatic brilliance is thus irrelevant to his bid to establish hierarchical authority over his own generation of epigones.

3. The fact that Jiang had, as he put it, "never done military experience and ha[d] no experience in this area" turned out not to be fatal because neither Qiao nor Li nor any conceivable alternative contenders for power had any more military credentials than Jiang did.[18] Jiang's post-1989 retirement of thirty aging generals and promotion of thirty new generals, his relatively generous budgetary treatment of the PLA since Tiananmen, his frequent inspection visits to military bases, and the promotion of a back-to-the-barracks form of military leadership emphasizing technological expertise rather than political initiative all seem to have facilitated a depoliticization of the PLA so successful that Jiang could dispense with any active generals on the PBSC for the first time since the early Maoist years.

4. Finally, the assumption that because Jiang has fathered no significant new policy initiatives in the eight years since becoming "core," he is somehow politically inconsequential, likewise seems to be based on false premises, confusing policy with power. Jiang's emphasis has been on consolidating power, a process in which a high-profile policy resume may be of limited utility.

What, then, can legitimately be inferred from this most recently elapsed succession? It *may* prove true that the CCP leadership *as a whole* is weaker than during the Mao or Deng eras, due to the delegitimization of Marxist-Leninist ideology, the difficulties of reform (growing inequality, budget deficits, corruption), and the advent of the market as an alternative source of economic direction. But not necessarily: the regime has also been bolstered by unprecedented growth rates despite the collapse of rival Communist Party states and by a dazzlingly successful foreign policy (plus a generous dollop of luck) that has resulted in the elimination of all serious national security threats and in the retrocession *(huigui)* of Hong Kong and Macao. In his political report to the Congress on the general theme of "building a socialist state ruled by law," Jiang tried to exploit these advantages, carving out a middle-of-the-road position that endorsed reform but in a more cautious and contained manner than Deng, promoting further economic reforms while reducing political reform to a list of clichés,[19] emphasizing urban industrial reform while neglecting agriculture, and promoting shareholding but with elaborate safeguards designed to avoid financial speculation and ensure continued party control.[20] To the intellectuals he promised more emancipation of the mind, removing the *tifa* (slogan) "oppose bourgeois liberalization" from the work report for the first time since the Twelfth Congress.[21]

Regarding foreign policy, for the first time Jiang encouraged active engagement in multilateral cooperation, departing from Deng's focus on bilateral, divide-and-conquer strategies. Jiang devoted increased attention to Taiwan policy during the last four Congresses. Although he reaffirmed his January 1995 "eight points" and insisted on the "one-China principle," Jiang introduced an interesting concession by referring to the PRC as "the main part of China," implicitly acknowledging that there is another part of China not under its control. Jiang's announcement of an armed forces reduction of 500,000 troops was probably aimed at the international audience (since 1994, PLA forces have shrunk below 3 million, according to the Institute for International and Strategic Studies in London, but this does not include People's Armed Police forces or militia).[22]

Though the war on corruption continued, as indicated by the heavy emphasis in Jiang's report and by the decision to prosecute Chen Xitong, no new institutional countermeasures or policy initiatives were adopted to deal with the problem. Meanwhile, the leadership's ideological delegitimation was finessed by trumpeting the "theory" of Deng Xiaoping *(Deng Xiaoping lilun)*, which has been written into the constitution as the party's guiding ideology, for the first time transcending the ideological commitment to Mao Zedong Thought made at the Seventh Party Congress.[23] Jiang's own remarks are also being collected and enshrined in the form of "Jiang Zeming expositions," so as to create a hierarchically structured theoretical framework of Mao Zedong Thought, Deng Xiaoping Theory, and Jiang Zemin's expositions.[24]

## CONCLUSION

Has the recently completed transfer of power further developed the institutionalization of successions processes in general in the PRC? Although firm conclusions would be premature, positive indications include the confirmation of a fixed term of office (e.g., Li Peng's retirement as premier), more explicit procedural criteria of selection and appointment (e.g., age limits, educational credentials, and demonstration of professional competence), and apparently open discussion of the succession issue in a formal group context rather than decisions in secret cabals.[25] As "the leadership core of the third generation," Jiang Zemin had no direct experience of the revolutionary seizure of power and rose in the regime hierarchy not because he learned how to play the power game in the context of a minority party in a hostile environment, but as he himself said, as a career bureaucrat in a ruling party: "I climbed the stairs step by step. I worked for 23 years at the basic level and 19 years in leadership organs. My experience extends to the Ministry of Machine Building, electronic industry, electrical construction and import-export work."[26] The "winner-take-all" mentality that framed the power struggles of Mao and Deng may be less pronounced in the case of Jiang and his cohort.[27]

Although Jiang's accession to power thus appears in striking contrast to the abortive successions of Hu Yaobang and Zhao Ziyang, the comparison is perhaps not altogether valid because a succession may not have been previously intended at the time in question. In fact, a closer analysis of the three cases actually reveals a fundamental structural isomorphism. All are deliberate premortem succession arrangements in which there are two principal players: the incumbent leader and the heir apparent. In addition, there is a sort of "Greek chorus" consisting of the two dozen or so top-level elites qualified to participate in succession discussions and to advise the two principals. In this central bilateral drama, the heir apparent is expected to prove his political mettle in a kind of advanced internship, while the incumbent observes from behind the scenes and offers advice and correctives. The internship is of prolonged, indefinite duration and the lessons ill-defined and arbitrary, yet under no circumstances may the intern question the authority of the incumbent.

Though there is no mass audience, this little drama does not take place in a vacuum. It takes place in a variable international and domestic economic environment, which may enhance the credibility of either the incumbent (if favorable) or the successor (if unfavorable). Because the central drama is so closed and slow-moving, the temptation of the Greek chorus to kibitz, even to challenge established succession arrangements, is sometimes irresistible.

This basic structure was the same in all three cases, as well as in the succession of Hua Guofeng in 1976 and the abortive successions of Liu

Shaoqi and Lin Biao during the Cultural Revolution. The immediate socioeconomic environment of peace and burgeoning prosperity in 1997 might be deemed more favorable than the ambiance of, say, the Liu Shaoqi or Zhao Ziyang succession crises, but the context was largely fortuitous. At the outset of Jiang's internship, the outlook was by general consensus extremely bleak, and even after Deng spurred a revival of growth and reform in 1992, the resulting inflation could have been a political liability. In addition, many have noted that Jiang's regency was much longer than that of Hua Guofeng, giving Jiang nearly eight years to establish himself. This is true, but it would be a mistake to say that unsuccessful candidates such as Liu Shaoqi (1959–1966) or Hu Yaobang (1982–1987) fell from lack of time to consolidate their positions. Although Jiang did succeed in building a strong united front with the incumbent generation, in contrast to Hu or Zhao, this unity hardly immunized him from challenges, as indicated by the successive fall of the "Yang brothers gang"—Chen Xitong and Qiao Shi. It has also been argued that after 1989, Deng could no longer politically afford to dump an heir apparent, but the same logic should have prevented Mao from going after Lin Biao following the purge of Liu Shaoqi or Deng from sacking Zhao Ziyang. Certainly, it did not inhibit Deng from criticizing Jiang.

If there is no basic structural difference, why was Jiang's succession so much smoother? I believe it was essentially due to Jiang's ability to learn from recent political history how to play this privileged but very tricky role. First, recognizing the key part that incumbent-generation elites had played in derailing the candidacies of Hu and Zhao, Jiang endeavored first and foremost to ingratiate himself with the likes of Chen Yun, Wang Zhen, and Bo Yibo.[28] Second, when his kudos in this direction went so far as to arouse the misgivings of his original patron,[29] Jiang promptly jumped back on the reform bandwagon, never mobilizing his own constituency but making repeated self-criticisms and even offering to resign in favor of his most obvious rival.[30] Thus he courted and ultimately regained Deng's favor. Third, rather than articulate his own distinctive platform of cutting-edge reforms, Jiang avoided identification with new policy initiatives. He nonetheless remained in the public eye by preoccupying himself vigorously with his ceremonial duties: changing in and out of PLA uniform, civilian suit, or Mao jacket as the occasion demanded, Jiang undertook more inspection tours during these years than any other Politburo member. By 1992 he had toured each of China's provinces, autonomous regions, and province-level cities at least once, including pilgrimages to Mao's cave in Yenan and to the Jinggangshan base area. Though this strategy alienated him from the intellectuals, who considered him empty and "slick" *(hua),* it deprived prospective rivals or challengers of any substantive target to shoot at.[31]

Thus, although certainly more consistent with the original premortem scenario than the succession of Deng Xiaoping after Mao Zedong's death,

Jiang Zemin's accession was not, in my view, the predictable outcome of well-institutionalized formal procedures so much as the mastery of subtle informal rules of the game still being contrived while the game was in progress. This does not mean, however, that institutionalization is not taking place. First, ideology has all but disappeared as a criterion for discriminating among succession candidates or ousting losers like Chen Xitong or Qiao Shi. In this way the latter, though still shut out of the ruling circle, are not necessarily cast into political oblivion but have some incentive to play by the rules and bow out gracefully. Second, though Jiang did not allow formal procedural criteria to constrain his own freedom to maneuver, he usually legitimated his political decisions in terms of procedural rationality and took care not to publicly violate existing procedural conventions.[32]

All things being equal, then, I expect that Jiang will indeed retire as CCP general secretary at the Sixteenth Party Congress in 2002, in accord with the "rule" invented to legitimate the removal of Qiao Shi. He should be joined by his generational cohort, consisting of the leading troika (Jiang, Li Peng, and Zhu Rongji) and nearly two-thirds of the full Politburo members.[33] Deng Xiaoping's generation demonstrated, however, that retirement need not be politically disabling. Because the current senior generation will wish to engineer their own succession so that they can still supervise their appointed "interns," Jiang may well retain his chairmanship of the Central Military Commission, Zhu Rongji may move up to the NPC chairmanship, Li Peng may become chief of state, and so forth.

This remarkably smooth transition and the passing of nearly the entire "shadow cabinet" of revolutionary veterans has left Jiang and his "third generation" in a strong position to make whatever distinctive contribution to Chinese political history they may have had in mind. Although substantive policy commitments once were a liability, since the succession Jiang has clearly identified himself with Deng's reformist legacy, launching at the Fifteenth Congress a bold, indeed risky proposal for reform of the nation's urban industrial base—a task for which the technocratic career credentials of the third generation leadership seem ideally suited. It is to be carried out within essentially the extant political-administrative framework, notwithstanding the restructuring and downsizing introduced at the March 1998 Ninth NPC, and is squarely ensconced in Deng's legacy of economic reform and political authoritarianism. The restructuring per se may be both feasible and worthwhile. Despite the vulnerability of the Korean *chaebol* to the Asian financial crisis, China's great power ambitions will surely require just such a large-scale, heavy industrial sector—a requirement that "growing out of the plan" neglects—and the relatively conservative CCP efforts to consolidate state-owned enterprises (SOEs) appear more promising than the approach taken in many of the former Soviet bloc countries.[34]

The prospects for this reform depend on how vigorously it is implemented, which is not yet entirely clear (see Chapter 8). The initial proposals were hedged by so many conditions and qualifications that at least two alternative outcomes are possible. Under the first scenario, the treadmill option, this reform, like its predecessors in 1994–1996, will remain frustratingly incomplete. The reforms will be so constrained by concern for maintaining party control and preserving social stability that there will be no effective break from the status quo. In the wake of the Asian financial crisis and its likely constraints on capital and exports, this scenario is least risky and perhaps most likely: Jiang and his team continue to run in place until their tenure elapses in 2002, then retire in favor of younger, bolder leaders. Despite the hemorrhaging of many SOEs, China continues to grow rapidly without entering the World Trade Organization, unemployment and corruption remain within manageable bounds, and the nation has a chance to catch its breath after the turbulent reigns of Mao and Deng. The problem with this scenario, from Jiang's point of view, is that he will become a colorless, historically forgone transitional figure. The systemic problem is that such a period of protracted passivity and policy drift will tend to erode the leadership credibility of a revolutionary party.

The alternative scenario, genuine reform, is fraught with much greater uncertainty, but some preliminary predictions seem warranted. First, it seems likely to entail much higher urban unemployment at a time when China still lacks an efficient labor market or comprehensive social security net. According to Michel Bonnin, writing in Chapter 9 of this book, by mid-1997 there were 5.56 million registered unemployed. By the end of the year, there were 11 million laid-off workers (*xiagang zhigong*) and 11.9 million "workers in difficulty." Under such circumstances the number of those who are (or perceive themselves to be) worse off under reform may come to exceed those who are better off, creating a risk of social instability. Second, the recently announced experiments with property rights reform, however economically successful, seem likely to generate enhanced opportunities for cadre corruption, always a highly inflammatory phenomenon. Third, the current regime's rigid insistence on the bureaucratic authoritarian status quo and on beefing up the apparatus of public security repression to deal with any dissent from the top down lowers the risk of protest while at the same time removing any "safety valve" through which dissent might be articulated and dealt with in some reasonable fashion. Taken together, these factors create a rather explosive mix. These risks may be worth taking if SOE reform offers a realistic prospect of gains in terms of gross domestic product (GDP) growth and the technological upgrading of China's large-scale heavy industrial base, an issue still under active debate.

Although generally endorsing "political structure reform," the new leadership team has announced no specific plans beyond extending the ambit of the "rule of law" and possibly expanding village electoral reform to the rural township *(xiang)* and county *(xian)* echelons.[35] Yet the envisioned economic reforms also have indirect political implications of quite far-reaching significance. The downsizing of government and the reduction in numbers of state cadres, though driven by budgetary rather than political considerations, would make trade unions, youth and women's organizations, and science and technology, education, culture, sanitation, and sports institutions independent of the government and free to operate on their own funding. Already, according to a document disseminated by an incensed Deng Liqun in 1995, "the embryo of a bureaucratic bourgeoisie and a comprador bourgeois has emerged. . . . There are now (semi-independent) newspapers, including *Nongovernmental Entrepreneurs Daily*, *Factory and Managers Daily*, that directly reflect their interests and demands."[36] Meanwhile, many intellectuals took the view that the debate on political structure reform that was aborted in 1989 might gradually resume in the context of the post-Congress "thaw," to assume a quite prominent position on the agenda of the next Party Congress. This expectation has not yet been fulfilled by late 1999.

## NOTES

I wish to thank Hung-mao Tien and Yun-han Chu for their helpful comments on an earlier draft of this chapter.

1. Jiang presented a draft version of his report to leading cadres at the Party School on May 29. The draft was then circulated among some 4,000 people of diverse provenance to accommodate the interests and objections of varied political forces. Several key points of the draft were deliberately leaked to Chinese media beginning in early summer by Jiang's advisers; at the end of August the report was finally discussed at a session of the Politburo held at Beidaihe.

2. *Guangjiaojing* (Wide angle), September 1997, 6–7.

3. Cf. *Renmin ribao* (People's Daily), September 18–19, 1997.

4. *Qianshao yuekan* (Advance guard monthly), October 1997, 16–17.

5. Cf. Lee, *From Revolutionary Cadres to Party Technocrats;* also Li and White, "The Fifteenth Central Committee."

6. Wan Xueyuan, former head of the Communist Youth League in Shanghai, was appointed by the center to be governor of Zhejiang in 1993 but was then rejected in a legally required election by the Zhejiang People's Congress. Wan subsequently was appointed director of the Bureau of Foreign Experts, a much lower position.

7. See Liu, "The Current Power Struggle in the CCP," 68–91.

8. Military representation in the Politburo has declined from 40 percent in the Ninth Congress, to 31 percent in the Eleventh, to 11 percent in the Thirteenth, and to 8 percent in the Fifteenth Congress.

9. Even so, Wen Jianbao shifted his allegiance to Zhao Ziyang upon Hu's political disablement, even accompanying him when he met with the protesters at Tiananmen. With Tian Jiyun, Wen is among the few surviving Zhao protégés.

10. In a report impossible to corroborate, Zhao Ziyang, after unsuccessfully appealing to attend Deng Xiaoping's funeral or the Hong Kong reversion ceremonies, is said to have sent a letter to the Fifteenth Congress calling upon the leadership to reassess the June 4, 1989, Tiananmen incident. Although the authorities successfully blocked dissemination of the letter at the Congress and denied its authenticity or even existence, rumors have spread. Zhao was reportedly placed under strictest surveillance, losing his freedom to golf or entertain friends, even having his phone lines cut; some two dozen guards were permanently stationed outside his gate. *China Focus* 5, no. 11 (November 1, 1997).

11. Xia, "Qiao Shi xiatai neimu," 10–13.

12. For example, in a speech at the reception of a German delegation in September 1996, Qiao Shi emphasized the overriding importance of opposing the left. Jiang Zemin reacted swiftly, informing the *Renmin ribao* editorial staff that Qiao's remarks represented only his personal opinions, not those of the Standing Committee or the center. Xia, "Qiao Shi," 10.

13. At a 1991 conference marking the seventh decade of the CCP's founding, Jiang gave the following definition: "A socialist economy with Chinese characteristics must primarily hold fast to the principle of socialist public ownership of the materials of production . . . must primarily practice the principle of 'to each according to his work' . . . must establish an economic system and operative mechanisms that are adapted to the development of the socialist planned commodity economy, and to the combination of the planned economy with regulation of the economy by market forces." But in his political report to the Fifteenth Congress, Jiang reneged: "The public ownership system can be manifested in a variety of forms" and "the stock system . . . can be used by capitalism, and can also be used by socialism. You cannot make generalizations about the stock system falling into the category of public ownership and private ownership." The shift was justified in terms of Deng's "principles," now lauded as "the party's guiding ideology."

14. *Qiu shi*, the official party journal, in issue 14, carried a commentary describing Jiang as having the "revolutionary courage and great boldness of vision of a proletarian politician" in making this speech. On July 13, *Renmin ribao* and other official media reprinted the article, burdensomely entitled "Hold High the Great Banner of Deng Xiaoping Theory for an All-Round Advancement of the Cause of Building Socialism with Chinese Characteristics into the 21st Century." Yet many on the left were disturbed by the ideological implications of shareholding and there was a spirited media debate until the Fifteenth Congress, which seems to have resolved the matter.

15. For different versions of the power struggle, cf. *Jingbao yuekan* (Mirror monthly), October 1997, 26–27; *Zhengming* (Contending), October 1997, 79; and *South China Morning Post,* October 9, 1997. A policy so spontaneously approved naturally had exceptions. At the provincial and ministerial level, three nominees exceeded the age limit: Zhang Quanjing, head of the CC organization department; Shu Huaide, deputy secretary of the Central Commission of Political Science and Law; and Han Zhubin, minister of railways. Zhang and Shu were then withdrawn, but Han (who has a Shanghai background) was made deputy secretary of the CDIC. At the senior level there were two prominent exceptions: Jiang Zemin and Hua Guofeng.

16. That team included Wang Hanbin, Ni Zhifu, Chen Muhua, Fei Xiaotong, Sun Qimeng, and Liu Jieqiong. They are slated to be replaced by Vice Premier Zou Jiahua and State Councilors Li Tieying, Li Guixian, and Peng Peiyun, respectively. Li Tieying will assume Wang's role in charge of legislation; Peng Peiyun will

replace Chen Muhua in charge of women's affairs. *South China Morning Post*, January 3, 1998, 7.

17. On September 28, the *Renmin ribao* editorial stated: "Any collective leadership must have a core, and it will be unreliable if it has no core." According to *Xinhua*, Jiang "remained unruffled in the face of turmoil and coped with the situation calmly in the manner of a statesman who 'remains calm before the collapse of Mount Tai.'"

18. Xi Wen, in *Zhongguo zhi chun* (China spring), May 1991, 15.

19. Jiang's work report includes a separate chapter on political reform, but it is basically a summation of old clichés: develop democracy with Chinese characteristics, enhance the legal system, enforce separation of government and enterprise, reduce and simplify the bureaucracy, perfect democratic monitoring systems, maintain stability and unity, and so forth. He also mentions strengthening the NPC and adopting a cooperative system of multiple political parties. The bottom line is that political reform must center on invigorating the CCP leadership.

20. China will continue to control the 1,000 large SOEs while adopting a more flexible policy toward the others. Shareholding will be permitted, but the regime is cracking down on any stock exchanges other than those at Shanghai and Shenzhen. The practice of allowing staff members and workers to hold shares of enterprises, once popular across the country, has been stopped for fear it will lead to loss of state assets and trigger financial problems. Experiments in this respect were permitted only in twenty-four selected foreign economic and trade enterprises for the first year. After an inspection tour of Zhucheng, Zhu Rongji reportedly instructed that increment equity participation, not stock sales, should be the goal of the stock cooperative program.

Li Lanqing, who is in charge of foreign trade and economic cooperation, issued twelve requirements in the summer of 1996 for experiments at selected points: (1) enterprises selected for experiments should, after examination, be changed into limited liability companies; (2) the recruitment of shareholders should be confined to full-time staff and workers in the company; (3) the guiding position of the state sector should be insured; (4) the difference between the amount of shares purchased by management and those purchased by workers should not be too big; (5) enterprises should not be able to give shares to staff and workers as presents; (6) shareholding staff members and workers could only have stock certificates with their names on them, and such certificates should be managed in a concentrated manner; (7) shares held by staff and workers could not be listed or traded; (8) companies should buy back shares held by staff and workers upon their departure from the company; (9) stock ownership certificates purchased in the name of legal persons could not be redistributed to individuals; (10) shares of staff members and workers should not have fixed dividends; (11) boards of directors should be established; and (12) corporations should maintain balance sheets and profit and loss statements and establish boards of supervisors. *Ming Bao*, July 26, 1997, a10. Li Peng and Zhu Rongji warned regional leaders again after the Fifteenth Congress not to "kick up a whirlwind" of forming joint-stock companies or selling off state assets. *South China Morning Post*, September 17, 1997, 7.

21. This is significant, for it was Deng himself who initiated this *tifa* (slogan) in an informal speech to propaganda officials on July 17, 1981, denouncing a tendency toward "bourgeois liberalization on the ideological, literary and artistic fronts," the core of which was to oppose Communist leadership. He made these comments after students from certain universities ran for district-level delegates to the NPC, when the campaign against *kulian* (the movie script "Bitter Love") was

in full swing. Since then, this has been an ideological staple, included in the work reports of the Twelfth, Thirteenth, and Fourteenth Congresses. Yet neither Jiang's message to the nation after Deng's passing nor his eulogy at Deng's memorial service mentioned either "opposing bourgeois liberalization" or the June 3–4, 1989, incident.

22. It is important to remember, however, that coincident with the downsizing of the PLA has been the advent (in 1983) and subsequent growth of the People's Armed Police. Estimated to total some 600,000 in 1989, the PAP has subsequently grown to around 1 million and is well armed. Report by Chong-pin Lin, as summarized in *MAC News Briefing*.

23. Plainly, Mao has been eclipsed by this move, as indicated by rudimentary content analysis. Whereas Jiang made forty references to Deng Xiaoping's theory and twenty-two to Deng Xiaoping in his report, he mentioned Mao Zedong only four times and made fourteen references to Mao Zedong Thought.

24. The latter include Jiang's "five remarks" on the PLA; his "four principles" regarding cultural and propaganda work; the "three strict" requirements for cadre development; the "eight points" for Taiwan policy; the "four self" regarding anti-corruption work; the "theory of twelve relationships" on the economy; the "theory of running the country in accordance with law" on the legal system; the sixty-four-character spirit of starting an enterprise in a spiritual civilization; the "theory of patriotism" for united front work; the remarks made in Shanghai and Changchun regarding SOEs; and the "theory of new international relations" on foreign policy. *Guangjiaojing* (Hong Kong), October 16, 1996, 6, 9.

25. The key meeting was reportedly an expanded meeting of the Politburo convened just before the convention of the Congress in early September, at which Jiang mobilized group pressure to force the resignation of Qiao Shi.

26. V. Jin Di, in *Guangjiaojing* (Hong Kong), July 1989, 13 ff.

27. I wish to thank Peter Lee of the Chinese University of Hong Kong for this insight.

28. This ingratiation was achieved not through policy reversals but via ideological rhetoric and elaborate personal attentiveness. As the child of a revolutionary martyr who unequivocally supported the Tiananmen crackdown both during and after June 4 (without being personally involved), Jiang already had a good start, and he benefited from his alliance with Li Peng, long a favorite of the revolutionary veterans.

29. By the fall of 1991 Deng had reportedly come to feel that Jiang exercised too little initiative and enterprise in reform policy, that he was "excessively careful and anxious," had moved too far to the "left," and "could be somewhat bolder." See Tang, in *Kaifang* (Opening), 16.

30. Deng undertook his historic *nanxun* from January 18 to February 21, 1992. Jiang's course reversal was immediate. In his speech at the Spring Festival on February 4, he conspicuously called for strengthening reform. In March 9–10 he convened a Politburo session in support of Deng's *nanxun* platform, warning in particular against the danger of "leftist" deviation. In his June 9, 1992, speech to the Central Party School Jiang again criticized "leftist" deviation and echoed Deng in pronouncing a market economy to be neither socialist nor capitalist.

According to the Hong Kong media, Jiang offered to resign at least three times prior to the Fourteenth Congress. After the Fifth Session of the Seventh NPC in April 1992, Jiang suggested at a Politburo session that he not be renominated, recommending Qiao Shi for the general secretary position. In July 1992 he wrote a long letter to Deng saying he did not consider himself qualified, that he had indeed gone too far to the "left," and that he wished to resign. And in August 1992 at Beidaihe, he again recommended Qiao Shi as his successor and offered to step down. He also made self-criticisms in Politburo meetings in March and June 1992. *Zhengming* (Contending), November 1992, 8.

31. This strategy was reportedly the brainchild of Jiang's confidant Zeng Qinghong, a deputy party secretary in Shanghai who accompanied him to Beijing upon his promotion. Pointing to the fate of Hu and Zhao, who remained in the capital and spearheaded reform on the front line, Zeng advised him to remove himself from the strife-torn capital and place someone else (Zhu Rongji) on the front line to assume operational responsibility. See Xi Wen, in *Zhongguo zhi chun* (China spring), May 1991, 15.

32. Thus not only Li Peng but former foreign minister Qian Qichen (69) relinquished their government positions in deference to term limitations, though both remained on the CCP Politburo (Qian also remains a vice premier until that term expires in 2003).

33. This group would comprise Wei Jianxing and Li Lanqing in addition to Jiang, Li, and Zhu in the Politburo Standing Committee, and Ding Guangen, Tian Jiyun, Chi Haotian, Zhang Wannian, Jiang Chunyun, Qian Qichen, Wei Jianxing, and Xie Fei, who are full Politburo members.

34. Cf. the excellent book by Naughton, *Growing Out of the Plan.*

35. For an excellent empirical analysis of ongoing local electoral reform, see Manion, "The Electoral Connection," 736–749.

36. "Several Factors," FE/2744 S2/1–13.

# Emerging Patterns of
# Political Conflict in Post-Deng China

## *David Bachman*

In recent years, with some notable exceptions, the study of elite politics in China in the United States has fallen into disfavor for several reasons.[1] First, the Chinese political process remains largely opaque, and scholars find themselves overly reliant on Hong Kong publications that have a mixed track record with regard to their accuracy. Second, the prolonged wait for Deng Xiaoping's death and the seeming stagnation of politics at the center also discouraged the study of elite politics. Succession politics has been discussed since the mid-1980s, and there seemed little new to say. Third, many of the individuals involved in the post-Deng period were less than fascinating, and some verged on the repugnant to many Americans, China scholars included. Why waste time studying largely faceless and uninteresting individuals?

Fourth, it was not clear that politics at the center explained all that much about elite politics. The reach of the center was widely held to be shrinking, and the elite was sufficiently divided such that, at best, only marginal adjustments could be made in the general direction of policy evolution. Localities, as long as they complied with a few key central goals, could experiment and follow many of their own ideas. Although the center insisted on maintaining political order, rapid growth, and birth planning, it appeared that much of the rest of the political-economic agenda was negotiable or even up for grabs. Fifth, along those lines, local political units were more accessible and in some ways more amenable to prevailing theoretical trends in American political science. For careerist reasons, central politics had become a less strategic choice than focusing on localities. Sixth, as archives have opened and research materials have become increasingly available, especially in the former Soviet Union and gradually in China itself, the analysis of elite politics has proven dependent on an extremely small portion of the evidence (the proverbial tip of the iceberg).[2] Why undertake serious study of the elite when in the future, the documentary record will show potentially serious flaws in virtually any study because of very limited information? Finally, many Americans, including many China scholars, believe there will be a democratic transition in China in the future, so why study a doomed system? Ending up in the position of a Sovietologist writing on the origins of the Brezhnev Doctrine in the late 1980s and early 1990s is a truly unappealing idea.

Despite the partial validity of at least some of these reasons, good reasons still exist to speculate about the future of elite politics and to analyze at least some of the ongoing elite political infighting. If for no other reason, our students ask us to do it all the time. There remain interesting puzzles about the nature and use of power in the late Deng period and anomalies about power and leadership in the early Jiang regime. For example, the conventional wisdom is that Deng Xiaoping was able to overcome stiff resistance to further reform only with his *nanxun* of early 1992. But how his travels concretely altered power calculations, what sources of authority he tapped into, and what mechanisms of power this travel activated have not been made entirely clear.

Moreover, the difficulties in getting reform back on track should be contrasted with the ease with which Yang Shangkun and Yang Baibing were eased from power later in the same year. Some accounts of the difficulty stress the contention among the military, Deng, and Jiang Zemin over policies toward the United States and Taiwan. At least according to some, the political leadership was forced to adopt a harder line thanks to military pressure. But what kind of pressure was it, and what brought it on? Why would a Deng who could replace the two Yangs now be vulnerable to military pressure? At the same time, however, if Deng and Jiang were vulnerable to military pressure, how do we account for China's repeated statement that it will ratify the Comprehensive (Nuclear) Test Ban Treaty?

Clearly, modernizing China's nuclear weapons and developing tactical nuclear weapons would seem to be central to military interests, as a central component of the revision of military doctrine.[3] Yet it would appear that Jiang Zemin and perhaps Li Peng prevailed over these military interests. The dramatic departure of Qiao Shi from the Central Committee at the Fifteenth Party Congress was almost uniformly unexpected. Finally, as Andrew Walder has argued, although China's history of mass protests may only be paralleled in the former state socialist systems by that in Poland, in China the public engaged in mass politics only when the elite was split or when the foremost leader at least temporarily legitimated mass politics.[4] Thus, there remain some intriguing anomalies, interesting contradictions, areas of lack of knowledge, and more potential for big surprises than we had anticipated.

Although rational choice approaches to politics have risen to the dominant position in the study of political science in the United States, most of the time such approaches are used to "explain" past events. As has been noted, rational choice models do not take account of alternate explanations.[5] A committed rational choice theorist can always make the data or case with the theory or dismiss discrepant data by arguing that theories cannot be disproved by data but only by better theories. Even so, rational choice perspectives *should* have more predictive power than other types of approaches. I have had some limited success drawing on institutional choice perspectives (as well as empirical materials and logical deductions) in analyzing the future orientations of post-Deng China, and I propose to continue in this vein in this chapter.[6]

Herein I discuss what I see as the structure of power and the central lines of cleavage and conflict among the top leaders in China today. I will address emerging issues and concerns and try to move from the center of the political system to broader segments of the politically aware and ultimately to ordinary citizens of China. Most attention will be focused on the elite because I believe the elite hold the key to the system. In terms of authorizing change, trying to legitimate rule, and structuring political and other incentives, they are a positive force, but in blocking change, denying access to the political agenda, and trying to exercise hegemony over the entire system, they have also had a negative impact.

## THE STRUCTURE OF POWER

### The Ruling Triumvirate

Jiang Zemin continues to show that he is perhaps the luckiest politician in recent Chinese history. But at some point, his own skill has to be appreciated as contributing substantially to his luck. With his maneuvers to remove Qiao Shi from the Central Committee, coupled with the retirements of Liu Huaqing and Zou Jiahua, Jiang has been able to build himself into the center of the political system and to make much of the system revolve around him. Although he has yet to use this structural position to influence policy profoundly—except perhaps with regard to moving to stabilize and improve Sino-American relations—he has built what looks like a stable position of power for himself and perhaps his supporters.

At the center of the Jiang system is an inner triumvirate of leaders—Jiang (b. 1926), Li Peng (b. 1928), and Zhu Rongji (b. 1928).[7] Although there are tensions among all three, it is clear that they have learned to work together, and as a result, they form the nucleus of the leadership. Within this group, however, Jiang holds key advantages that make it unlikely that Li and Zhu could unite to topple him.

Li Peng remains quite unpopular with elements of the party and much of urban society. By being removed from the premiership and taking over the chairmanship of the National People's Congress (NPC) Standing Committee, Li has lost a substantial portion of his political base. Thus he has been somewhat cut off from his former institutional base in the State Council, where there has been significant turnover as a result of the First Session of the Ninth NPC. It is unclear how long it will take Li to build up a new support base in the NPC. The obvious pathway is to push the development of the legal system and the institutionalization of the NPC itself, but it is far from clear whether Li and his aides are so inclined at present. Since it is hard to believe that Li is more conservative than Peng Zhen, who is celebrated as one of the fathers of the legalization movement, it should not be impossible to imagine that Li could also further the legal system to improve his political position, but whether this will happen is uncertain. Li has power and influence, and has proven himself to be able to protect his political position, but he is not well positioned to campaign for the top position, and perhaps his time is past.

Zhu's position may be the most exposed. With his network and reputation as a very demanding boss damaged as a result of the Hundred Flowers Campaign, Zhu's political base is relatively weak. He will be seventy-two in 2000 and probably not therefore in a position to reach for the top position unless Jiang self-destructs. Moreover, he is highly vulnerable. As premier, Zhu will be the official most responsible for the issue of state-owned enterprise (SOE) reform in a time of slowing Asian economic growth and likely greatly diminished capital inflows. Although enterprise reform in the long run will be beneficial to the Chinese economy, the short-term costs of unemployment and social disruption will be borne immediately—and unevenly, as Edward Friedman shows in Chapter 14.

Further, a slowing economy and a commitment to keeping inflation under control may leave Zhu very little policy leeway. The recent announcement that China will spend $750 billion on infrastructure through the year 2000 to keep the economy going suggests that deficit spending and increased borrowing will be the preferred way to try to finesse enterprise reform. Borrowing and deficit spending are by nature inflationary (though a real labor market would lower labor costs, at a tremendous political price). Thus, Zhu is likely to be the person held most responsible should the economy produce problems, which it almost certainly will. Scattered worker protests have already occurred over the past year, especially in Sichuan, with many more factories barely staying alive and workers waiting to be paid.

Although Zhu is in an exposed political position, he does have a few things going for him. The first, and perhaps most important, is his superior competence. Zhu is widely credited for bringing inflation under control without seriously slowing economic growth, at least through the end of 1997, and for getting the Shanghai economy moving again after its relative stagnation in the early and mid-1980s. It would be a mistake to assume that Zhu is fully committed to free markets, but he understands the Chinese economy better than any previous premier (which may not be saying much) and is widely regarded by others in the elite as highly skilled in this area. Second, those who pass muster with Zhu's demanding standards are believed to inherit at least some of their patron's reputation for competence and skill. Thus, for the highly intelligent and ambitious economic official on the rise, hooking up with Zhu may be a high-risk, high-return strategy. Third, Zhu has shown he can work with Jiang, and mutual role expectations may be well established. Fourth, Zhu likely will be able to replace a number of Li Peng's followers in the State Council, and although he may not be able to fill all those spots with his followers, he will weaken Li Peng's base. This may have already taken place with Zou Jiahua's retirement and Chen Jinhua's departure from the Central Committee.

Finally, Zhu's behavior seems to suggest that he places China's interests above his own personal interests. This impression may be a vital requirement for Zhu to try to advance in the system—particularly if it is merely a facade. Coupled with competence, this seeming disinterestedness in personal power is one of the great keys to real power in Chinese political history. In fact, as a legitimating claim, it is probably second only to founding the dynasty or regime. Of course, if Zhu does sincerely place China's interests above his own, he may find it impossible to take proactive measures to rise to the top position in China.

Jiang Zemin's position is above, but in between, those of Zhu and Li. The key issue regarding Jiang's power is whether anything should prevent Zhu and Li from combining against Jiang. I believe that neither Li nor Zhu trusts the other enough to work in concert against Jiang. For reasons that I would be hard pressed to specify, I believe that neither could live as coleader with the other, and a major power struggle would develop that might threaten the regime or might lead a third party to step in and suppress both men. Jiang is likely to try to rule by consensus and, if that fails, supramajority rule, thus limiting his exposure on critical areas. He will be in a position to dump additional difficult assignments on either Zhu or Li, making them more vulnerable. In addition, Jiang could play Zhu and Li off each other, further limiting their ability to present a united front against him. He also could throw Li Peng to the wolves should some reassessment of Tiananmen become either necessary or expedient, blaming the bloodshed on an out-of-touch Deng, a manipulative Li, and the already purged Chen Xitong.

In more formal terms, assuming that it is each leader's preference to be the top leader, then Jiang Zemin is the second choice for both Zhu and Li, with Zhu being Li's least preferred outcome and vice-versa. Jiang's second choice may not matter, unless he suffers incapacitating illness and growing infirmity. Given Li's and Zhu's weaknesses, Jiang's leadership may be stable. In any case, Jiang is working to keep Li and Zhu divided. Furthermore, the growing institutionalization of the NPC competes with the existing prerogatives of the State Council. Without an institutional base in the NPC for Li, his prospects are limited. Should Zhu lose control over the authority of the State Council, his prospects are limited as well. Institutional competition neatly serves Jiang's purposes, particularly because it is clear that neither institution will emerge fully successful from the competition.

### The Outer Elements of the Inner Circle

The four other members of the Politburo Standing Committee (PBSC) do not seem to carry the political weight of the big three. Li Ruihuan (b. 1934) has greater seniority on the Politburo Standing Committee than does Zhu Rongji, and there was some initial speculation that Li was slated to become premier. But although Li may have more of the common touch than other top Chinese leaders, his competence and skill are open to question. He too is a survivor of the elite power struggle, but his position is not indispensable, nor is it clear that his political network is all that powerful. Wei Jianxing (b. 1931) and Li Lanqing (b. 1932) are specialists, and it is unclear that either has a base of power outside his field of specialization. Only three or four years younger than Li and Zhu, neither is necessarily in a good position to advance as a potential successor on other than an interim basis.

Hu Jintao (b. 1942) is the fourth member of the outer/inner circle. Hu's elevation to the Politburo Standing Committee in 1992 was surprising, and he appeared to be the early favorite to succeed Jiang's generation of political leaders. Provincial party leadership positions in Guizhou and Tibet are not usually fast-track appointments, but unless the declaration of martial law in Tibet in March 1989 is seen as a positive signal, it is far from clear that anything distinctively positive can be claimed for his rulership. But as a Qinghua graduate, Hu has some ties to Zhu, and as a bureaucrat in the Ministry of Water Conservancy and Power, he is connected to Li. He also had a more typical fast-track appointment in the Youth League, particularly when it was a recruiting and training ground for Hu Yaobang. His political heritage lacks only clear ties to Jiang, but this may be critical. Whether Hu is able to live up to his lofty position remains to be seen, particularly with several potential competitors in his generation on the Politburo. Even so, his accession to the vice presidency of the People's Republic of China (PRC) marks him as the most favored "younger" figure to rise to the top when Jiang's generation retires.

## THE POLITBURO AND MULTIGENERATIONAL SUCCESSION

As of 2000, the twenty-four-member Politburo ranged in age from 74 (Jiang Zemin) to 56 (Li Changchun), with one-third born before 1930 (including both military members of the Politburo) and with five members born in 1940 or after.[8] According to Hong Kong accounts, Jiang manipulated the Beidaihe meetings in the summer of 1997 to create pressure for Qiao Shi to resign, to smooth succession issues, and at the same time, to exempt himself from hints that the new party constitution would limit membership in top bodies by age.[9] Whether Jiang will hang on to power in 2002 remains to be seen, but many of the current members of the Politburo, perhaps all those born before 1932, will face pressures to step down and retire. This, of course, raises the issue of the immediate succession to Jiang and his cohort and a less obvious generational succession issue.

In 1992, Hu Jintao appeared to be the front-runner of the "fourth generation" of Chinese Communist Party (CCP) leaders. In the 1997 Politburo, Hu faces potential competition from other members of approximately the same age, with Huang Ju (b. 1938), Wu Bangguo (b. 1941), Li Changchun (b. 1944), Jia Qinglin (b. 1940), and Wen Jiabao (b. 1942) and perhaps Zeng Qinghong (b. 1939) as possible or likely challengers. With the exception of Li and Jia, these members have closer relations with Jiang, based on career ties, than does Hu.

Jiang is in the advantageous position of having multiple potential protégés to play off against each other. Because both Jiang and Zhu Rongji share ties with many of the "Shanghai gang," both men's positions are strengthened by having multiple contenders for succession. Each can pit others against each other to strengthen his own position, so long as most of the potential candidates for succession do not conclude they have no prospects and give up. Should they drop out of the competition, they may become opposed to the Jiang leadership system.

The key conclusion here is that there will be intense competition among the younger members of the Politburo. This competition may not be direct—in fact, it is more likely to take the form of preparing for a power struggle, by shoring up resources, than actual struggle. But at the very least, competition among the younger Politburo members will become part of their functional responsibilities and will revolve around the following issues. The up-and-comers will work on maintaining and cultivating good relations with older Politburo members and especially Politburo Standing Committee members. They will cultivate their careers, and aspire to attain the background necessary to become the ranking specialist in such key areas of party administration as the economy, law and order, propaganda, and party organization, when older figures in these areas retire or when competitors falter. They will develop and expand their own bases of support, whether these are geographical or functional groupings or experiential social networks, such as the Qinghua alumni group.

None of these younger leaders stands out yet, with the exception of Hu Jintao and his vice presidency, and strategically it might be dangerous for them to do so at this time. Nonetheless, key aspects of intraelite politics will focus on the process of the younger members trying to distinguish themselves, either among the elite or to a broader attentive public, both in China and abroad. As in the case of the succession politics to Deng Xiaoping, seemingly exogenous factors will undoubtedly play a major role in how the power competition unfolds, but many of these developments are by nature unpredictable. The effects of some external shocks will be felt evenly across the elites, but others will have more personalized impacts. Coping and adapting to various unforeseen developments will be one of the great tests for the coming generation of leaders.

A broader point about generational succession should be noted. All the contenders for power in the succession to Jiang completed their college educations before the Cultural Revolution or were "graduated" without completing their course of study because colleges and universities were closed in the late 1960s. It is increasingly apparent that a college education is required to advance in the political system. But those who graduated from college before the Cultural Revolution have already entered the leadership and elite recruitment system. "The Cultural Revolution will have a profound effect on political recruitment, especially among the generation born in the late 1940s and 1950s." Between 1966 and 1972, slightly more than 210,000 people entered colleges and universities in China, and none entered between 1966 and 1969.[10] Those recruited after 1969 and graduating in or before 1980 received educational materials and practices influenced by the Cultural Revolution and were at least partially selected by Cultural Revolutionary criteria. It would be a mistake to assume either that all of these students were not very bright or that they were all leftist. Nonetheless, there is clear prejudice in the system against them (as the literature of the late 1970s shows), and there is some question whether they are considered trustworthy enough to be recruited to high office. Different consequences flow from the answer to this question.

If Cultural Revolution–era graduates are recruited into politics, their experience will give them a very different perspective than previous generations of CCP leaders, except perhaps the first generation. This Cultural Revolution generation would have had real experience with mass politics, at least as followers in the movements of the 1960s and 1970s, but perhaps as lower-level leaders of various organizations as well. Arguably, they will be more comfortable with the idea of mass politics than the older generations, whom they attacked. This may have profound consequences on the willingness of the current cohort to support political reform.

To be sure, many caveats apply. First, it is a mistake to equate the socialization experiences of an entire educational cohort with the specific perspectives of the small number of former students recruited into the upper reaches of the political system. Second, not all college graduates during the Cultural Revolution period were leftists or even extremely politically active. Clearly, some were educated in research institutes and were insulated at least partially from some broader political currents. Third, the views of some Cultural Revolution activists are different today than they were in the 1960s and 1970s. The life histories of such activists who either did not go on to college (such as Wei Jingsheng) or left China (such as Yang Xiaokai or Gao Yuan) demonstrate this change. Finally, before being recruited into party leadership, this generation would be under intense pressure to deny that anything positive came from the Cultural Revolution, mass politics, or any other central element of the Cultural Revolution and to downplay their activities during the 1966–1976 period.

Nonetheless, even if specific elements of the Cultural Revolution are denied, the broader experience of mass politics cannot be. A history of mass political participation and perhaps a certain confidence about leadership of mass politics may inhere in those members of the generation educated during the Cultural Revolution who pass party muster and begin to compete for leading positions.

If the Cultural Revolution generation of students is excluded from recruitment into top party positions, the Hu Jintao generation of leaders will be "succeeded" by those who graduated from college after the restoration of competitive college entry examinations in 1977. Although a number of older entrants were part of the first cohorts of college students after 1977, most of the post-1980 graduates now are in their late thirties or early forties. Presumably, they will be the best educated, best trained, and most "modern" cadres in the history of the PRC, some of whom have experience abroad, unlike the student cohorts of the 1960s and 1970s. They should be more comfortable with international trends and technology and more cognizant of China's technical shortcomings. What political and other skills they might bring to leadership positions are unclear.

The educational experiences of different potential leadership cohorts are likely to have profound effects on the nature of the Chinese political system, certainly greater than any previous generational turnover in the history of the PRC. While the succession to Jiang will involve the "fourth generation" of leaders, the real change will come from subsequent generations of leaders.[11] Arguably, their socialization experiences differ so vastly from anything that previous generations experienced that they cannot help but fundamentally affect major aspects of Chinese politics. A key and probably unresolvable issue is whether playing the political game to get ahead in Chinese politics is a more powerful solvent than the concept of generational succession in homogenizing these Chinese politicians.

Predicting how various generations of party leaders will relate to each other is difficult. Some consciousness of generational differences and perspectives can be easily imputed to the elite. No doubt older generations will express grave doubts about the Cultural Revolution generation and perhaps its more Western-tainted successor generation. At the very least, it is unlikely that the third and fourth generations will give way quickly and easily to the fifth (Cultural Revolution) and sixth (competitive examination) generations. This intergenerational conflict may strengthen intragenerational ties if each cohort retains some solidarity in the face of divide-and-rule tactics. The fifth generation is likely to feel the most politically embattled, and, other things being equal, the least wedded to the status quo. Whether they can form an effective cross-generational alliance with the sixth generation may be the key to their ability to rise within the system and transform it.

## SOME FURTHER OBSERVATIONS ABOUT THE PURSUIT OF POWER

Other things being equal, younger politicians in the localities should be likely to advance more quickly than those in the center, who serve in party, State Council, or other national hierarchies in Beijing. Local "prefectural" positions offer more flexibility—there is a greater variety of tasks to perform and, more importantly, a greater chance to show one's ability at an earlier age than would be possible within a particular ministerial hierarchy, where the range of tasks is likely to be narrower and more specialized and the bureaucratic structure more fully fleshed out. The ministerial track offers fewer opportunities to draw favorable notice from truly powerful figures within the ministry. As a result, central ministries may be more conservative for organizational reasons and localities more dynamic and entrepreneurial, regardless of the state of central-local relations.

But although starting a career in the localities may be a good way to get ahead in the system, politicians who have ascended to the center after careers spent mostly in localities have not been overwhelmingly successful. Tao Zhu, Hua Guofeng, and Zhao Ziyang are examples that come to mind. If a base of power in the center is essential for effective rulership, Huang Ju, Wu Bangguo, and Jiang Chunyun might have difficulty ruling effectively, even if they were named to succeed either Jiang Zemin or Zhu Rongji. Li Changchun's background is more diverse, though his career has been mostly regional. Hu Jintao's mixture of central and local posts may be an optimal pattern for building diverse networks of supporters, whereas Wen Jiabao, despite some experience in the localities, represents a central and ministerial career path.

There is no compelling reason to assume that prior patterns of success and failure within elite politics will continue indefinitely. Nonetheless, I believe it remains very difficult for someone whose career has occurred overwhelmingly in the localities—specifically, within one province—to function as an effective leader at the center. All politics may be local, but knowing the ropes and having a strong base in Beijing seems to be a prerequisite for rising to the very top of China's political system.

## THE MILITARY

Much of U.S. literature on the Chinese military has assumed that because Jiang and his colleagues have few contacts with the military, it may not be fully responsive to Jiang or any other leader. In this literary realm, evidence has been presented of a more assertive People's Liberation Army (PLA), demanding more forceful Chinese actions to stand up to the United States and to halt, if not reverse, a perceived drift toward Taiwanese independence.

Perhaps the PLA as a whole is less likely to be monitored closely by civilian party leaders. It may also be fairly autonomous with regard to its professional duties and corporate interests, as long as it professes loyalty to the regime and its leader. Nonetheless, these views ignore important points of leverage and control that Jiang Zemin in particular possesses. Many analysts seem to have forgotten that PLA generals are no less anxious to rise to top leadership positions—at least within the military hierarchy—than are civilian leaders within the political system. Jiang's chairmanship of the Central Military Commission (CMC) gives him critical leverage to play military politicians off against each other, to exercise patronage, and to control leadership selection within the PLA. Although he may have no influence whatsoever over broad PLA political and other interests, Jiang does possess the means to control those in the best position to represent and argue for PLA interests.

To increase the influence of Jiang and other civilian leaders over leadership within the PLA, civilians may push for fixed rotations in all commands, including the central PLA departments and especially the general staff department.[12] In this way, Jiang and his associates would be able to exercise control over generals anxious to succeed the current incumbents, although this action might make the incumbents more independent. In fact, if there is one thing that Jiang has done since the removal of the Yangs in 1992, it has been to play patronage politics within the PLA.

This dynamic may help to explain why China has said it will ratify the CTBT and has ceased nuclear testing, even though such testing appears necessary to create the weapons to support a new nuclear doctrine, to perfect multiple independent reentry vehicles (MIRVs) for China's missile forces, and to develop and refine tactical and theater nuclear weapons. Nonetheless, with the decision made, it will be very hard for China to start testing again.[13] Although I don't believe that the PLA would have supported such a decision, there have been few signs of PLA opposition to the policy, even though accounts from Hong Kong and elsewhere have regularly stated how assertive the PLA has become with regard to Sino-American and cross-Strait relations. Jiang's announcement that the PLA is supposed to get out of the state's business, made before CMC members in mid-July 1998, suggests that he is not afraid to tackle complicated PLA issues and interests. Also, because Deng was clearly out of the picture when the decision was made, international image concerns and payoffs to particular military leaders may have allowed Jiang to reach his decision, undoubtedly with Qian Qichen's support.[14]

A second major source of civilian leverage over the PLA is resources. China's military modernization requires the active support of numerous civilian hierarchies. Many observers assume that the PLA has been able to bid up its budget since 1988 because of its political clout. Although this may be the case, it is hard to argue, even with double-digit budget increases for almost ten years, that military modernization has progressed much. The problems in this area go beyond money and largely reflect the nature of civilian institutions. For example, if China's top young physicists look to jobs other than in the nuclear weapons industry, it is not clear what the military can do about it. Similarly, if the military industrial complex cannot hire the best engineers, it will encounter severe problems with military modernization. And if only poor peasants want to join the PLA, this too will slow modernization.

In short, real military modernization would require a much more interventionist state effort, with considerably higher salaries for recruits in the military and for scientific and technical personnel in the defense production and research and development sectors. Advancing these goals would require much higher educational spending and perhaps even a retreat from some elements of the population program—after all, what families would encourage their only sons to join the PLA? In short, to speed the pace of military modernization in China, a more powerful, centralized state would be required, with much greater capacity to guide and control money and personnel.

But of course, the Chinese state is moving in the opposite direction— toward greater allocation by markets, very low levels of taxation and spending as a percentage of gross national product (GNP), and so on. The PLA has clearly lost its bid—if indeed it ever tried—to redefine the nature of state power in China so that it will serve military modernization. At the same time, however, it is not entirely clear that military modernization can be or will be served without fundamental changes in the Chinese state, even if economic and industrial modernization take off. These changes would be so fundamental that we would have to speak of a post-Communist China with the rule of law, binding taxes, and other modern characteristics.

The PLA apparently has reconciled itself (at least partly) to its position in the allocation of resources. This position is higher than usually assumed: although military modernization might rank fourth among the four modernizations, it probably ranks second in terms of actual spending. Within this context, the civilian leadership can partially control the military two ways. First, civilian control might be achieved if intramilitary debates on prioritization within the PLA were to divide it, rendering it unable to present a united front. Forcing the PLA to prioritize among nuclear modernization, missiles, submarines, and air superiority fighters is an inherently divisive process. Second, civilians will be able to alter these priorities, intervening to reward some priority sectors and perhaps downplaying others by allocating extra or fewer funds, as well as influencing the process of allocation through selective promotions. In this way, at least in the short term, the civilians can divide and control the military.

Such tactics are obvious and may provoke a united PLA backlash, but short of force, it is not clear what a united PLA could do against the party-state leadership. It is hard to imagine that type of concerted PLA action. Even if the military directly ruled China, it might not be able to move the Chinese state in the directions needed to truly modernize the military. Thus, even in power, the PLA is likely to be divided.

## THE PARTY

The CCP is growing increasingly diverse and heterogeneous. Its penetration of society is less complete than in the past, and many key elements of party-state power, such as the Youth League, have been in decay for an extended period. Village elections are beginning to challenge the power of rural cadres, though their strength should not be overstated. In terms of education and experience, there is a growing gap between rural and urban party members.

What this means is that the CCP mirrors the complexity of Chinese society. In itself, however, a split within the party along urban-rural or any other lines of cleavage is not inevitable. Party leadership is dominated overwhelmingly by urban members and those with higher education. The likely result is continued decay of grassroots party organizations and a further disconnect between urban and rural areas, at least within the political system. One possible consequence is growing abuse of power in rural areas, provoking peasant unrest, particularly if there are more attempts to curb rural migration to urban areas. Whether scattered unrest could coalesce into a larger, more challenging social movement with urban links remains to be seen.

## SOCIETY

Since 1989, Chinese society has pursued an avid quest for prosperity. The political realm was a dangerous one in which to become active, and it was clear that for many, material rewards served as the carrot instead. In the past year or so, acts of dissent seem to have increased, and there are growing signs of restiveness within society (and the party, as the Fang Jue manifesto suggests).[15] But the nature of party rule makes the appearance of overt opposition all but impossible—except perhaps to those who are laid off—and makes the formation of an organized opposition leadership difficult, if not impossible. Leadership can emerge during the course of protests, but its ability to guide a movement in process is likely to be incomplete and over time, increasingly radical, if the spring of 1989 is any guide.[16]

As Walder has suggested, for opposition to appear widely in China, the elite must be divided. The elite seems aware of this fact, and efforts to keep elite disputes within fairly narrow limits appear to be working. It should also be noted that not all intraleadership disputes provide opportunities for mass involvement, as the 1989–1992 years suggest. But without intraelite conflict that paralyzes or divides the agents of coercion, there is little possibility for an extensive mass movement to get off the ground.

The key question then becomes: what issues or questions are likely to fracture this relative elite unity? The issue of Jiang's succession is not likely to be one such issue. Although the intraelite competition and conflict may be intense, it probably will run along individual, rather than factional, lines. As long as the stakes for both victory and defeat are relatively low, the consequences should not create opportunities for popular action. More controversial and divisive are questions related to state enterprise and banking reform. For both of these reforms to make substantial progress, the spread of legal norms and bureaucratic and market autonomy probably needs to take place and may further spill over into demands for democratization. Such reforms, even without democratization, are fundamentally redistributive in their political and economic effects and would have profound implications for employment as well. Even more potentially controversial are developments in Taiwan and relations with the United States. The spread of independence sentiment on Taiwan would pose a fundamental challenge to the leadership that would risk war with Taiwan and possibly the United States. But with respect to these issues, hard-liners in the elite probably will find substantial support from many in society.

Thus, many of the top issues on the political agenda have the potential to spin out of control, either through intraelite disagreements or through exogenous developments, such as Ch'en Shui-pien becoming Taiwan's next president. It is not just because Jiang Zemin and Li Peng are cautious individuals or lack the "vision thing," however, that China's state enterprise and banking reforms have proceeded gradually. The social and political costs of such reforms are readily apparent, and the regime is trying to go as fast as the political system, and society's capacity for change, can accept.

## CONCLUSION

Not surprisingly, politics will suffuse the reign of Jiang Zemin. He has cleverly taken advantage of his opportunities to create a system that gives him a great deal of leverage over key personnel issues and that enables him to divide and rule. His manipulative skills, however, have not been matched by any apparent vision of where he wants the system to go. In this way, he might be China's Leonid Brezhnev.

There will be continual jockeying for power within the Politburo and between military and political elites, in which Jiang should have the upper hand. This situation, however, will not differ too much from the political climate in the last five years of Deng's life. What will be different will be the nature of the emerging generational successions. The time frame is longer, and the dynamics of generational succession much less understandable and predictable. Nonetheless, I believe they pose profound consequences for China and a great challenge for the regime.

Finally, Jiang's consolidation of power should make broad social protest less likely, at least in the short run. But without a clear sense of direction for China's future, Jiang's consolidation may be temporary. As China faces more difficult choices regarding its economic future, in its relations with the world, and in its state-society relationships, the chances grow for elite cleavage, creating the potential for mass politics.

## NOTES

1. The major exceptions to this are Baum, *Burying Mao,* and issue No. 34 of the *China Journal,* 1–205, focusing on the nature of Chinese elite politics.

2. On some of the archival records becoming available, see the Cold War International History Project of the Woodrow Wilson Institute for Scholars of the Smithsonian Institution, available online at http://cwihp.si.edu.default.htm. In the Chinese case, journals such as *Dangde wenxian* (Party documents) or the 13 volumes of *Jianguoyilai Mao Zedong wengao* (Manuscripts of Mao Zedong since 1949) are helpful. For what these new materials are able to tell us that fundamentally revises our

understanding of Maoist China, see the writings of Lewis and his collaborators over the last ten years: *China Builds the Bomb*; *Uncertain Allies;* and *China's Strategic Seapower.*

3. On nuclear doctrine revision, see Johnston, "China's New 'Old Thinking,'" 5–42.

4. Walder, "Does China Face an Unstable Future?" Walder did not include a discussion of the top leader encouraging mass participation but conceded the point in the question-and-answer discussion of his paper.

5. For a profound critique of rational choice approaches to American politics especially, see Green and Shapiro, *Pathologies of Rational Choice Theory.*

6. Bachman, "The Limits on Leadership in China," 1046–1062; "Succession, Consolidation, and Transition in China's Future," 89–106; and "Succession Politics and China's Future," 370–389.

7. All biographical data for this essay come from *Who's Who in China,* 6.

8. Earlier work on political generations and politics in China includes Yahuda, "Political Generations," 793–805; Liu and Schwarcz, "Six Generations," 42–56; and Vera Schwarcz, "Behind a Partially Open Door," 577–604.

9. *Zhengming* (Contending), October 1997, 7–9.

10. For the data on college entrants and graduates in the 1960s and 1970s, see *Zhongguo jiaoyu nianjian,* 971 and 969, respectively. For analysis, see Orleans, "Graduates," 444–449.

11. "Fourth generation" is placed in quotes because what is likely to be called the fourth generation of leaders is really the fifth generation. If the first generation is identified as those born in the 1890s, like Mao, and the second as those born in the 1900s, like Deng, the third generation should have been those born in the 1910s, like Zhao Ziyang. So referring to Jiang Zemin as the core of the third generation of leaders deliberately glosses over the 1910s generation, since they were decimated by the Cultural Revolution or are in disgrace or dead, with Wan Li as a lone survivor who essentially has retired. Given the length of Deng's rule and Jiang's obvious desire to hold onto power till at least 2002, if not 2007, the generation born in the first half of the 1930s is also not likely to be well represented among the top leadership much beyond its current positions, though perhaps in 2003, Li Lanqing might replace Zhu Rongji.

12. For convenience, I refer here and in the following passages to civilian leaders and military leaders, suggesting more differentiation than may be the case between PLA generals and top party and state leaders.

13. The explicit demonstration of nuclear weapons in South Asia may reopen the issue.

14. On this issue, prior to announcement of China's intention to sign CTBT, see Johnston, "Prospects for Chinese Nuclear Force Modernization," 548–576, especially 566–576. I discuss the issue in less detail in "Structure and Process in the Making of Chinese Foreign Policy," in Kim, *China and the World,* 34–54, esp. 46–48.

15. For an analysis, see Wei Jingsheng and Liu Qing, "Signal from China," *Washington Post,* February 1, 1998, C9.

16. As is shown in Karma Hinton and Richard Gordon's documentary, *Gate of Heavenly Peace* (1994).

# ⊞ 5 ⊞

# The Problematic Quest for Stability: Reflections on Succession, Institutionalization, Governability, and Legitimacy in Post-Deng China

## *Frederick C. Teiwes*

---

The central paradox in analyzing present-day China, not to mention its future, is that at a time of unprecedented access to the public and the elite and a flood of published information, there is arguably less certainty about both the nature of elite politics and the position of the regime vis-à-vis society than during any previous period. In terms of elite politics, many foreign specialists on China have established well-developed contacts with important officials in the People's Republic of China (PRC), family members of Chinese Community Party (CCP) leaders at or very near the top, and Chinese intellectuals and scholars deeply interested in contemporary politics, yet what goes on "behind the curtain" remains elusive.[1]

In a sense, the situation resembles a diabolical combination of pre–Cultural Revolution leadership opaqueness and Washington- (or Canberra-) style calculated leaks and fanciful rumors, with "analysis" little more than informed speculation. For example, consider the circumstances of Qiao Shi's (largely unpredicted) removal from the leadership at the Fifteenth Party Congress. Was it the result of his more "liberal" policy views, the failure of a calculated attempt on his part to challenge his Politburo colleagues,[2] or (as this writer favors in some respects) simply that as the oldest of the "third generation" Standing Committee members, his retirement number had come up?[3]

Similarly, Chinese society arguably is more open to outsiders now than at any time in the past. Scholars are able to talk to disaffected people on street corners and can conduct research—albeit with difficulty—among a considerable range of social sectors and formal organizations. And much has become known about the swirling social tensions in the country.[4] But again, any assessment of the systemic implications of such tensions is highly speculative. We need look no further than the traumatic events of

1989, which came as a surprise to most observers, and the subsequent predictions of many experts that the regime would crumble.[5] The regime has not collapsed, and perhaps the best way to characterize the predictions of the CCP's prospects by most of the field at present, this writer included, is as a big hedging of bets.

Thus any assessment of the party's direction is necessarily an intuitive undertaking relying on personal impressions and the views of friends enmeshed in Chinese society as well as the flood of (perversely inadequate) published material. With this apologia in mind, I shall offer reflections on the topics of succession, institutionalization, governability, and legitimacy in post-Deng China, with particular attention to comparisons with previous periods of the PRC experience. It is the past that shapes the expectations of both elites and populace alike, providing both the negative and positive lessons that guide behavior. Undoubtedly the most crucial lesson of that past has been the need to avoid chaos (*luan*) and to preserve stability.

## SUCCESSION

"Succession struggles" are a staple of analysis for Chinese politics and Leninist systems more generally, but I would argue that there have been at best two-and-a-half such "struggles" in the history of the PRC.[6] The Gao Gang-Rao Shushi case in the early 1950s was the first, albeit a very brief and premature one,[7] and the second and clearest case of an ongoing struggle, with clearly defined factions and identifiable leaders, was the "Gang of Four"–old guard conflict during Mao Zedong's final years and immediately postmortem.[8] The "half case" is the conflict between Zhao Ziyang and Li Peng from 1988 to mid-1989, which reflected the conflict between the reformer and planner perspectives. Although there clearly was a high degree of tension between the two "camps," it remains unclear whether there was a full-scale assault on Zhao's position as leader of the "first front"—the group in charge of day-to-day affairs and policy development—while Deng Xiaoping and other senior revolutionaries exercised authority in semiretirement from the "second front."[9]

In all other cases, classic succession struggles did not exist: during Mao's time Liu Shaoqi's fall and Lin Biao's rise had nothing to do with a conflict between them, and on the balance of evidence, Lin's subsequent fall was the product of Mao's peculiar perceptions rather than any grab for enhanced power on Lin's part.[10] Likewise, with the possible exception of 1988–1989, succession struggles have not been the order of the day after Mao's passing and the elimination of the Gang of Four.

The post-Mao period, however, has had an abundance of succession "situations." In these instances, various forces came into play: a commitment to leadership stability in contrast to the disruptions of the Cultural Revolution; the desire for collective leadership to avoid the excesses of Mao's one-man rule; a deference to revolutionary status, which had largely been taken for granted in the pre–Cultural Revolution period; and the wish to arrange for an orderly, institutionalized succession, as had been put in place briefly during the 1950s, to guarantee the longed-for stability. The contradictions among these goals, the inevitable differences over the pace of reform, the reality of Deng Xiaoping's overwhelming power, and the resulting deep-seated ambiguity all contributed to less-than-smooth transitions.[11] Although many observers have treated the initial post-Mao period to the 1978 Third Plenum as a succession struggle between Deng and Hua Guofeng, this episode is better viewed as an almost inevitable process of restoring proper statuses within the party. Simply put, there was no way Hua could stand against Deng, and he knew it.[12]

Once Deng's position as senior leader became unambiguous after the Third Plenum, the attempts to institutionalize the process of collective succession ran into various problems beyond those of finding a consensus on far-reaching reform. Deng's unchallenged power and the broader influence and authority of party elders generally were among the most important reasons. In addition, transition was plagued by the fact that first front leaders lacked the revolutionary status of their seniors and were expected to justify their positions by performance and the fact that the principles of collective leadership and institutionalized roles meant a less subservient and more conflict-ridden relationship among them. The case of Hu Yaobang illustrates these points. Hu was an easy target because he was on the cutting edge of reform, but his problems were also due as fundamentally to alienating both Deng and the elders and meddling in Zhao Ziyang's and other leaders' economic portfolios. This was not a classic succession struggle: the "beneficiary," Zhao Ziyang, had no interest in the fall of another reforming leader and in fact tried to avoid the "successor" post of general secretary.[13]

The unexpected emergence of Jiang Zemin as the new successor during the Tiananmen crisis in 1989 was not free of the above considerations, but the new succession situation was subtly different. Paradoxically, certain of Jiang's notional weaknesses bolstered his position. Clearly, he had less of a "power base" than any presumptive successor since Hua Guofeng and arguably even less than Hua. Jiang had been imposed from above by a fading generation and had considerably less status than not only Hu Yaobang or Zhao Ziyang, but also his new Politburo Standing Committee colleagues Li Peng and Qiao Shi.[14] Yet this fact, together with the Tiananmen lesson of how leadership instability could contribute to a regime crisis, may have produced a situation in which the elders pulled together in support of Jiang and, in conjunction with their declining physical abilities, consciously reduced their interference in first front affairs.

The main exception, of course, was Deng's southern tour (*nanxun*) and the revitalization of reform in 1992. It was an implicit rebuke to the first front leadership and therefore to Jiang's stewardship but did not diminish Deng's support of Jiang as the "core" of the "third generation" party leadership. This designation as "core" was of special significance: although the leadership was still expected to be collective, Jiang took his place in conceptual terms as the successor to Mao and Deng, leaders of the "first" and "second generations," respectively—a considerable elevation from being first among equals with Hu and Zhao. No one seriously believes Jiang holds the same personal authority as Mao or Deng, but the core designation not only reflected the elders' belief that the ambiguity of first front leadership was a destabilizing factor, but also served to link Jiang symbolically ever more closely to the regime and facilitate his amassing of additional institutional powers.

From the standpoint of the first front leaders, it was not only the still-unchallengeable authority of Deng but the need for stability that guaranteed, at least provisionally, their support for Jiang. Although certainly repelled by Cultural Revolution chaos and supportive of stability and unity in broad terms during the 1980s, they had participated in the robust politics surrounding reform. Now, however, even leaders like Li Peng, who had obtained "victory" over Zhao Ziyang, were arguably much chastened by the fallout in Tiananmen Square and throughout the country. Further leadership disruptions might lead to similar threats to the regime. It is instructive that there have been so few visible signs (as opposed to unsubstantiated speculation) of anti-Jiang moves within the leadership. The closest case, which involved the "Yang family" (Yang Shangkun and Yang Baibing) at the time of the Fourteenth Congress, apparently was largely concerned with military affairs and was settled by Deng Xiaoping's decisive intervention on behalf of Jiang.[15]

Apart from this, the only other conceivable instances of challenges to Jiang's authority involved Chen Xitong, whose eventual purge for corruption may have resulted from power struggle considerations, and Qiao Shi. In my view, however, any tensions between Chen and Jiang at most signaled that the general secretary had little interest in protecting Chen against corruption charges; in fact, Jiang acted with great sensitivity in handling the case in order to avoid charges of his own factional bias.[16] As for Qiao Shi, although tensions may indeed have existed, leading Jiang to maneuver for Qiao's retirement, the fact that Qiao was particularly vulnerable on age grounds made this a relatively easy ploy rather than a no-holds-barred political struggle.[17]

Thus there is little solid indication of any real challenge to Jiang's position. Given this situation, the outcome of the Fifteenth National Congress was an entirely predictable reaffirmation of his status as "core." By the time of the Congress, of course, the transition of the basis of Jiang's position had passed from the initial imposition from above to what I have called the "normal politics" within the first front itself. Jiang's succession has been secured by his political skills. At the same time, he is vulnerable to a failure of those skills, although Beijing's preoccupation with stability suggests it would take some very substantial failures to prevent him from serving out his present term.[18]

The good news for Jiang is that his skills are considerable, in terms of the present elite mindset. He has operated as a consensus politician, both in terms of policy and in the sense of respecting the bureaucratic interests and turf of his colleagues, a conciliator devoid of the provocative initiatives of a Hu Yaobang or Zhao Ziyang.[19] A nonthreatening posture toward his colleagues is a definite plus, reaffirming the heartfelt desire for stability and unity. Significantly, although the succession struggle paradigm places high value on building factional networks and although the emergence of a "Shanghai clique" has drawn comment inside as well as outside China, the actual process seems more subdued on Jiang's part. Key "Shanghai clique" members on the Politburo, Wu Bangguo and Huang Ju, were favorites of both Deng Xiaoping and Chen Yun, and the Fifteenth Politburo as a whole has more members with career ties to Li Peng than Jiang.[20] In short, although Jiang undoubtedly has used the appointments power to further his own position, it has been done in a restrained manner.[21]

For the present Jiang Zemin's position seems secure, but it rests largely on a combination of office and political skill, a situation not unlike "normal politics" in other political systems. One aspect of his leadership, potentially more threatening for the party system generally than for Jiang personally, is that Jiang's position is almost entirely based on elite support. Many in the public see Jiang as a mediocrity, an opportunist prone to vacuous speeches of "transcentury significance" who lacks sincerity. Even more threatening for the leadership as a whole is that Li Peng is still widely hated for his role during the Tiananmen crisis in 1989. A crude assessment of popular attitudes concludes that there is a considerable reservoir of goodwill for Zhu Rongji, installed as premier in March 1998 to much acclaim, based on his perceived honesty and forthrightness, a mixed view of Jiang, and general disdain for Li. In terms of the larger collective succession, there is a tension between the elite's desire for internal stability that mandates Li's continuation in a position of authority short of retirement age and the greater popular support that would be secured for the regime by his "early" retirement. This conflict, of course, relates to the question of legitimacy, to be taken up later.

A second aspect concerns the issue of governability: do the qualities that have sustained Jiang's succession aid or inhibit effective governance? More broadly, do the qualities underlying the collective succession of the larger leadership group contribute to governability in a general sense? Finally, there is the question of institutionalization, in one sense a prop to Jiang's position, but by its very incomplete nature a factor underscoring his limitations. How much clout Jiang actually carries in top-level decision-making defies clarity: the notions of "core" and collective leadership push in different directions. Although there are suggestions of a political retirement norm, there is no certainty as to whether this applies to the "core." And, of course, there is still no truly institutionalized procedure for the transfer of power. I turn now to these and related issues of institutionalization.

## INSTITUTIONALIZATION

One cannot but agree with Kenneth Lieberthal's observation that "the Chinese political system is strewn with organizations that have not become institutions."[22] Lieberthal may underestimate the degree to which organizations have developed sufficient regularity to shape the behavior of their members, but he is certainly correct that throughout the PRC, and not just at the apex, power is highly personalized. Crucially, there are no (or only highly erratic) legal restraints on such power—China remains far removed from the rule of law despite the recent attention to legal reform.

Nevertheless, an inexorable trend has moved toward an institutionalization of sorts. In Mao's time, the only limit on the chairman was his self-restraint or disasters caused by his foolish initiatives; throughout the system, meeting Mao's expectations by and large swept all considerations of decency, not to mention law, aside. Deng Xiaoping concluded that the lack of effective institutions had brought about Mao's disasters and moved to introduce various procedures and limits concerning the exercise of power, yet he too ultimately operated by a more restrained form of fiat.[23] Jiang Zemin, however, cannot act in the same manner because of his lack of revolutionary status and because his power is so closely linked to his office. Meanwhile, regular patterns have proliferated that do regulate behavior, but at present critical areas exist where these norms fall short of true institutionalization. I now examine some of the most significant of these.

Perhaps the most successful aspect of institutionalization has been the evolution of a retirement system. As part of the effort to curb personal power and infuse the system with new blood, Deng Xiaoping emphasized the need to end life tenure, whereby officials stayed in their posts regardless of capacity as long as they did not fall afoul of some political deviation. As this system took hold at various official levels, the variant of retirement to the second front was undertaken by Deng and other party elders from the mid-1980s.[24] By the time of the Fourteenth Party Congress in 1992, leaders in their seventies were routinely retiring from top posts (with the exception of military figures—see below); thus, both Yao Yilin and Song Ping left the Standing Committee at the 1992 Congress. As indicated previously, retirement is one explanation for the exit of Qiao Shi at the Fifteenth Congress. Indeed, according to unverified Hong Kong reports, there was spirited discussion at the Beidaihe meetings regarding a formal retirement system for Politburo members setting an age limit of 70, along with related proposals to limit the number of terms that could be served (for example, two for the general secretary).[25] The apparent fact that there has been no formal decision along these lines indicates the current limits to institutionalization, but regular practices that shape behavior do appear to be emerging.[26] Thus Qiao Shi's case is consistent with such "regularized" practice since, apart from Jiang Zemin, not only the new Standing Committee but the entire Politburo consisted of members under age 70.

Probing deeper, however, the limitations to institutionalization are more in evidence. Assuming there is an internal understanding on retirement at age 70, the exception for the general secretary is interesting. I believe this has less to do with the office than the person and the political situation. As the "core," one only marginally older than his senior peers, Jiang is crucial to the system at this juncture less because of his skills than because competition for the succession (if not necessarily a struggle) would be deemed a threat to stability.[27] Certainly, there is the expectation that Jiang will gracefully step down when the Sixteenth Congress convenes in 2002. One must wonder, however, whether the "core" will see it that way, especially if the elite views his current five-year stewardship as a success.

Another indication of the extent of institutionalization concerns the number two man, Li Peng. Leaving aside Li's low standing with the public, the regularized practices of the state system required him to stand down as premier and thus pave the way for Zhu Rongji to assume the role, even though, paradoxically, much of Li's real clout over the past decade came from the formal powers of the premier,[28] and from his status as second-ranking Standing Committee member since the Thirteenth Congress in 1987, which was linked to his position as premier. To be sure, in March 1998 Li took over as National People's Congress (NPC) head from Qiao Shi, but his power undoubtedly must be more personal than institutional under the new arrangement.

At another level, the whole emphasis on both stability and the recruitment of younger talent also points to the limits. True institutionalization regulates the competition for power; it creates a situation where there can be genuine struggles for office that are not life-and-death battles or, in Tang Tsou's term, "games to win all."[29] In contrast, the present CCP approach is to limit conflict by political management rather than binding rules. Thus, the party has made efforts to smooth the transition to the "fourth generation" by designating, if not formally, a "core-in-waiting" in

Hu Jintao at the Fifteenth Congress,[30] a move reaffirmed by Hu's March 1998 appointment as PRC vice president, in direct constitutional succession to Jiang Zemin's leading state position. Should this come to pass at the Sixteenth Congress when Hu would be 60—and thus ideally poised to serve two five-year terms as leader before reaching retirement age—the succession may be orderly enough. But will it involve a genuine test of Hu's abilities or simply his skill at avoiding making enemies? If Hu's performance in the intervening period is not all that convincing, there are no mechanisms apart from disruptive internal challenges to stability to alter the order of succession.

The implicit problem of the danger of mediocrity can also be seen in the Politburo more generally.[31] Although I have noted elsewhere both the importance of performance for first front leaders and the impulse to preserve continuity at the top, the results of the Fifteenth Congress strongly suggest the additional fear of disruption through personnel change. Except for the disgraced Chen Xitong, all the members of the Fourteenth Politburo apart from those over 70 were retained or promoted.[32] Arguably, this is not terribly significant given the frequency of change in administrative positions, but this very observation raises questions about the Politburo as notionally the highest policymaking institution of the system.

One of the key institutional relationships for a developing society undoubtedly is that between civilian authority and the military. The army's ties to the party-state have been unusually close in the PRC, a relationship marked during the Mao and Deng eras by strict institutional subordination that was paradoxically profoundly personal at the same time.[33] For although "the Party [did indeed] control the gun," what this meant in practice was generals saluting first Mao and then Deng regardless of what their policies meant for military interests.[34] Clearly, this state of affairs involved enormous military respect for Mao as the architect of armed struggle and for Deng as one of the great People's Liberation Army (PLA) heroes of the revolution.

The situation could not be more different for Jiang Zemin, who lacks any military credentials despite his formal position as commander-in-chief. In recent years, Jiang has strengthened his support in the PLA through a deft combination of careful support of a range of military interests and use of the power of appointment, but the degree to which military support for Jiang and the civilian leadership as a whole is based on traditional subservience to the party remains unclear, as does the extent to which it is contingent on the willingness of the leadership (in contrast to Deng Xiaoping) to tend to army interests.[35] Perhaps it is best to say that the PLA leadership does retain the traditional loyalty to the party, but that it is hardly the reflexive support of the Mao and Deng eras and could be missing in extreme circumstances. For the present, the evidence suggests military satisfaction not simply with policy outcomes but more broadly with a policy process that gives the PLA ample opportunity to argue forcefully for its institutional interests.[36]

In any case, the military differs from other organizations when it comes to institutionalization. The personal ties to surviving old revolutionaries are stronger, and the sense of separateness of "the Party's army" is greater. This difference is evident from a whole set of arrangements in the reform era, from Deng Xiaoping staying on as Central Military Commission (CMC) head after giving up all other posts, to an 80-year-old Yang Shangkun confirmed in daily charge of military affairs at the rejuvenating Thirteenth Party Congress, to septuagenarians Liu Huaqing and Zhang Zhen brought out of retirement to assume guiding positions at the Fourteenth Congress. Although the Fifteenth Congress has been viewed as a step toward greater civilian control through the exclusion of military representatives on the Standing Committee, that was a partial development at best. The two military additions to the Fifteenth Politburo, Chi Haotian and Zhang Wannian, buck the trend for new members by pushing the upper limits of the under-70 standard,[37] and Deng Xiaoping's personal chief of staff, Wang Ruilin, gained a seat on the CMC. Despite an undoubted trend toward military professionalism, old practices die hard. It makes an intriguing mix—traditions that call for obeying the party but disparage those without revolutionary credentials and a professionalism that argues for a limited role in politics but at the same time promotes a contingent relationship demanding service of corporate interests. Strict institutionalism it is not.

Even as the above suggests a slow if erratic process of institutionalization of practices within the elite, the arbitrariness of official interaction with society presents a far different picture. Related to this is the inability to curb clearly illegal activities, because political calculation and the need for intraleadership stability outweighs the law where the interests of elite actors are involved, even at the cost of weakening regime legitimacy. This is the story of repeated anticorruption crackdowns throughout the reform era: despite the theoretical support of Deng Xiaoping and Chen Yun for such measures and scattered severe penalties, well-connected figures have generally been protected. When a determined effort to deal with the problem was undertaken by Hu Yaobang in 1986, it became one of the contributing factors in his fall.[38] As already suggested, perhaps the most remarkable aspect of the Chen Xitong case was the delicacy with which it was handled. While Chen was officially expelled from the party at the Fifteenth Congress and presumably denied his many mistresses and houses in Beijing, the popular belief was that he was still living quite well in internal exile, a cynicism unlikely to have been substantially altered by Chen's mid-1998 sixteen-year prison sentence after a closed trial. Even the regime's trumpeted anticorruption efforts only serve to illustrate the distinction between "them" and "us"—with detrimental consequences for both governability and legitimacy.

## GOVERNABILITY

In contrast to institutionalization, governability is an amorphous and problematic concept that has eluded systems other than the PRC. Over the years there have been claims that the highly institutionalized U.S. polity is ungovernable, whether because of structural gridlock or an inability to reach a consensus on resolving major social problems.[39] How governable is India, the one country arguably comparable to China in terms of developing nature and size—a democratic country that regularly imposes central rule, has a social system that in important respects is quasi-feudal, has been ruled for most of its independent history by a family dynasty, and has seen several heads of that dynasty assassinated? And what of post-Communist Russia, which is in its own way coping with a transition from state socialism? Russia today, it has been argued, is one of the weakest states imaginable—one that has allowed the collapse of productive forces, cannot control its own borders, lacks an infrastructural capacity, is dependent on external Western aid, and has stood by while its military apparatus has decayed.[40] In view of this, for all the PRC's enormous problems, it may not be in such bad shape after all, and the issue of regime collapse that implicitly underpins many discussions of both governability and legitimacy may be premature.

In historical terms, however, the regime over the last decade has been in a more precarious position than at any time previously. The Maoist state was a strong if blunt state, able to impose its will throughout the country to bring about far-reaching change, even if communications limitations and the interests of various organizations and subordinate leaders created room for adaptation and avoidance.[41] Fundamentally, the party center— and Mao personally—set an agenda that was executed even when it caused horrific damage to the people and nation, as in the famine caused by the Great Leap Forward[42] or the bizarre madness of the Cultural Revolution that damaged virtually all vested interests.[43]

Part of Deng Xiaoping's post-Mao agenda was to avoid such disasters by limiting arbitrary power, ending political movements, and recruiting technical expertise into leading positions, even as he retained nostalgia for the pre–Cultural Revolution years when "the Central Committee uttered one word and the whole country acted accordingly."[44] In fact, Deng realized this was no longer possible and instead sought a middle way where party leadership would provide the necessary muscle to enforce the state's more rationally determined policies. In short, the dictatorship was still required, but it could no longer use old methods. The recent question has been whether a relaxed dictatorship allowing a greatly expanded "zone of indifference"[45] can provide effective governance.

Party leadership was crucial in Deng's eyes, as in those of the current leadership, but effective governance also required the development of adequate technical and institutional means to achieve the state's goals—something at the heart of the debate over state capacity.[46] In technical terms, the current state holds an advantage over its Maoist predecessor. Although the Maoist state could reach into any sector of society and enforce its will, it lacked the means to know what was going on to a significant extent.[47] The great expansion of transportation and communications, as well as the development of modern statistical methods, has not solved the problem but has alleviated it significantly.

More elusive has been the development of adequate institutional means to support the new reform orientation. It is important, however, to acknowledge the complexities in moving from the old planning system to a market economy. Such difficulties involve not only the clash of different interests and the difficulty of altering deeply ingrained habits but also the need for trial and error in the design of methods. The attempt to address one of the major deficiencies of state capacity—the massive decline in the ability of government, particularly central government, to extract sufficient financial resources to carry out its programs and exercise macro control—has highlighted the pitfalls of reform. Shaoguang Wang's recent analysis of the 1994 fiscal reform indicates both a substantial step forward and the unsurprising limitations of the process. Wang concluded that there was "a notable move away from the old bargaining system" that has been such an inhibition on institutionalization, with the result that the new system is "much more comprehensive, unambiguous, and transparent, and rule enforcement mechanisms are more reliable." But the aforementioned factors of habit, trial and error, and conflicting interests mean the result is "not truly rule-based."[48] Progress is possible but difficult, with fear of instability repeatedly slowing the pace of reform.

Many observers take a bleaker view of the regime's ability to govern. In reaching his assessment that "China's capacity to resolve [its formidable list of problems] is growing ever more limited," John Bryan Starr focused on political resistance to party and central authority. He noted such diverse "new forces" as military officers, regional politicians, and successful entrepreneurs, as well as disaffected social groups that have been "staging local dress rehearsals for a nationwide demonstration of opposition."[49] In each of these aspects, the assessment seems exaggerated. Military officers, a pampered group despite efforts to curb PLA involvement in business, have already been discussed. As for regional politicians, clearly

there has been a long-running tug-of-war between the center and the localities, and it may well be that the notable number of provincial leaders
on the new Politburo and an increase in provincial representation on the
Central Committee reflects an increase in overall local clout within the
system.[50]

Nevertheless, the real tensions that exist should not be considered the
prelude to the breakup of the nation or even a less dramatic form of non-
cooperation. The center still retains substantial powers of appointment and
resource allocation that are well understood by lower levels, and to the extent one can judge, even parochial officials have a high patriotic attachment to China. Relations between the center and localities, then, are best
understood as the negotiation of viable relations in a huge and diverse political system.[51] Although the specific modus vivendi worked out on any
particular issue may enhance or detract from central state capacity, there is
little threat to a unified state. The real problem at present is that, due to the
primacy given to economic growth by Beijing and the lack of adequate coordinating devices among the localities, many key problems such as environmental degradation cannot be adequately addressed.[52]

As for successful entrepreneurs, these are hardly a significant anti-
regime force. Quite to the contrary, they maintain a symbiotic relationship
with the party-state. The detailed work of David Goodman in Shanxi
shows such entrepreneurs firmly enmeshed in the CCP's web. Despite considerable variation in the attitudes and motivation among such types, all
are dependent in a myriad of ways on the official structure. They range
from the owner of a boiler factory of bad class background whose efforts
to join the party have been rebuffed, but whom the local party committee
bailed out when his business hit hard times to avoid untoward employment
consequences, to the manager of a state chemical industry enterprise making a huge salary without having ownership rights, to the majority owner
of a coke washing plant (with Taiwanese minority owners) who sought to
avoid CCP membership but was impressed into becoming the party secretary of his plant. For such people, a rupture in party rule would introduce
uncertainty and threats to their own livelihood; whatever the attitudes of
this "class" toward the party-state in the long run, they are "on board" for
the immediate future.[53]

And finally, although demonstrations and riots are a sign of widespread and potentially explosive discontent, such outbreaks have been too
scattered to be a "dress rehearsal" for a nationwide challenge. The situation is different from 1989 in two respects. First, the leadership seemingly
has learned its "lesson" from 1989 and, the evidence suggests, is prepared
to crack down forcefully before any demonstrations get out of hand or link
up nationwide.[54] Second, although dissidents continue to petition the leadership,[55] the commitment to political change of potential student and

intellectual "counterelites" seems considerably weaker than in 1989. According to one foreign observer based at Beijing University, although interest continues in various "liberalizing" trends as reflected in attendance at lectures on law, for example, there was virtually no response to the 1997 release of Wei Jingsheng, who was apparently regarded as yesterday's man. More graphic are the reflections of an Australian diplomat who was told he was crazy when he warned his embassy of impending disaster in 1988, but who now characterizes the current situation as one of living for the moment, making as much money as one can because who knows what will happen a few years down the track.[56] The difference is that in 1989, apart from hard-core pro-reform intellectuals (not to mention loose cannons among those on Tiananmen Square), the movement was fueled by idealistic students who believed in the possibility of change, whereas today Deng Xiaoping's assertion that "to get rich is glorious" is truly the dominant ideology.

But if the immediate threat to the regime can be controlled, in the longer term the quality of leadership could be decisive as to whether the PRC is truly governable. Assessments of leadership quality are probably at the most speculative end of this inherently speculative exercise. Yet one must note that the leadership bears some uncanny similarities to that of the Brezhnev leadership in the Soviet Union, which gave us the "era of stagnation." First, the Brezhnev period was one of unusual personnel stability, a time when rather than plunging knives into the backs of colleagues, Soviet politicians allowed their daggers to rust in their scabbards.[57] To use CCP terminology, "stability and unity" were such priorities after the Stalinist and Khrushchevite past that they took precedence over effective government.[58] In addition, the current CCP leadership, like its Brezhnev counterpart, is packed with engineers.[59]

Whether such background characteristics necessarily produce stagnation, or, given the Gorbachev experience, whether leaders with more legal and political background produce better results is a moot point, but the similarities with the Brezhnev leadership are striking.[60] Although the technocratic credentials of the current leadership might provide the skills needed for economic development and, to follow the insightful argument of Li Cheng and Lynn White, strengthen the elite's sense of its right to rule, such leaders, with their inherent bureaucratic isolation from the populace, are arguably ill-suited to managing the politics of a difficult transition and bridging the gap between "them" and "us."[61]

Whatever the influence of background characteristics, it does appear that the present leadership's preferred mode for dealing with the PRC's huge list of problems is to muddle through, albeit with "Chinese reform characteristics."[62] Throughout the reform era the regime has moved a significant distance toward structural (nonpolitical) reforms, but in fits and starts, with an eye always peeled for dangers to stability. The emphasis on the market and state-owned enterprise reform at the Fifteenth National Congress and Zhu Rongji's government streamlining in 1998 have been packaged as decisive leadership action, but skepticism remains as to whether the measures actually implemented will be decisive or a familiar partial outcome. The larger question is whether muddling through will suffice over the longer term as reform enters a more difficult phase. Notwithstanding the magnitude of the problems and explosiveness of the tensions, I would be tempted to say yes, except for one factor—the issue of regime legitimacy.

## LEGITIMACY

It is one of the great ironies of PRC history that the state during the Maoist era, for all its horrors and absurdities, was more legitimate than that during the post-Mao period. Unlike governability, legitimacy in its Weberian usage is a precise concept but one difficult to operationalize, particularly in a system such as the PRC. The key to legitimacy, of course, is that the state's claims for obedience are accepted by society as based on right rather than force or calculation; the problem, apart from measuring such popular attitudes, is that different segments of society may have very different attitudes in this regard.[63] Nevertheless, and notwithstanding evidence of not only elements of society violently opposed to the regime but also considerable social dissatisfaction even during the "golden age" of the 1950s, overall indications suggest a population that either actively supported the Maoist regime or passively accepted its "right" to rule.[64] This support seemed to result from a combination of factors: the legitimacy conferred on new dynasties; the benefits gained as a result of ending decades of civil war and the process of economic construction; the party's monopoly of the distribution of material rewards and symbolic status; nationalist pride that China had "stood up"; and, not least, the ever-present indoctrination in an official ideology that, especially for many intellectuals, was persuasive and in any case was the only conceptual view of the world allowed.

Perhaps the best evidence of Maoist legitimacy comes from the two great crises caused by the chairman—the Great Leap Forward famine and the Cultural Revolution. There has long been evidence of riots and rebellions that had to be put down by military force during the famine,[65] but more impressive is the overall passivity of the peasantry while anywhere from 15 to 46 million or more people died, a situation leading a provincial first secretary of the period to reminisce that "the peasants were too accepting [of the situation]."[66] At a personal level, the hold of the regime over the thinking of its citizens at this cruel juncture was driven home to me in a conversation with a highly intelligent and sophisticated intellectual, someone who not long before the famine had been sharply criticized as a rightist, who recalled refusing food packages from relatives abroad despite his and his family's malnutrition out of patriotic feelings and an acceptance of the nature of the crisis as defined by official propaganda. His was not, he observed, an isolated case. Even at its lowest ebb, the regime retained a remarkable degree of credibility.

Arguably even clearer is the CCP's (or at least Mao's) legitimacy during the Cultural Revolution, which can be seen in the naive idealism of the youthful Red Guards who answered Mao's call. Even though with time such groups and other actors increasingly engaged in calculated maneuvers to advance their own interests, the activities of young students and hardened cadres alike reflected either a belief in Mao's radical message or an acceptance of the view, to adopt Weber's expression, that to disobey the chairman "would be abhorrent to the sense of duty."[67] But the crucial point is that, for all the social tension and chaos generated by the movement, for all the threats to production and official institutions, at no time was there a challenge to the regime itself.

The events of early 1967 are instructive. At a time of escalating violence, when PLA installations as well as civilian units were under "rebel" attack, the generals begged Mao to give the order to bring things under control. Two things stand out: the clear assumption that once the order was given, society would quickly come to heel; and that duty demanded inaction, despite the costs to the state and the PLA as an institution, as long as Mao withheld his consent.[68] The political and social distance between the events of 1967 and the nervous prophylactic measures enforced in Beijing and elsewhere by the current leadership, for fear of the slightest disturbance at the time of its presumptive greatest moment with the return of Hong Kong, is beyond measure.

In the period from the Cultural Revolution until 1989, regime legitimacy ebbed in a prolonged process. Although the very madness of the Cultural Revolution and the Red Guard's sense of being used for political games eroded the regime's support, it was the Lin Biao affair and the incoherent efforts to explain how the chairman's "best student" could become his potential assassin that brought about a sharp drop in credibility. Yet the major challenge posed by the 1976 Tiananmen demonstrations was not to the regime as such or to Mao (despite some pointed statements by people involved), but to those individuals who were seen as opposing two of the CCP's leading lights—Zhou Enlai and Deng Xiaoping.

The popular delight at the fall of the "Gang of Four" a few months later indicated a fundamental willingness to accept party rule stripped of its Cultural Revolution perversions.[69] In the process, however, something had been lost due to the bitter experiences of the preceding decade and the resulting questions about systemic deficiencies that had allowed them to happen. It is no accident that various leftist intellectuals of the early Cultural Revolution period now emerged as some of the more radical reform advocates. More broadly, the oft-mentioned "crises of faith, confidence, and trust" in the population as a whole became a major concern for the leadership and a key factor driving change forward.

If the Cultural Revolution had jeopardized the legitimacy of the system, the unfolding process of reform further eroded belief. The tension between traditional socialist values and the new emphasis on initiative and markets, along with the sharply enlarged "zone of indifference" and the fact that many people perceived unfairness and personal loss despite overall rising prosperity, clearly led to ideological disorientation within the public in a process perceptively analyzed by David Kelly as the "evaporation and dismemberment" of Marxism.[70] Yet despite all that, the CCP at the moment of its greatest peril in 1989 still retained legitimacy in important if contingent respects.

Most important, it was apparent in 1989 that most support for the student demonstrators came from people (including student spear carriers) who really wanted, as one put it to me, little more than having "the government listen to the people." The remarkable sight of students kneeling on the steps of the Great Hall of the People to present their petition is instructive. Some observers argued at the time it was a theatrical attack on the leadership, saying, in effect: you are no better than the feudal emperors. Yet, as a wise friend observed, a more likely interpretation is that the petitioners realized that they must show such "proper" respect for authority if broad popular support was to be sustained for the protests.[71]

Another factor was the deep impression of ideology even on the minds of those most committed to reform. Thus Yan Jiaqi remarked shortly after going into exile in 1989: "Something very heavy weighed on our minds, because this thing, Marxism, had already taken root among the younger generation . . . and could not be shaken. When [Fang Lizhi criticized Marxism], I felt there was reason in what he was saying, but I didn't dare let my faith be shaken."[72] The guns and tanks of 1989, however, shook that faith as never before, and the current regime, notwithstanding some research suggesting "a moderately high level of popular support," cannot be considered legitimate in the way the Maoist regime or even the pre-Tiananmen Deng regime could.[73] But rather than regarding this regime as "illegitimate," it might make more sense to see it as "beyond legitimacy." Certainly the old belief is gone; although it is too facile to say nobody believes in Marxism any more, clearly very large sections of both the public and (perhaps especially) elites find it irrelevant.[74] The widespread perception of the Fifteenth National Congress line is that it is Alice in Wonderland ideology, and as one observer commented, "they know it." Yet the regime persists, and not just by force.

Among the factors sustaining the regime, one of the most basic is simple inertia, that the regime is just "there." As a Beijing friend put it, "the Chinese people [as always] have no choice." But most crucial is the concern, heightened since 1989, for stability. This is not just a leadership preoccupation but something deeply and widely felt, including by many active in the 1989 demonstrations.[75] Ironically, although the elite's concern for stability may lead to unpopular acts such as retaining Li Peng in a leading position or to temporizing on needed reforms, society's fear of chaos provides potent support for even an unloved party-state. In addition, economic results are often cited as the critical link for whatever legitimacy the regime retains, and they certainly matter, particularly for that growing minority doing well economically. Overall, however, the majority is roughing it, and as of mid-1998, signs of an economic slowdown suggest a significant weakening on this front.

Nationalism also buttresses the regime as old ideologies become more and more irrelevant, but the question remains how solid and lasting a basis of support it provides. One Beijing friend speculated during the handover of Hong Kong that the government enjoyed 80 percent public approval, but that it would soon fall back to its "normal" 30 percent. Meanwhile, a highly analytical young party intellectual considered the shelf-life of nationalism quite limited as a prop for the regime, estimating that it will wear thin in five to ten years. Of course, such opinions are as speculative as my own, but they do not give the current leaders anything to cheer about.

Two other supports can be mentioned. First, the ubiquitous symbols of the regime and the collectivist ethos associated with them are part of everyday life. Thus David Goodman, admittedly in old revolutionary base areas in Shanxi, found thirty-year-old cadres saying, quite naturally, "I come from an 8th Route Army family."[76] The most notable aspect of this phenomenon is the fluctuating "Mao craze" of recent years. Although such veneration of Mao has many meanings, especially as a form of safe criticism of the current leaders, many Chinese still regard the late chairman with awe and considerable national pride.[77] How much such symbols might mean if the regime comes under challenge is unclear, but they do mean something in the present circumstances. Second, there is widespread belief in economic development and the concomitant importance of political stability, which differs from—indeed opposes—living for the moment and facing the future when it arrives. Instead, it is a belief—as reflected in the views of a Chinese postgraduate overseas who regards himself as a "developmental fundamentalist"—that the crucial objective is to build the country, the government has a critical role over the next ten to fifteen years in achieving that goal, and there is an unprecedented need for stability during that period. Again, this attitude does not provide an open-ended grant of legitimacy but serves as a very important prop for the regime in the intermediate term.

There is one final matter to consider. The preceding discussion has been framed largely in terms of the grant of popular legitimacy, but it is at least as important whether the elite itself will continue to grant legitimacy to the present regime. One only need look north to Boris Yeltsin in Russia to find a lifelong Communist turned vociferous anti-Communist. Indeed, there is evidence to indicate quite different degrees of elite commitment to the existing order based on different generations. Consider 1989. Whatever differences there were among the old revolutionaries and the party elders, they had no doubt that the regime must be defended and that Deng Xiaoping must be obeyed.[78] But at the next lower level—the first front— was the unprecedented case of a top leader, Zhao Ziyang, refusing to carry out the wishes of the preeminent leader and endorse martial law.[79] Meanwhile, cadres of various levels joined in the march of bureaucratic units (*danwei*) that supported the protests against their own official apparatus.

Should another crisis emerge, with the old revolutionaries gone, could the elite present even a shaky united front against society? It is questionable that a regime "beyond legitimacy" with its own people would pass this internal test, notwithstanding its apparent present determination to crack down on disorders.

## CONCLUSION

In its present form the CCP has relatively good prospects for the short and intermediate terms barring a major crisis, but a far more problematic situation for the longer term. Succession politics have been carefully managed, not only for the "third generation" with Jiang Zemin safely installed as "core" but a "fourth generation" with Hu Jintao waiting in the wings as "core designate." Whether all this comes to pass smoothly and whether it leads to effective government are other questions, but the arrangements reflect the party's preoccupation with stability.

Institutionalization has also proceeded within the elite, although with limitations leaving a large scope for personal authority and unregulated deals. The key institutional relationship between the party and army seems established, although it is as much contingent as rule bound. The real shortcomings are the lack of law, the arbitrariness in dealing with the Chinese people, and the problem of "them" and "us," all of which produce resentments that add to the long list of problems making governance difficult. Yet it would be bold to conclude that these problems or the effectiveness of the regime in dealing with them are worse than in other developing countries or that the populace's concern for stability seemingly weakens any challenge to the system. Although the basic inclination of the current leadership seems to be to muddle through toward further reform, one should never underestimate the political viability of such an approach—particularly when there are no organized forces gathering against the state.[80]

The long-term danger for the regime comes from its lack of solid legitimacy, a situation which in turn arises from its self-legitimization using an outmoded ideology that relatively few can accept as having contemporary validity. All the "substitute" supports—fear of chaos, nationalism, belief in economic development, and the like—can sustain the system for a time. Ultimately, however, the lack of respect for the CCP's core claim to authority means that concrete discontents will not simply be written off as instances where "the government screwed up" but will be linked to that very devalued claim. Put another way, there is an inchoate expectation that somehow the system will change by 2010, that the authorities will become less heavy-handed, and even, perhaps, that competing political parties will emerge by the end of the period. Although few will be prepared to take to the barricades over such expectations, the very fact that they exist enhances the possibility of such change and makes the status quo less tenable.

Apart from the possibility that the regime will sustain itself with minimal political change through a combination of good luck, the happenstance that leadership will make needed decisions, and ongoing repression of social discontent, two broad outcomes are plausible in the period ahead. The first is precisely the great crisis: 1989 revisited. In my view at least, this result seems relatively unlikely given the leadership's determination not to allow matters to get out of hand and the population's own acceptance of the need for stability, but it is not possible to know what will happen in a severe economic slowdown, financial collapse, or heightened social tensions. If such a crisis did occur, the chances of a leadership split or the collapse of the regime as in the Soviet case are reasonably high. What is likely to emerge in such circumstances would also follow the Soviet example—a new political class from the old *nomenklatura*[81]—which would jettison the official ideology but hopefully provide better leadership than its Russian cousins. The second possibility is gradual evolution toward a truly reformed polity, with the CCP somehow reinventing itself as a competitive political party. In such a process, the CCP most likely would retain a dominant position for a considerable period. This would be a further stage of the ongoing transition and something elements of the "fourth" and subsequent generations, for all their authoritarian impulses, will be willing to consider.[82]

## NOTES

This paper has benefited from personal discussions with and seminar presentations by Anita Chan, Keith Forster, David Goodman, Danny Kane, David Shambaugh, Warren Sun, Pamela Tan, You Ji, and especially Chris Buckley, as well as various unnamed Chinese friends, and from a comparative Soviet/Russian perspective from Graeme Gill, Roger Markwick, and T. H. Rigby.

1. The outstanding study by Lieberthal and Oksenberg, *Policy Making in China,* is a case in point. For all the detail on bureaucratic structure and processes, the way in which issues were settled at the apex of the system remained largely impenetrable.

2. A view based on reported questioning of Jiang Zemin ally Ding Guangen's pre-1949 career, speculatively on Qiao's initiative.

3. At 73 Qiao was older than any other Standing Committee member except Liu Huaqing who, as Deng Xiaoping's designated military representative at the Fourteenth Congress, was clearly a special case. Li Peng, Li Ruihuan, and Zhu Rongji were all under age 70 at the Fifteenth Congress, whereas Hu Jintao is in his mid-fifties, and newly elected members Wei Jianxing and Li Lanqing are in their mid-sixties. Jiang Zemin, although 71, as the leader was in a different position and in any case was Qiao's chronological junior. For further discussion on the general issue, see below.

4. See, for example, the work of Dorothy Solinger on the floating population and Thomas Bernstein on peasant disaffection.

5. A rare exception in print was Anita Chan's perceptive article, "Challenge to the Social Fabric."

6. See Rush, *Political Succession.* On China, see, for example, Shirk, *Political Logic of Economic Reform,* 14.

7. See Teiwes, *Politics at Mao's Court.*

8. For a brief treatment, see Teiwes, *Leadership, Legitimacy, and Conflict,* 113–118.

9. For a brief assessment of Zhao's decline that deals tentatively with this still unknowable issue, see Teiwes, "Paradoxical Post-Mao Transition," 65, 92–93. For a detailed discussion of the issues involved, see You Ji, "Zhao Ziyang."

10. See Teiwes and Sun, *The Tragedy of Lin Biao.*

11. Although he clearly lacked Mao's power, in my view the evidence is overwhelming that Deng could enforce his agenda whenever he was willing to take a strong stand. See Teiwes, "Paradoxical Post-Mao Transition," 62ff. For a contrary view, see Fewsmith, *Dilemmas of Reform* and "Reaction, Resurgence, and Succession."

12. See the preliminary analysis in Teiwes, *Leadership, Legitimacy, and Conflict,* 118–127. A far more detailed analysis, providing a more subtle understanding of the leadership politics of this period, is under preparation jointly with Warren Sun and Chris Buckley.

13. See Teiwes, "Paradoxical Post-Mao Transition," 87–88, 92–93.

14. It is unclear to what extent Jiang was Deng's personal choice that was subsequently ratified by the other party elders or the product of a more active consensus, but the best evidence suggests he had both Deng's and Chen Yun's strong backing.

15. For an account positing a somewhat broader political challenge, see You Ji, "Jiang Zemin," 13–14. My assessment is based on discussions with well-connected party historians who claim the affair was a result of Yang Baibing's attempt to freeze Jiang out of military affairs on the grounds he was a novice and Jiang's

appeal to Deng that he could not function in his position as chairman of the CMC under such circumstances.

16. This assessment draws on the analysis in You Ji, "Jiang Zemin," 14–17. For a different view emphasizing Jiang-Chen conflict, see Li and White, "Fifteenth Central Committee," 236–237.

17. Hong Kong press reports, always of dubious reliability, offer several versions of maneuvers concerning Qiao Shi's position during the lead-up to the Fifteenth Congress; see Baum, "Fifteenth National Party Congress," 149–151, for a summary. The point argued here is that although it is conceivable and may have been Qiao's perception that the general interest in stability would affirm his position on the Standing Committee, he had little choice but to retire once the age question was raised. See below for further discussion of the larger issue.

18. Of course, uncertainty would be introduced if Jiang were to die before the completion of his term, particularly in view of the apparent animosity between Li Peng and Zhu Rongji, the number two and number three figures in the leadership. A debilitating struggle in such a situation between Li and Zhu cannot be ruled out, but I believe that Hu Jintao, as the "core designate" (see below) would become general secretary and, more certainly given the state constitution, PRC president because of his position as vice president since March 1998. Of course, in view of his lesser seniority, Hu would probably exercise less authority than Jiang, depending on the timing of the succession.

19. On the significance of consensus politics in the post-Mao period generally, see Teiwes, "Paradoxical Post-Mao Transition," 82ff. On Jiang's consensual approach, see You Ji, "Jiang Zemin," 4–6, 18–20.

20. The information on Deng and Chen's attitude toward Wu Bangguo and Huang Ju comes from sources in the central organization department as reported in You Ji, "Jiang Zemin," 28. The assessment of Politburo career links is based on an analysis of official profiles released at the time of the Fifteenth Congress.

21. For an alternative account emphasizing the limits to Jiang's power in leadership appointments, see Li and White, "Fifteenth Central Committee," 239–241. There is no necessary conflict between the two views, in that the "normal politics" of the post-Deng period precisely involves significant limits on the power of the leader. The point argued here, however, is that even with his ultimate authority constrained, Jiang can be confident in his security of tenure, barring major regime reversals, in significant measure because of his consensual style.

22. Lieberthal, *Governing China*, 183.

23. See *Selected Works of Deng Xiaoping,* 302–325.

24. For an overview, see Manion, *Retirement of Revolutionaries.*

25. *Sing Tao Jih Pao,* September 15, 1997, in FBIS-CHI-97-258; and *Cheng Ming,* September 1, 1997, in FBIS-CHI-97-268. As for Jiang's state position as PRC president, a constitutional two-term limit does exist.

26. Of course, by themselves retirement systems and term limitations are not necessary for institutionalization; the U.S. presidency was an institution before and after the two-term limitation. In the Chinese context, however, the tradition of personal power makes such regularized limitations a key to institutionalization.

27. You Ji, in "Jiang Zemin," 22, makes the perceptive observation that Chinese "power struggles" more often than not are "just quiet fight[s] for acceptance."

28. On these powers, see ibid., 5.

29. See Tsou, "Chinese Politics at the Top."

30. See the official September 19, 1997, *Xinhua* profile of Hu at the time of the Fifteenth Congress, in FBIS-CHI-97-262.

31. A presumptive case in point is Jiang Chunyun, whose appointment as vice premier was opposed by more than a third of NPC delegates in 1995 but who retained his Politburo seat at the Fifteenth Congress. See Starr, "China in 1995," 20, where Jiang is incorrectly identified as Jiang Chunying.

In contrast to the entire foregoing emphasis, many see both events surrounding the Fifteenth Congress and recent leadership politics generally as involving, in Michel Oksenberg's phrase, "enormous infighting." See the contributions of Oksenberg, Edward Friedman, and others in the "Chinapol" discussions of September–October 1997, as well as Richard Baum's article in the *Asian Wall Street Journal,* September 10–11, 1997. The argument here is not to deny intense maneuvering for appointments, particularly new positions on top bodies, but to highlight the restraints resulting from the preoccupation with stability.

32. See Teiwes, "Paradoxical Post-Mao Transition," 86ff, especially 89n, on the stability factor in previous reform-era Politburos.

33. For overviews, see Shambaugh, "The Soldier and the State"; Shambaugh, "Building the Party-State"; and Joffe, "Party-Army Relations."

34. Although this is a controversial view for the "Lin Biao period," extensive evidence in support is provided in Teiwes and Sun, *The Tragedy of Lin Biao.* On Deng Xiaoping and the military, see Teiwes, *Leadership, Legitimacy, and Conflict,* 123–124; and Teiwes, "Paradoxical Post-Mao Transition," 67–68.

35. For a summary of Jiang's relations with the PLA and an analysis emphasizing the army's developing professional corporate identity, see You Ji, "Jiang Zemin," 7–12, 22.

36. Cf. the discussion in Li and White, "Fifteenth Central Committee," 263, which emphasizes the similar technocratic orientation of the civilian leadership and military professionals.

37. Chi at 68 and Zhang at 69 were considerably older than other new Politburo members, who ranged from 53 to 62, with State Council general secretary Luo Gan the only other recruit over 60.

38. See Teiwes, "Paradoxical Post-Mao Transition," 87.

39. Consider also the comments during the early 1998 Australian Constitutional Convention of the respected former independent parliamentarian Ted Mack: "Australia is like a great Gulliver tied down by 1,000 Lilliputians. Ravaging business tycoons, takeover merchants, union leaders, special interests, remote bureaucracies, complex regulations, indecisive and sometimes inept and even corrupt and lying politicians, and many others, have combined to tie down the body and debilitate it." *The Sydney Morning Herald,* February 4, 1998, 17.

40. This argument was made in a stimulating presentation by Markwick, "What Kind of State Is the Russian State?"

41. For an argument challenging the view of an all-powerful Maoist state, see Shue, *The Reach of the State.* For a rebuttal congenial to my own views, see the review article by Unger, "State and Peasant."

42. See the gripping account of the damage in Becker, *Hungry Ghosts.* An analysis of the politics of Great Leap Forward excesses, including an epilogue on the retreat from the leap in 1960–1962, is Teiwes with Sun, *China's Road to Disaster.*

43. Although much of the disruption of this period came "from below" and was uncontrollable by the state, this was ultimately due to Mao's unwillingness to give clear and consistent directives to curb the "revolutionary masses."

44. For a discussion of the tension between such nostalgia and reform, see Teiwes, "Restoration and Innovation."

45. See Womack, "Modernization and Democratic Reform," 424–425.

46. The key contribution to the debate is Wang and Hu, *Zhongguo guojia nengli baogao*. Divergent views were presented at the "State Capacity in East Asia" conference organized by the State and Society in East Asia Network, Copenhagen, September 27–29, 1996. Significantly, David Shambaugh's summing-up listed a range of aspects in which the PRC had demonstrated impressive state capacity, but during the discussion he declared it was a rash assumption that the regime would still be around in 2010.

47. Of course, fundamentally, as in the Great Leap Forward, the problem was more political than technical, involving the unwillingness of other actors to tell Mao truths he did not want to hear. See Teiwes with Sun, *China's Road to Disaster,* especially chap. 4.

48. Wang, "China's 1994 Fiscal Reform," 801–802, 815–816. For a less positive assessment of another key policy, enterprise reform, see the contribution of Nicholas Lardy in Chapter 8.

49. Starr, "China in 1995," 13, 18–22.

50. Three of the six new full Politburo members are provincial secretaries, making a total of five, or a larger number than at any time except for the Cultural Revolution and initial post–Cultural Revolution period. In addition, provincial representation on the Central Committee increased by 6 percent in comparison to that during the Fourteenth Central Committee. See Li and White, "Fifteenth Central Committee," 252, 254–255.

51. The work of David Goodman provides this more subtle assessment; see, for example, his "Politics of Regionalism," *China Deconstructs.*

52. Lieberthal, *Governing China,* 285–286, 315–317, provides excellent discussions of both issues. The priority given to economic results means that higher levels pay relatively little attention to the activities of subordinate levels as long as they produce the required resources, something that in turn means little concern with the environmental impacts on others of the productive activities of a locality, as in the case of upstream areas dumping pollutants that create problems for downstream areas.

53. Goodman, "In Search of China's New Middle Class."

54. Of course, this does not mean there are no hesitations in specific cases; see Thomas Bernstein's discussion of the handling of 1993 peasant demonstrations in Sichuan in "In Quest of Voice," 70–77. On the nationwide aspects of the 1989 crisis, see Unger, *Pro-Democracy Protests.*

55. High-profile calls for change, including letters to both domestic and international authorities, have increased in the period since Deng's death, and the regime has, in the words of the U.S. State Department's annual human rights survey for 1997, "exhibited some limited tolerance of public expressions of opposition." It, however, was only a slight tactical reduction in repression, and the dissident community remains very small.

56. The above is based on private conversations in November 1997 and January 1998.

57. This characterization was raised by Graeme Gill in personal conversation sometime in the 1980s. Again note the contrast between this period and notions of brutal infighting within Communist leaderships.

58. This is perhaps an appropriate occasion for self-criticism of my 1979 assessment (see *Politics and Purges,* 487ff, esp. 491), which not simply predicted the post-Mao pursuit of stability, but with reference to the Brezhnev regime, suggested it would lead to more effective government. Although this was certainly true insofar

as comparisons to the later Maoist period are concerned, it neglected to canvass the costs of too much stability. In the event, the pre-Tiananmen reform period produced a fairly tumultuous politics despite the ongoing concern for stability. The question is, to what degree is the even further heightened preoccupation with stability impeding dealing with pressing problems?

59. An analysis of Xinhua profiles of the Fifteenth Politburo membership indicates that at least eighteen of the twenty-four full and alternate members have engineering or other technical backgrounds. Cf. Li and White, "Fifteenth Central Committee," 231.

60. See Myron Rush's devastating assessment of Gorbachev, "Fortune and Fate." It is also of interest that the current Russian leadership, although drawn from the same broad pool of the Communist Party *nomenklatura,* differs significantly from its Soviet counterpart in that a balance of social science and engineering backgrounds exists, as opposed to the earlier dominance of engineering and the hard sciences; see Rigby, "New Elites for Old." One would not, in any case, be overly impressed with the performance of the Yeltsin regime.

61. Li and White, "Fifteenth Central Committee," 234.

62. This was Richard Baum's third-most-favored future scenario after "neo-conservatism" and "neo-authoritarianism" in his early 1996 laying of the odds; see "China After Deng."

63. For the concept by the man himself, see Weber, *Theory of Social and Economic Organization,* especially 124, 324–325. For a discussion canvassing some of the issues involved while applying the concept to the party leader, see Teiwes, *Leadership, Legitimacy, and Conflict,* chap. 2.

64. See, for example, Domenach, *Origins of the Great Leap Forward,* pt. 1; and Perry, "Shanghai's Strike Wave."

65. As revealed in the PLA's *Bulletin of Activities.* See Cheng, *Politics of the Chinese Red Army.* Notably, the most serious rebellions took place in national minority areas, where legitimacy was not granted by the minority populations.

66. Interview, Beijing, 1997. A similar assessment is offered by Becker in the course of his numbing description of the famine in *Hungry Ghosts.*

67. See the analysis in Wang, *Failure of Charisma,* for Red Guards. Andrew Walder's paper to the "State Capacity in East Asia" Copenhagen conference (see note 46), (September 1996), "When States Unravel," makes a similar case for cadres and work teams during the early days of the movement. Although such behavior was common, it was clearly accompanied by belief.

68. On these developments, see Teiwes and Sun, *The Tragedy of Lin Biao,* 72–75.

69. For a detailed discussion of the Tiananmen incident, see Baum, *Burying Mao,* 32–36. On the popular joy at the "Gang's" fall, see Garside, *Coming Alive,* 165–166.

70. Kelly, "Chinese Marxism."

71. For an analysis critical of the students for taking on too much cultural baggage, see Perry, "Intellectuals and Tiananmen."

72. Quoted in Kelly, "Chinese Marxism," 19.

73. See Jie, Yang, and Hillard, "Level and Sources of Popular Support."

74. There are, of course, conservative ideologues such as Deng Liqun who firmly do believe in socialism. Deng, according to a source with first-hand knowledge, has "declared war" on Jiang Zemin, but given Deng's marginalization, this will cause Jiang no loss of sleep.

75. This impressionistic conclusion is supported by the survey data of Jie, Yang, and Hillard, "Level and Sources of Popular Support," 53, which found 93

percent of a Beijing sample preferring an orderly society to a freer one prone to disruption.

76. See Goodman, "In Search of China's New Middle Class."

77. On recent manifestations of the Mao cult, see Barme, *Shades of Mao.*

78. See the purported differences between Deng Xiaoping and Chen Yun over the use of force, with Chen as the moderate; Baum, *Burying Mao,* 10.

79. Cf. Yang Shangkun's exasperated remark to Zhao during the spring 1989 deliberations: "Comrade Xiaoping did speak on this question, . . . So are you for Comrade Xiaoping or against him?" Tong, "Death at the Gate of Heavenly Peace," 71.

80. One might consider the Soviet Union in its declining period when there were significant forces, whether social such as national minorities (where the problem was substantially more explosive than in the PRC) and striking workers, or by 1989 organized political groups gathering against the regime. Yet without Gorbachev actually encouraging or facilitating such developments, it is unlikely the fatal crisis of the regime would have arisen, at least within anything like the same time frame. See the collected articles in *The National Interest,* especially those by Rush, Kontorovich, and Fairbanks.

81. See above, note 60.

82. For a stimulating discussion of possible developments in this direction by even the present "third generation," see Oksenberg, "Will China Democratize?"

# PART TWO

⁘  ⁘

# The People's Liberation Army and Its Political Role

# ▦ 6 ▦

# The People's
# Liberation Army and Politics:
# After the Fifteenth Party Congress

## *Ellis Joffe*

As a guide to the People's Liberation Army's (PLA's) political role, the Fifteenth National Congress of the Chinese Communist Party (CCP) and its aftermath should be viewed from two angles. From a narrow one, not much is new. The Congress confirmed the trends that had marked the PLA's role in the transition from the Deng Xiaoping to the Jiang Zemin era. Changes were minor and did not alter the direction of events. Developments after the Congress have not diverged from these trends.

Viewed from a wide angle, however, the PLA's political role is undergoing a major transformation. Arising out of the political changes that began to take shape in China toward the end of Deng's rule, as well as from changes in the PLA, this transformation is steering party-army relations away from patterns that had existed for more than forty years under Mao Zedong and Deng and during the revolutionary period before that. How far away will be worked out in the coming years, but it was already clear before the Congress that these relations had shifted.

## PARTY-ARMY RELATIONS: A NEW MODE

The most important feature of this new relationship is the acquisition by the Chinese military of an unprecedented potential for wielding political influence. To be sure, this potential is tempered by a growing military professionalism and by countervailing political factors. It has manifested mainly in the military's new capacity to influence high politics and policies, not in routine involvement in political or administrative affairs. The military's imprint on policymaking is unprecedented but selective. Nonetheless, such a potential hardly existed under Mao and was limited under Deng. Therefore, its acquisition constitutes the most striking difference in the political position of the military between then and now.

The significance of this difference stems from the basic importance of the military on the Chinese political scene. "Political power," Mao said during the revolutionary struggle, "grows out of the barrel of the gun," and this statement remains true almost fifty years after the revolution. In China's one-party authoritarian regime, the position of the paramount leader ultimately depends on the support of the party-army. This maxim was applicable to Mao and Deng, although their dependence was offset by other leadership strengths. It is clearly applicable to Jiang, who is vulnerable as a new figure and lacks the countervailing strengths of his predecessors. For him, military support is vital for political survival.

In the most extreme case, military chiefs control the forces that may be used to oust the party leader. However, this is hardly an ever-present concern for Jiang because the possibility of a coup is remote in the current Chinese scheme. The combination of Chinese political culture with the tradition of the PLA and its professionalism forms a powerful barrier against a military coup, which, if it occurs, will be only in the most dire circumstances. Nonetheless, Jiang needs the support of the military in circumstances that are far less extreme. He needed their support to ensure his ascent to the top, and he needs it to continue his rule effectively. Unless all players in the political system are unequivocally aware that the military is behind him and his programs, Jiang's position will be unstable, and he will not have vital leverage in the pursuit of his policies.

The military shows its support in various ways. PLA chiefs and organs frequently praise Jiang, declare their loyalty to him, and show him respect in public ceremonies. They educate the troops to do the same and make such efforts public. They avoid any action that might undermine his position, such as criticizing his policies, and they refrain from showing support for a potential rival. But their support has not been provided gratis to the successor to Mao and Deng, giving the military the potential for influence that they lacked before.

Routine aside, crisis situations might arise (as they had in the past), requiring action by the military. Mao and Deng needed the military in such situations, but Jiang might need them much more. They might be called upon to intervene in a leadership conflict in support of the paramount leader, as they were on the eve of the Cultural Revolution; to maintain public order in a time of turmoil, as they were during the Cultural Revolution; or to remove a rival leadership group, as in the case of the "Gang of Four." They might be employed to put down major antigovernment demonstrations, as in the Tiananmen crisis, or to suppress a rebellious provincial figure, a possibility that is not entirely unrealistic given the growing power of China's local leaders. Since under Jiang the response of the military in such situations would not be automatic, uncertainty also opens new possibilities for political influence.

The PLA, in short, has become a pivotal player in Chinese politics. But since it may be said that the PLA has always been such a player, what is new? The answer is that the terms of the political game have changed substantially and so has the role of the armed forces. This has occurred in three ways. First, whereas under Mao and Deng military support for the paramount leader against opponents at the top and on the ground was ax-iomatic, under Jiang it is conditional and may be transferred to a rival. Second, under Mao and Deng the PLA's bargaining power and imprint on major decisions were limited, but under Jiang both have grown greatly. Third, whereas under Mao and Deng the party exercised control over the military hierarchy, under Jiang the PLA is becoming a separate entity sub-ject to minimal organizational control by the party. The following sections explain these changes and their effects.[1]

## THE PLA AND JIANG ZEMIN: CONDITIONAL SUPPORT

The first change pertains to Jiang Zemin's relations with the PLA. The Fif-teenth Party Congress ceremoniously confirmed him as paramount leader after Deng, but Jiang falls into a different category from his predecessors. Although he defied widespread predictions that he would not survive after Deng's death and in fact has gained considerable strength since then, Jiang's position is far less secure than Mao's or Deng's ever was, which both stems from, and is reflected in, his vastly different stature in the PLA.[2]

Mao's stature in the PLA was unique because it derived from his per-sonal authority, which was accepted like a "mandate of heaven" by all other leaders in their public behavior and was unassailable. This authority enabled him to disregard institutional boundaries and, like an emperor, to rule everything. Most prominently, no boundaries existed for Mao with re-gard to the PLA and with good reason. As founding father of the Red Army and its leader throughout the revolutionary years, Mao regarded himself as eminently qualified and justified to intervene in military affairs in later years as well and always acted as an active commander in chief of the PLA. The PLA leaders fully accepted this situation. To them, Mao was not only the nominal chairman of the party's Central Military Commission (CMC), but China's supreme military authority in fact.

This relationship had several implications for the political position of the PLA. First, the PLA lent the support of its chiefs to Mao and his poli-cies without reservation, even when they disagreed with him on specific is-sues. Second, Mao could use the PLA as his personal power base in elite struggles, confident that his personal authority would ensure its positive response, even if the situation required deeper involvement, including the use of troops. Third, because of Mao's personal authority, the PLA had little leverage to sway him or to dissent from his orders. This does not mean that its chiefs were meek yes-men; in inner councils they voiced their opposing views. But from the little that has been revealed by disputes that became public, it appears that when Mao made up his mind, he prevailed. Because of his stature, military leaders lacked the power and probably the will to defy him. Under Mao, the PLA did not become an independent political player.

Neither did it under Deng Xiaoping, despite the differences between Deng's stature as paramount leader and Mao's. His return to supreme power in 1978, after the second of two Mao-induced periods in the political wilderness, obviously pointed to his preeminent status but not to his unquestioned superiority. He still had to prove himself, and unlike Mao, his personal authority also depended very much on the success of his policies. As these policies reaped remarkable success, Deng's stature soared. Deng's own special relationship with the PLA played a crucial part. This relationship was forged during the Sino-Japanese War, when Deng served as the respected political commissar of what later became the PLA Second Field Army, and during his tenure as a key figure in the administration of the southwest region in the early years of the new regime, when Deng worked closely with military leaders who would later move to the capital with him.[3]

This bond accounted for the protection Deng received from PLA commanders when he was hunted by Red Guards in the mid-1960s, for the backing he got from PLA commanders when he made his bid for power in the late 1970s, and for their reluctant readiness to intervene in the Tiananmen crisis of 1989 and to fire on the demonstrators. It also accounts for the steady support of PLA leaders for Deng's reforms, which he could take for granted as an invaluable asset in his unyielding efforts to implement the new policies.

Deng's standing in the PLA likewise was vital in toning down the sectoral demands of its commanders. Even though Deng named military upgrading as one of the nation's "four modernizations," it came last on the list, which meant that, despite the PLA's dire needs, precedence would be given to economic development. As a result, the military budget was more or less frozen during the 1980s and during that time declined by about 10 percent as a share of national expenditure. Although there was some compensation in the form of massive manpower cuts, efficiency campaigns, and limited involvement in profit-making enterprises, allocations to the PLA were far from adequate for its daily requirements, let alone for weapons upgrading. This situation could have been fertile ground for PLA alienation. But although there were periodic complaints about the low level of military financing, PLA leaders did not make any move that could weaken Deng, such as publicly withdrawing support or aligning with rival leaders.

Jiang Zemin's position, when he was thrust into power in 1989, was completely different. Although it has improved steadily over the years, it cannot compare to that of his predecessors. When Jiang became paramount leader, his personal qualities were hardly notable. His greatest disadvantage was that he lacked the three most important sources of personal authority on which Mao and Deng drew: personality, past achievements, and a network of connections. As a member of the postrevolutionary generation, he inevitably missed out on the years of struggle during which illustrious records were created and long-lasting loyalties formed. According to most observers in China, his presence did not inspire much awe or respect.

Jiang's political career had been relatively short. Before his ascent, he had been mayor of Shanghai and before that a nondescript technical administrator. Unlike Mao, he had not articulated a grand vision, and unlike Deng, he had no original blueprint for China's development. Along with his unproven leadership abilities, his personal authority appeared shaky at best. For this reason, support for Jiang did not flow naturally from members of China's ruling elite. It had to be granted, and Jiang was decisively dependent on their readiness to accept him as leader. This dependence has waned considerably since then, but it is still critical. To remain in power, he needs the support of the principal personalities who head the vast hierarchies making up the Chinese power structure. And the most important of these are the armed forces.

Under Mao and Deng, such support was forthcoming without question regardless of the circumstances because of their standing with the military. Jiang does not have such standing and consequently does not enjoy such support. His command of the armed forces derives first of all from his chairmanship of the CMC, but unlike Mao and Deng, he clearly lacks the personal qualifications to hold this position. Even by his own admission, Jiang was not fit to assume the top post in the Chinese military establishment. The reasons were glaring: he had no military record, no military experience, no particular knowledge of military affairs, and no connections in the armed forces. He came to the PLA position only by virtue of his elevation to paramount leader, and Deng reportedly had put pressure on the veteran PLA chiefs to give Jiang the essential backing. This backing did not come naturally and has remained conditional.

From this fact derive two essential features of Jiang's relations with the military. First, because he cannot rely on the automatic backing of the military, Jiang's political position is not completely secure, since other players know that in a major crisis support may not be forthcoming. Second, Jiang can gain such backing by making concessions to PLA leaders, placing them in a position to exert unusual political influence.

Since 1992, however, Jiang has done much to neutralize these features and to strengthen his position in the PLA by drawing on two invaluable assets. First, Jiang has institution-based authority, stemming from the nature of his official duties. As paramount leader, he occupies pivotal positions—since 1992 he has been general secretary of the CCP, chairman of the CMC, and president of the People's Republic of China. As CCP and CMC leader, he stands at the apex of the two most important hierarchies in the Chinese political system, and from his presidency he accrues luster and international exposure. These posts give Jiang substantial power. Despite the supreme importance of personal authority in Chinese political culture, official position is also highly significant because traditional culture emphasizes the centrality of hierarchy and subordination to powerholders. Those at the top command much symbolic prestige, in itself a source of power.

Jiang's official status also has permitted him to place trusted officials in key posts. The loyalties and obligations stemming from this advantage have always been a core component of power in China's authoritarian political system, which is still moved above all by personal ties between the leader and his supporters. They are absolutely crucial to a leader like Jiang, whose personal authority is not upheld by charismatic leadership traits or connections that reach far into the past. Personal traits cannot be created, but connections can.

Jiang began to create connections in the PLA shortly after ascending to the top post. Since then, he has carried out sweeping changes at the upper echelons of the PLA.[4] Nonetheless, until the Fifteenth Party Congress, Jiang's position as supreme commander of the PLA was weakened by the presence of two veteran military leaders, Admiral Liu Huaqing and Gen. Zhang Zhen, whom Deng had brought out of semiretirement and appointed as vice chairmen of the CMC. As longtime leaders enjoying great prestige in the PLA, their task was apparently to ease Jiang's way into the top military echelons in the face of suspicious commanders, but their relationship with Jiang was uneasy from the beginning. While towering over him in military stature, they treated Jiang publicly with the respect due their senior in his capacity as chairman of the Central Military Commission and supported him without reservation. At the same time, however, Jiang presided over meetings attended by China's foremost military leaders and presumably had to defer to Liu and Zhang on matters concerning the PLA and beyond.

As long as the two old veterans remained in office, they overshadowed Jiang's standing in the military. This was most obvious in the appointment and retirement of high-ranking officers, which could not have been carried out without their approval. After reportedly trying for some time to ease Liu and Zhang into retirement, Jiang finally succeeded in doing so at the Fifteenth Congress. In the future, he will stand alone as the leader who appointed officers to their new posts, and these officers will be in his debt.

Liu and Zhang's replacements at the Fifteenth Party Congress as the two senior officers on the CMC—Chi Haotian and Zhang Wannian—not only belong to Jiang's generation and cannot outshine him as veterans of the revolutionary wars but owe their promotion to him.[5]

In addition to weaving a network of supporters, Jiang has been a PLA-friendly leader in other respects as well. He shows great respect to military leaders and to the PLA as a whole and has cultivated the retired leaders of the PLA, the "elders" who continue to exercise influence over their former subordinates, some of whom have risen to top commands. He has been unusually generous with promotions—in one fell swoop in May 1994 Jiang promoted to the rank of general eighteen lieutenant generals and major generals who held key posts. When making frequent and well-publicized visits to military units, he reportedly shows personal concern for soldiers' well-being. He pays great respect to the traditions of the PLA and consults with PLA leaders on critical issues such as Taiwan.[6]

Most important, Jiang is an ardent advocate of military modernization and has sharply raised allocations to the PLA for that purpose. Of course, the pressing needs of the PLA played a part, not only to purchase new weapons but also to improve the plummeting living standards of the troops. The increased allocations also stem from the economic upsurge of the 1990s and the obligation of the leaders to make good on their promise that the PLA would benefit. But an important reason has doubtless been Jiang's desire to show his goodwill toward the PLA in the most tangible way. The increase in official spending, when adjusted for inflation, has been only about 4 percent, although actual spending has doubled since 1986. The PLA's real budget, however, is four to five times the official figure according to the best estimates, given the hidden allocations and the PLA's earnings from commercial enterprises, research institutes, and weapons sales.[7] Thus, under Jiang the money at the disposal of the PLA has increased significantly.

The second thing going for Jiang in enhancing his standing with the armed forces is the tradition of a respectful PLA. As an institution, it has never strayed from subordination to party leadership. Although the personal authority of the paramount leader played a part, this deference also stemmed from the PLA's acceptance of party supremacy. As leader of the party, Jiang commands the obedience of the army also by virtue of his position, regardless of his individual traits.

Along these lines, the growing professionalism of Chinese officers has strengthened military respect and obedience as the armed forces step up their modernization, with three significant consequences for Jiang's leadership.[8] First, it instills an ethos of compliance with orders emanating from higher levels, without which no modern army can function effectively. Second, it turns officers away from political pursuits that interfere with their specific tasks, which are becoming increasingly complex. And finally, it discourages them from intervention in political struggles, which can only end by dividing commanders of the PLA and jeopardizing its existence as a national army. As every senior Chinese officer knows from personal or recounted experience, the PLA's intervention in the Cultural Revolution—the antithesis of professional behavior—almost destroyed it.

On balance, Jiang's support in the PLA derives from his institutional standing and the tradition of the PLA rather than from his personal authority. As a result, this support is limited and is contingent on performance. Because it is not likely that Jiang or his successor will enjoy the authority to command unlimited support, both of them will be dependent on the military as Mao and Deng never were, a new stage in the relationship between the paramount leader and the PLA.

## THE PLA AND POLICYMAKING: A GREATER IMPRINT

The second change in the role of the military pertains to national policymaking. This role has increased in scope and substance. Under Jiang, the military gained the capacity to influence areas from which they had been previously excluded and to exert a much greater influence than before in other areas.

Under Mao, policymaking was a one-man show, less so on internal issues and more so on foreign policy and security. Under Deng, policymaking was a much more open process. Due to political expediency and personal inclination, Deng tended to bring his senior colleagues into the process, but he also had the stature to be the ultimate source of major decisions. The picture of leadership is different under Jiang. He does not tower over his colleagues, and his standing does not endow him with the privilege of claiming final wisdom on all affairs of state. As a result, the policymaking process under his chairmanship is undoubtedly more open and dispersed among his senior colleagues.

In this process, the military is particularly well placed. Not only does it have leverage over a paramount leader who is critically dependent on its support, but it also occupies an advantageous position with respect to other influential leaders. In contrast to the Mao and Deng eras, leaders in the Jiang era do not have their own constituencies in the PLA stretching back to revolutionary days, but they require its support to advance their own interests. This gives PLA chiefs unusual leverage over policy.

Such leverage is presumably brought to bear first of all in the Politburo. Until the Fifteenth Party Congress, the military also had a representative—Liu Huaqing—on the Standing Committee of the Politburo, but the Congress did not renew this representation. Although this suggests that the influence of the PLA has been weakened, in fact it has not. First, because Deng placed Liu Huaqing on the Standing Committee in a personal capacity to help Jiang establish his authority, there was no reason to put a military man on that body once Liu retired and Jiang had made substantial progress consolidating his rule. Second, the PLA chiefs probably wanted to distance themselves from an overly intimate involvement in the daily running of the country, especially in areas that do not impinge directly on their interests. Third, the military, in fact, does have a representative on the Standing Committee—Jiang himself. As chairman of the CMC, Jiang will not oppose PLA views on matters that had been previously discussed in the military forum but will push for their adoption by the Standing Committee.

Furthermore, the military can exercise influence themselves through its representatives on the Politburo—the two senior military leaders Chi Haotian and Zhang Wannian. At the Fifteenth Congress they replaced Liu Huaqing, who retired, and Yang Baibing, who had remained in the Politburo for reasons of face even after he was dismissed as director of the general political department and general secretary of the CMC in 1992. Since Yang obviously had no influence after that point, his replacement by a top PLA leader has, in fact, increased the weight of the military on the Politburo.

This does not mean that PLA leaders intrude into all areas of national policy. As professional military men, they probably do not claim a singular prerogative to make decisions in matters on which they have no particular expertise. Besides, other Politburo members are unlikely to accept such intrusion passively. Furthermore, in the history of political-military relations at the highest level in China, PLA leaders have not had any known special influence on decisions outside their professional sphere, except in their capacity as national leaders who rose above strictly institutional concerns. Since that generation of military leaders has passed from the scene, the likelihood of inordinate military intervention in matters that do not directly relate to the armed forces is remote. The removal of a military representative from the Standing Committee of the Politburo after the Fifteenth Congress reflects this detachment.

In military affairs, PLA chiefs enjoy much more autonomy than in the past. Under Mao, after the PLA had embarked on its first period of modernization in the early 1950s, a de facto division of labor inevitably developed to some extent at the highest level, and the military chiefs took charge of the PLA's daily work. Mao remained its real supreme commander, however, and when he chose to intervene, he did so with impunity. Deng was also an active commander in chief, and although he was much more considerate of professional military sentiments, he still made the final decisions.

In contrast, Jiang has neither the qualifications nor the authority to be an active commander in chief who is deeply involved in guiding the PLA, and he has not attempted to do so. Professional decisions are made by its leaders in the CMC or in other organs, and Jiang follows their lead and gives his approval.[9] Because Jiang makes no pretense to effectively command the PLA and because he surely does not want a confrontation with its leaders, this arrangement is satisfactory to both sides and seems to be working smoothly.

In foreign affairs, the military not only acquired a new capacity to exert influence but also is driven to do so as never before.[10] This drive derives from two factors that did not carry the same force in earlier periods. The first factor is nationalism. Always the most powerful factor in Chinese foreign policy, nationalism acquired new force after the collapse of the Soviet Union and the disintegration of Communist ideology, events that changed the preoccupation of Chinese leaders. As never before, Chinese leaders were confronted with the question of China's role in the world as a rising superpower and not as a secondary player in the political game between two superior powers. And the demise of Communist ideology shifted the emphasis entirely away from China's defunct global revolutionary mission to an exclusive concern with its role on the world scene.

The new nationalism is a direct result of this single-minded preoccupation. It is driven by the view that China is in constant danger of encroachments on its independence, which are reminiscent of past imperialist humiliations and obstruct the pursuit of its rightful place in the world. It is shared by all Chinese leaders but has particular relevance for the military.

The military see themselves as chief protectors of China's territorial interests and national honor. This self-image cannot be separated from the pride and patriotism that are universal hallmarks of the military profession. In the PLA, nationalism has a particularly sharp quality because Chinese officers function in an intensely patriotic milieu, which continuously inculcates them with nationalistic values and imbues them with a sense of mission as protectors of these values. Their sense of mission has grown stronger because Jiang Zemin has yet to prove his revolutionary credentials. Under Mao or Deng, the military would hardly venture to claim a unique role in the defense of nationalistic objectives. Jiang, however, still must demonstrate that he is a worthy standard-bearer of Chinese nationalist aspirations. Until then, the military will tend to view him with some suspicion and presumably consider it necessary to keep a close watch on foreign policymaking to ensure that Jiang does not compromise China's core principles.

The second factor propelling the military into foreign affairs is the international situation that has emerged after the end of the Cold War and the collapse of the Soviet Union. These changes have caused changes in China's strategy and have placed new responsibilities on its military leaders.

During the Cold War, the overriding concern of Chinese leaders was with the perceived threat from the superpowers—the United States in the 1950s, both the United States and the Soviet Union in the 1960s, and the Soviet Union until the late 1970s. During this period, the sole mission of the PLA was to defend China against an invasion based on the Maoist doctrine of "people's war." Essentially, war would be fought on China's territory, and its conventional armed forces would be developed (or undeveloped) accordingly—as a massive, technologically backward, but highly motivated and well-led force.

The PLA's mission began to change in the mid-1980s, when the Chinese officially acknowledged what they had already believed for several years: that China no longer faced the threat of a major war. If war were to break out in the future, they said, it would be limited and local. This momentous change signaled the virtual abandonment of Maoist doctrine—except in the unthinkable eventuality of a full-scale ground invasion of China—and a recognition that the PLA had to prepare for war outside its borders. For this, a new force-building policy was formulated: the development of rapid reaction units that were more mobile, better trained, and better equipped than the rest of the army. This policy was accelerated in the 1990s, with emphasis on the navy, air force, and elite ground force units.[11]

After the collapse of the Soviet Union, these concepts acquired broader and more direct relevance. The elimination of a threat that had constrained them for years, along with a reduced U.S. presence in the Pacific, presented the Chinese with fresh opportunities for pursuing a vigorous foreign policy in their neighborhood. Together, the new nationalism and the PLA's improved capabilities raise the possibility that China might become involved in conflicts that will draw its armed forces into hostilities. Given the desire of Jiang's administration for a stable external environment, such a possibility is remote, but Taiwan remains a potentially volatile issue. Core questions of China's sovereignty and national honor combine with military force to create an explosive mix that catapults the PLA straight to the center of the policymaking arena. As the Taiwan Strait crisis of 1995–1996 demonstrated, PLA chiefs believed themselves essential to ensuring China's firm nationalistic stand, as well as to deciding the military actions designed to terminate Taiwan's moves toward independence.

A new area that carries the potential to enhance the military's role is India. In May 1997, India carried out several nuclear tests that were both preceded and accompanied by hostile statements toward China. Although China's initial reaction has been restrained, if the assertive nationalism that has fueled India's militant posture is translated into moves that threaten Pakistan, China might feel compelled to respond. For instance, it might strengthen military ties with Pakistan or deploy troops on its border with

India. Over the long haul, the latent rivalry between China and India for supremacy in Asia might escalate into military confrontations—for example, in the Indian Ocean or on the India-China border. If Taiwan is the first front for the Chinese military, India might loom as the second one.

## THE PLA AND THE PARTY: SEPARATE WAYS

The third change in the PLA's role pertains to relations between the PLA and the party as organizations. At the heart of this change is the fact that the close integration existing between the two during the Maoist period and to an attenuated extent under Deng has given way to an increasing separation. Consequently, the dichotomy between them as two entities with different and sometimes conflicting interests is growing.

This shift does not mean that the army's ultimate subordination to the party and its leader is in doubt. It does mean, however, that political controls in the armed forces have been weakened. As a result, the party's presence in army units is less intrusive, and army commanders have more leeway to pursue their specialized missions—within the broad framework set by the party but without undue interference on the ground.

The clearest evidence of this reduced presence is that party committees largely have been silent as supreme decisionmaking organs in military units. Also, there has been an increasing division of responsibilities between military commanders and political commissars in carrying out military decisions. Since it was primarily through these two functions of political work that the party had intruded most markedly into the PLA and kept a tight grip on it, their attrition is a clear indication of the PLA's growing separation from the party.

This distance is hardly surprising, since it is driven by three powerful factors. One is the drastic decline in the importance of the CCP as the traditional epicenter of the Chinese political system. Although the party still occupies this position in theory, under the new politics the system has become much less rigid due to decentralization and the loosening of central authority over bureaucratic and regional power centers. Furthermore, with the de facto end of ideology, erosion of power, and corruption, the party has lost much of its effectiveness. These developments have greatly eroded its power and legitimacy: the party decline could only undermine the authority of party members in the armed forces, especially the formerly omnipresent political commissars and other full-time functionaries. Since the hierarchy of these functionaries runs parallel to the military chain of command and is supposed to supervise it, its weakening has surely strengthened the distinctive professional identity and insular character of the military organization.

Nothing has strengthened this identity more than the second factor: the modernization of the PLA, which has turned to readying itself "to fight a modern war under high-tech conditions." After laying the groundwork in the 1980s, the Chinese embarked on an accelerated upgrade program in the early 1990s and have pursued it in a sustained and comprehensive fashion. They have closed the long-standing gap between doctrine and operations by abandoning Maoist concepts of the "people's war" and preparing for realistic limited engagements that will employ modern forces and conventional strategies. They have improved their rapid deployment forces, air force and navy, by buying small quantities of new weapons from Russia, mainly modern aircraft, submarines, and air defense systems. They have advanced their logistics, force structure, training procedures, and joint service operations, and they are increasing and refining their missile delivery systems.

All these efforts have not yet brought the PLA much closer to the level of the most modern armies. Of course, it continues to suffer from major deficiencies that will take years to rectify.[12] But the Chinese leadership is determined to build armed forces commensurate with the long-term aim of gaining preeminence in East Asia and a pivotal global role. To this end, it will have to mount a steady long-term effort that will transform the PLA into an ever more complex and effective fighting force. To succeed, the armed forces must continuously cultivate an officer corps that is competent professionally and preoccupied with its specialized missions. The military leadership is well aware of this requirement and has moved it to the top of the PLA's priorities. As a result, the professional officer corps, which under Deng began to emerge from two decades of Maoist stagnation, has entered a period of flowering under Jiang, even as the party is wilting and its representatives in the armed forces have lost much of their vigor.[13] The party still "commands the gun," but the gulf between it and the military has never been as large.

The third factor fostering this gulf is the PLA's massive involvement in economic pursuits. Growing rapidly since the late 1980s, this investment has spawned a huge empire that embraces every major profit-making activity. Its potential effects on party-army relations are wide-ranging and include an attachment of military units to economic projects at the expense of political activities; the participation of party functionaries in financial undertakings to the neglect of their duties; the disregard of party directives by officers who put profits first; the disintegration of revolutionary élan in the money-making climate of a modernizing China; the erosion by corruption of the ethic of duty and devotion; the formation of alignments among officers based on common economic interests; and the gaining by the military of income independent of government allocations.[14] Although these effects are detrimental to military professionalism, they have also most probably loosened party controls in the army.

Chinese military leaders are well aware of these effects, and since the mid-1990s they have tried to reduce the PLA's economic projects, both by curbing its activities and by bringing them under tighter control. These efforts have probably limited the damage to the PLA's military standards. For example, the leadership has withdrawn elite rapid reaction forces from economic pursuits but let them share in the profits generated by second-line units. These efforts are not likely to prevent the loosening of party controls, since the PLA continues to be an economic enterprise with huge independent funds at its disposal. Nonetheless, looser party controls have not (and probably will not) cast doubt on the subordination of army units to the party leadership. Orders are transmitted by the leadership to the military high command and then passed down to the PLA. As long as PLA chiefs themselves follow orders and the military command and control system is effective, the obedience of the army to the party leadership is assured.

Nonetheless, the separation of party and army has enhanced the freedom of the PLA to conduct its affairs according to military imperatives alone, with two implications for its political position. First, by downgrading the latent conflict between professionalism and politics, the PLA has strengthened the internal cohesion of the armed forces. Second, by highlighting the role of the military chiefs as leaders of an institution with distinct and specialized interests, it has strengthened their hand in dealings with the party leadership.[15]

## CONCLUSION: IN OR OUT OF POLITICS?

Given the changes that have occurred in party-army relations, it is appropriate to speculate on the most basic question of all regarding the role of the PLA: will it stay in or out of politics under Jiang? To start, the PLA is a party-army with professional characteristics. Thus, it will stay both in and out because its role will be different under different circumstances. Jiang's leadership has given rise to new considerations, however. The PLA may intervene in elite politics against the paramount leader, something it has never done before, but it will probably not intervene with force in political struggles, something it has done before.

Only an extreme emergency is likely to change this. Such an emergency might arise, for example, in the event of a paralyzing leadership struggle motivated by personal animosities rather than by policy failures. This is an unlikely eventuality in Chinese elite politics, but were it to occur the PLA probably would intervene on behalf of the established leader against a challenger. Or, if the regime is threatened by mass demonstrations provoked not by economic collapse but, for example, by demands for rapid political change, the leadership and the PLA will be inclined to let the People's Armed Police, much improved since the Tiananmen incident, handle the demonstrations. If the police prove incapable of managing crisis, the leadership will surely turn to the PLA, and the army will probably intervene to protect the party.

PLA behavior will be determined by specific circumstances. Because Jiang, unlike Mao and Deng, cannot count on the unqualified support of the military in all circumstances, he must deliver the goods. His leadership must demonstrate the capacity to ensure economic advance and social stability, as well as to satisfy the demands of the military—that is, provide the funds and conditions for modernization. If the economy takes a sharp and prolonged downturn followed by widespread unrest, or if the PLA's needs are neglected, it might withdraw its support from Jiang. Such retreat might manifest anywhere along the spectrum from backing a rival to intervening with force, but since the use of force is a remote possibility in top-level Chinese leadership conflicts, military intervention might commence with pressure for drastic policy changes and culminate in the transfer of support to a rival. No political leader after Deng can survive without such support, adding a novel dimension to the potential power of the military in Chinese elite politics.

Also novel is that the PLA is less likely than ever before to serve as an instrument in political struggles. Mao and Deng had used it despite the reluctance and even resistance of PLA leaders. The PLA had never moved in force into the political arena on its own initiative but only because Mao or Deng had ordered it: Mao during the turmoil of the Cultural Revolution and Deng, during the Tiananmen demonstrations. They were able to do so because of their personal stature on the Chinese political scene and in the PLA, even though senior commanders opposed the interventions. Lacking this personal stature, Jiang and his successors will find it immensely difficult, if not impossible, to compel the armed forces to intervene. Furthermore, the new commanders are less political than their predecessors and will be even more reluctant to intervene. China's leaders will be circumspect in calling for PLA intervention, and PLA commanders will not respond to such calls as a matter of course.

## NOTES

1. These sections draw on my paper, "The Military and China's New Politics."
2. On Mao and Deng as paramount leaders, see Nathan and Ross, *The Great Wall and the Empty Fortress*, 124–129.
3. See Goodman, *Deng Xiaoping and the Chinese Revolution*, especially 37–48.
4. These have included members of the CMC; the defense minister and chief of staff; the directors of the three general departments in the PLA headquarters—

general staff (whose head is the chief of staff), logistics, and political departments; commanders of military regions, military districts, and group armies; commandants of military academies; commanders of the People's Armed Police and the Central Guards Bureau (charged with the protection of the central leadership); commanders of the navy and air force; and the director of the Commission for Science, Technology, and Industry for National Defense. See Shambaugh, "China's Commander-in-Chief," 216.

5. Shambaugh, "China's Post-Deng Military Leadership."

6. Shambaugh, 211–232, note 43.

7. Shambaugh, "China's Military in Transition," 287–288.

8. Mulvenon, *Professionalization.*

9. Swaine, *The Role of the Chinese Military,* 15.

10. Ibid., chap. 3.

11. Godwin, "From Continent to Periphery," 464–487, note 6; and Whiting, "The PLA and China's Threat Perceptions," 596–615.

12. *Jane's Defense Weekly,* December 10, 1997, 24–32.

13. See Mulvenon, "Professionalization."

14. Cheung, "China's Entrepreneurial Army," 168–197, note 4; and Joffe, "The Chinese Army and the Economy," 24–43.

15. Cf. Mulvenon, "Professionalization," 76–77.

# The Modernization
# of the People's Liberation Army:
# Implications for Asia-Pacific
# Security and Chinese Politics

## Michael D. Swaine

In this chapter I examine the implications of China's military modernization program along two critical dimensions: externally, for the security of the Asia-Pacific region, including Taiwan; and internally, for the military's changing role in Chinese politics, especially leadership politics in the post–Deng Xiaoping era. Each of these areas will be examined in a separate section.

In the first section, on regional implications I (1) present the strategic logic behind China's current effort at military modernization and describe the major elements of the modernization program; (2) estimate the kinds of military capabilities that will likely result from China's modernization program by the years 2010 and 2020; and (3) assess the general impact of such developments on the Asia-Pacific strategic environment, the security of Taiwan, and the interests of the United States and its allies in the region.

In the second section, on domestic implications I (1) identify and summarize the major changes that have occurred in the leadership structure, internal organization, and belief system of the Chinese officer corps since the early 1980s, largely as a result of China's military modernization program; and (2) assess the consequences of such changes for the present and likely future role of the People's Liberation Army (PLA) in domestic politics, particularly civil-military relations at the elite level.

## PLA MODERNIZATION AND ASIA-PACIFIC SECURITY

China's long-term program of military modernization has been motivated largely by the need to reduce growing weaknesses and vulnerabilities in the Chinese Communist regime's traditional defense doctrine, military training, and force structure. Shortcomings in all these areas emerged in the early 1980s as a result of major changes in China's internal and external strategic environment.

For over three decades, from the late 1940s through the late 1970s, the security of the People's Republic of China (PRC) was adequately provided by a force structure and operational doctrine derived from both the limitations and advantages of China's developmental experience. Specifically, the existence of a huge population, low levels of technology and education compared to modern industrialized states, and a relatively small and dispersed industrial infrastructure both required and permitted an operational doctrine centered on massive ground forces, deployed to carry out a defense-in-depth strategy and trained to wear down a technologically superior opponent through the fluid tactics of infantry envelopment and guerrilla warfare. This doctrine was expressed in the general concept of people's war, developed during the long Communist war of resistance against Japan and the subsequent civil war with the Nationalists.

To this general force structure and defense doctrine was added, in the mid-1960s, a minimal, low-tech nuclear deterrent force consisting of a small number of unsophisticated intermediate- and long-range, liquid-fueled ballistic missiles, each armed with a single high-yield and relatively inaccurate nuclear warhead designed to deter potential adversaries by threatening the destruction of a small number of countervalue targets such as cities. At the same time, China's ability to withstand external pressures or a crippling attack from a major power such as the Soviet Union or the United States was increased by deliberate decisions to avoid excessive dependence upon external sources of raw materials and essential goods for the Chinese economy and to disperse key industrial facilities across the Chinese heartland, from the northeast (formerly Manchuria) to the interior southwest.[1]

This defensive force structure and doctrine, designed to deter attacks on Chinese territory, not to project Chinese influence and presence beyond the Chinese heartland, was paired with a diplomatic strategy keyed to external balancing through shifting strategic relationships with the superpowers. This strategy primarily involved Chinese efforts to establish formal or informal alliances or understandings with the Soviet Union and then the United States, with China as the third player in a complex strategic triangle.[2]

Beginning largely in the 1970s, however, major changes occurred in China's internal development conditions and external strategic environment that eventually convinced the Chinese leadership that their past defense doctrine and force structure were largely incapable of ensuring Chinese security into the twenty-first century.[3]

Within China, the combination of continued population pressures and the mounting inefficiencies of a generally autarchic development strategy wedded to a highly rigid, repressive, and centralized political and economic system had resulted in increasing domestic disorder and impoverishment by the 1960s and 1970s. The utopian and highly disruptive policies of the Great Leap Forward and the Cultural Revolution of the 1950s and 1960s worsened this situation, weakening the faith of ordinary citizens and officials alike in the leadership qualities of the Communist Party elite and the accuracy of their development strategy. This development, in turn, greatly eroded the legitimacy of the Chinese communist state. In the military realm, the major shortcomings of China's economic system and rigid bureaucracy increasingly prevented or slowed the modernization of various critical elements of the Chinese armed forces. Most of the few advances in military capabilities attained in the 1960s and 1970s had come about through the marginal improvement of largely obsolete Soviet weapons designs of the 1950s and early 1960s. By the late 1970s and early 1980s, most Chinese leaders recognized that a strong and stable state and society could not develop through a continued reliance on the failed autarchic and utopian economic and political policies of the past.[4]

The response to this situation came in the form of the market-led economic reform and open door policies of the 1980s, intended to ensure long-term economic growth and social stability and also to generate the technological and financial foundations for a more capable military force. Indeed, the legitimacy and stability of the Communist regime came to be based increasingly upon the continued ability of the leadership to maintain relatively high economic growth rates and ensure improvements in the people's livelihood. This imperative placed an unprecedented priority on policy pragmatism, not the utopian concepts of the Maoist era.

While providing the wherewithal to overcome basic internal structural deficiencies, the adoption of the reform policies at the same time created strategic vulnerabilities in two critical areas. First, the reform and open-door policies resulted in China's increasing dependence on foreign markets, maritime trade routes, and external energy supplies, which contributed to a growing sense of strategic vulnerability to external political and economic actions and thus increased the need to acquire an unprecedented capability to control events beyond China's borders. Second, the sense of vulnerability was heightened by the fact that the reforms had ended the dispersed and less vulnerable pattern of industrial facilities of the Maoist era, leading instead to the concentration of China's major economic centers along the eastern and southern coastline, which were more vulnerable to a potential attack from maritime powers. This development placed a premium on the need to develop capabilities to deter or defeat adversaries before they could reach the Chinese mainland.

China's strategic vulnerabilities were increased further in recent decades by several external developments. Most important, the economic and technological capabilities of major Western industrial states and Japan increased exponentially during this period, largely because of market globalization and privatization. As a result, the advanced industrial states, and particularly the United States, achieved major technological advances in the military arena that greatly increased the lethality, accuracy, range, and general battlefield awareness capabilities of conventional and nuclear weapons and their various support systems. Specifically, rapid advances took place in areas such as weapons technology and accuracy, warhead design, delivery systems, surveillance, interception, battlefield command and control, electronic warfare, precision-guided munitions, coordinated air-land operations, and missile defense systems.[5]

The capabilities of many of these advanced military technologies and systems were demonstrated to the Chinese high command by the 1991 Gulf War, when U.S.-led forces defeated an Iraqi force armed with Soviet- and Chinese-designed weaponry.[6] At that time the upper levels of China's increasingly professional officer corps became highly cognizant of the enormous (and possibly growing) gaps between the technological capabilities of many Western (or Western-supplied) armed forces and those of the PLA.

In addition, partly because of trends in economic globalization and technological advances of the 1970s and 1980s, states or territories along China's southern periphery such as South Korea, Japan, Taiwan, Vietnam, and India have emerged as independent, strong, and stable nation-states with growing economic and military capabilities. Many of these states have established strong political and security links with countries other than China, including the United States, and have become increasingly integrated into the international economy. This development suggests that, although the Chinese state has managed to incorporate traditional periphery areas such as Tibet, Xinjiang, Manchuria, and parts of Mongolia into the Chinese nation, it now confronts a major challenge to any efforts to establish greater control over its periphery. Indeed, the traditional, oft-used Chinese option of direct military force against peripheral areas now presents enormous political, economic, and military dangers to the Chinese state, not only from the actions of major powers such as the United States and Russia but from many of the states themselves.

### Strategic Deficiencies

Together, the above developments suggested that the traditional Chinese military establishment of the 1970s was hopelessly inadequate to provide for China's security needs in the twenty-first century.[7] Although the PLA was large, by the early 1980s its force structure, operational doctrine, organization, and personnel all lagged significantly behind modern (much less state-of-the-art) levels in a variety of key areas by as many as fifteen to twenty years. For example, the PLA Air Force (PLAAF) possessed rudimentary or nonexistent offensive counter-air, close air support, battlefield interdiction, in-flight refueling, night operations, and airborne early warning and command and communications (C²) capabilities. The majority of its aircraft had a very limited range and generally suffered from obsolete airframe, engine, weapons, and avionics designs.[8] Likewise, the PLA Navy (PLAN) was essentially a coastal force, containing many outmoded submarines and surface combatants, with poor antisubmarine warfare, air defense, command and communications (C²), and electronics systems and very limited amphibious assault and at-sea replenishment capabilities.

Chinese naval and air force electronics and electronic warfare systems were outdated and inadequate. Little progress had been made in developing a new air defense network, for example.[9] China's ground forces were grossly oversized and infantry-heavy (comprising over seventy infantry divisions) and plagued by low mobility, obsolete weaponry, poorly educated officers and soldiers, and a limited ability to interact with PLAAF and PLAN forces in combined arms operations. The vast majority of PLA personnel (including most officers) still had only a rudimentary, if any, education. Many ordinary soldiers could not write or drive a car, much less understand and implement sophisticated doctrines or operate complex weapons systems.

China's strategic forces also displayed significant weaknesses. They were technologically obsolete; were armed primarily with large, high-yield warheads; and suffered from having poor command, control, and communications systems and inadequate early warning, attack assessment, battle management capabilities. As a result, most analysts believed that China's nuclear missile, submarine, bomber, and C³I capabilities could be seriously damaged if not destroyed entirely by an opponent's first strike. Although the Chinese might be able to launch a second strike against large cities, it is unclear whether they could attack targets of opportunity or launch coordinated strikes.[10]

Organizationally, the PLA continued to exhibit many features of a Soviet-style, ground force–centered military, including excessively large ground units, vertically structured lines of communication with little horizontal contact across units or between services, and excessive (largely political) controls over information and ideas. All these features greatly stifled innovation and initiative. They plagued the defense industry system as much as they did combat and support units in the field.

China clearly required a military establishment capable of attaining a greatly expanded level of political and military ends, including

- the defense of Chinese sovereignty and national territory (especially critical coastal facilities) against attacks from highly sophisticated military forces;
- the use of military power as a more potent and versatile instrument of a more extensive regional and global set of foreign diplomatic policies;

- the ability to better cope with a range of potential long-term security threats or concerns along China's periphery, especially in maritime areas;[11]
- in general, the attainment of power projection and extended territorial defense capabilities commensurate with great power status in the twenty-first century.[12]

These diverse security requirements provide the foundation for China's emerging post–Cold War defense doctrine, which comprises such modern concepts as "local or limited war under high-technology conditions," "active peripheral defense," and "rapid power projection." These concepts, first enunciated by the Chinese leadership in the early and mid-1980s,[13] assume that local or regional conflicts or short, low-intensity wars[14] could break out virtually anywhere on China's periphery, demanding a rapid and decisive application of force through high-tech weaponry and requiring the acquisition of sea denial capabilities, joint offshore capabilities, and joint territorial defense capabilities.

Thus, changing strategic conditions and requirements have led to a significant transformation in China's strategic outlook and resulting force requirements. China has had to shift its perspective from that of a continental power requiring a minimal nuclear deterrent capability and large land forces for "in-depth" defense against threats to its northern and western borders, to that of a combined continental-maritime power requiring a more sophisticated conventional and unconventional force structure with medium- and long-range force projection, mobility, rapid reaction, and offshore maneuverability capabilities and a more versatile and accurate nuclear weapons inventory.

### The Modernization Program

In the area of conventional weapons systems, key modernization programs have focused on the creation of the following:[15]

- a smaller, more flexible, better motivated, highly trained, and well-equipped ground force, centered on rapid reaction combat units with airborne drop and amphibious power projection capabilities;[16]
- a modest (by great power standards) blue water naval capability, centered on a new generation of frigates and destroyers with improved air defense and fire control, more modern nuclear and nonnuclear submarines, a more capable naval air arm, improved submarine warfare and antisubmarine warfare capabilities, and probably at least one carrier battle group;[17]
- a more versatile, advanced air force, with longer-range interceptor/strike aircraft, improved air defense (with airborne early warning

[AEW] aircraft), extended and close air support, and overall improved power projection capabilities, including long-range transport and lift and in-flight refueling capabilities;
- a combined arms tactical operations doctrine utilizing more sophisticated C$^3$I, early warning, and battle management systems, and both airborne and satellite-based assets; and
- a relatively large number of accurate, solid-fueled, conventionally armed ballistic and cruise missiles with both fixed and mobile capabilities.

With regard to unconventional weaponry, key modernization programs focus on improving the survivability of nuclear missile forces by reducing pre-launch time; acquiring less vulnerable basing modes; and making overall improvements in versatility, accuracy, range, guidance, and control.[18] Specific examples of such efforts include:[19]

- land- and sea-based intercontinental ballistic missiles (ICBMs) with improved range, accuracy, survivability, and penetration against limited missile defense;[20]
- a new generation of solid-fuel, short- and intermediate-range ballistic missiles;
- smaller warheads, which theoretically allow a multiple independent reentry vehicle (MIRV) capability (Beijing might perceive a need for a rapid increase in the number of deployed warheads to overwhelm an Asia-based theater missile defense [TMD] or U.S.-based antiballistic missile [ABM] system); and
- an improvement in China's nuclear weapons C$^3$I through the acceleration of space capabilities and the continued importation of advanced communication technologies, like fiber optics and microwave equipment.

This nuclear modernization program is apparently intended to serve two broad goals: the maintenance of a deterrence capability against both nuclear and conventional threats from the major powers and the development of a tactical nuclear weapons capability for possible use in limited conflict scenarios.[21] At the same time, China's official nuclear defense strategy continues to stress a "no first use" doctrine and prohibits the use of nuclear weapons against nonnuclear powers.[22]

During the 1990s, and especially since 1995, China's military modernization program has made significant progress in upgrading many weapons systems and capabilities.[23] The PLAAF purchased forty-seven advanced long-range interceptors (Russian Su-27) and reached a co-production agreement to assemble and eventually manufacture approximately 200 additional aircraft; purchased ten long-range transport aircraft (Russian IL-76) and might have reached agreement to import an additional fifteen; and purchased twenty-four transport helicopters (Russian Mi-17). In addition to developing a prototype of a foreign-assisted, multirole fighter-bomber (J-10), PLAAF improved the design of the J-8II fighter and converted several to midair refueling; converted five H-6 bombers to in-flight refueling tankers, with foreign assistance; and installed C-601 antiship missiles on more than twelve H-6 bombers. In general, it improved airborne naval strike and ground attack capabilities and made incremental advances in air defense systems.[24]

PLAN added approximately twenty principal surface combatants, including, most notably, a few hybrid-designed advanced guided missile destroyers (Luhu-class) and guided missile frigates (Jiangwei-class) containing foreign systems and purchased at least two advanced destroyers with sophisticated antiship missile capabilities (Russian Sovremenney-class). Besides new types of fast attack (Houxin- and Houjian-classes), coastal patrol (Huludao-class), and resupply craft (Dayun-class), PLAN produced additional amphibious and mine warfare ships, including large capacity tank landing ships (Yukang and Yuting-class LSTs). Finally, it improved indigenous (Ming-class) and hybrid foreign-assisted (Song-class) submarines, purchased four advanced diesel antisurface and antisubmarine warfare submarines (Russian Kilo-class), and developed a prototype for an indigenous naval fighter-bomber (JH-7).

To make ground forces more effective in fighting limited wars, the military reduced their overall size, trained and equipped several divisions as rapid reaction units, improved living conditions for troops (i.e., food, wages, and housing), and improved training at the small unit (squad to battalion) level. It also expanded combined arms and joint training exercises, primarily to the regimental level. To better equip soldiers, the PLA acquired more modern trucks and a few light attack helicopters and modern artillery and purchased several armored, amphibious combat personnel vehicles from Russia.

Strategic forces serially produced and deployed improved land-based, mobile, solid-fueled, short-range, surface-to-surface ballistic missiles (M-11 and M-9); deployed ten to thirty-five medium-range ballistic missiles (DF-21); and continued development of a new generation of antiship missiles (AshM and C-801) and submarine-launched ballistic missiles (JL-1/CSS-N-3). Advances in research on MIRV capabilities and improvements in C$^3$I capabilities may also have been made.

The above information suggests that China has made significant advances in its military modernization program in the 1990s. The most notable advances in indigenous weapons and support systems have occurred in the areas of ballistic and cruise missiles, the mobility and response time of selected units, logistics, C$^2$ and air and naval support of ground forces associated with combined arms operations, and some surface and subsurface naval combatants. The most significant advances in sophisticated systems and high-tech subsystems, however, have largely taken place as a result of expensive acquisitions from foreign, primarily Russian, sources.[25] Moreover, all these advances occurred from a relatively low baseline and are still far from the capabilities required by China's overall modernization program.

China's military modernization effort confronts significant and, in some cases, enduring obstacles or problems that will likely impede continued progress over the long term, possibly forcing efforts at radical restructuring or redesign or major tradeoffs in resource allocations. Specifically, China's military research and development (R&D), manufacturing, and organizational structure is plagued by a variety of problems that will likely hinder the full implementation of China's military modernization program. In addition to insufficient funds and lagging production due to the diversion of energies away from defense production,[26] these include

- insufficient funding;
- lagging defense production;
- excessive adherence to self-reliance as a guiding principle;
- lack of horizontal integration;
- separation from the civilian commercial sector;
- lack of skilled experts, managers, and labor;
- poor infrastructure; and
- technology absorption problems.[27]

At present, priority areas for the future include serial production of an indigenous fighter-bomber; submarine-launched cruise missiles and intermediate-range ballistic missiles; long-range, land-attack cruise missiles; long-range, over-the-horizon radar and downlink capabilities; space-based, real-time surveillance capabilities; and more accurate guidance systems for short- and medium-range ballistic missiles.

As the lists above indicate, China's military modernization program places particular stress on acquiring air and naval medium- and long-range detection, surveillance, and power projection capabilities. The acquisition of such capabilities clearly poses significant implications for the security environment in the Asia-Pacific region, especially over the medium and long term.

Assuming that Beijing can sustain or even accelerate somewhat the current tempo of its modernization program and overcome the kind of persistent development problems mentioned above, one might expect the following general military capabilities by the years 2007–2010:[28]

- the ability to conduct limited air and sea denial (as opposed to sea control) operations up to 250 miles from China's continental coastline;[29]

- the ability to strike a wide range of civilian and military targets in East, Southeast, and South Asia with a large number (perhaps 1,000 or more) of nuclear or conventionally armed short- and medium-range ballistic missiles;[30]
- the ability to transport and deploy one to two divisions (i.e., approximately 15,000–30,000 fully equipped soldiers) within 100 miles of China's continental borders, via land, sea, and air transport;
- the ability to survive a preemptive strike against China's nuclear facilities and retaliate with a small number of improved accuracy intermediate and long-range land- and sea-based ballistic missiles; and
- the ability to overwhelm any likely space-based or air-breathing missile defense system deployed in Asia.

Projecting these trends for another ten years or so, to the year 2020, one might expect the following:

- the ability to routinely patrol a single, noncarrier surface and sub-surface battle group within 1,000 nautical miles of China's continental coastline;
- the ability to conduct both sea and air denial operations within 500 nautical miles of China's continental coastline;
- the ability to attempt a naval blockade, with air support, of islands within 200 nautical miles of China's continental coastline; and
- the ability to transport and deploy three–four divisions (i.e., approximately 45,000–60,000 fully equipped soldiers) within 200 miles of China's continental borders, via land, sea, and air transport.

## IMPLICATIONS FOR SECURITY IN THE ASIA-PACIFIC REGION

The acquisition of even rough approximations of the above capabilities poses several significant implications for the security situation in the Asia-Pacific region. First and foremost, an increased Chinese air and naval presence of the type summarized above could have a significant psychological impact on the security perceptions of the United States and its allies and friends in the region. If Asian countries cannot develop military forces to effectively counter new Chinese capabilities or lose confidence in the ability of U.S. forces to counter such capabilities, they might gradually become more pro-Chinese in their foreign economic and diplomatic policies or less supportive of U.S. Asian policies. Without a continued strong U.S.

presence, Asian alarm over growing Chinese capabilities could fuel a destabilizing arms buildup in the region as countries such as Japan, the Philippines, Indonesia, India, and Vietnam seek to establish or maintain a military advantage over China in key areas. Such developments could significantly increase Chinese tensions with Japan over the U.S.-Japan security alliance, with the Association of Southeast Asian Nations (ASEAN) over the Spratly Islands, and with the United States and Western European states over continued access to Asian resources, technology, and markets.

In addition, the acquisition by China of the capabilities described above could significantly increase the costs and risks involved in deploying U.S. forces in East Asia, especially over the long term. For example, the acquisition of significant Chinese sea denial or control capabilities could erode the aggregate capabilities of the forward U.S. naval presence in the region and constrain Washington's freedom of action in a crisis. Specifically, such capabilities could seriously complicate the U.S. calculus regarding whether, when, and how to deploy its forces in the region to deter or reassure friends and allies. This problem would worsen if the United States were to reduce the physical presence or qualitative capabilities of its forward presence in Asia; either reduction could seriously undermine confidence among regional states.

Obviously, such developments pose extremely important implications for the future security of Taiwan. Some analysts believe that, as a result of the 1995–1996 tensions over Taiwan, China's weapons programs now place an increased emphasis on acquiring capabilities designed to strengthen the credibility of Beijing's military options against the island, and to deter the United States from deploying aircraft carriers in an effort to counter such options.[31] By as early as 2010, the type of increased Chinese capabilities summarized above could lead China's leaders to attempt a variety of military actions against Taiwan. These might include another, more intensive round of military intimidation through various exercises and missile "tests," a naval blockade, a limited direct missile or air attack, and even perhaps limited ground incursions, in an attempt to establish a fait accompli in Beijing's favor that the United States would find difficult to counter.

The Chinese leadership is unlikely, however, to attempt such actions unless it believed that Taiwan were about to achieve permanent independence. Moreover, it is important to note that the ability of China to prevail in any attempt to employ military force against Taiwan, even by the year 2020, is by no means certain. As suggested above, China's *relative* military capabilities vis-à-vis both Taiwan and the United States will be a far more important indicator of China's willingness to employ force than the sort of absolute capabilities projected above.

## PLA MODERNIZATION AND CHINESE POLITICS

Enormous changes have occurred in the leadership structure, internal organization, and belief systems of the PLA during the reform period that pose major implications for the role of the PLA in areas of both policy and civil-military relations at the elite level.

### The Military in Transition

Chinese military officers today display both a greater sense of institutional mission separate from the party and a much greater resistance to involvement in domestic political affairs than their predecessors. A new generation of more professional military leaders has largely replaced China's military politicians of the past. These successor officers are younger,[32] better educated, and more professionally trained than their forebears.[33] Most have passed through one of the increasing number of China's military academies and institutes, where a much greater stress is placed on purely military skills as opposed to political correctness. China's senior officer corps is increasingly specialized in functional expertise, with a clear differentiation among political, military, and technical cadres.[34] Moreover, most members of the current high-level military leadership are too young to have served during the highly politicized guerrilla war period. Instead, their key formative experiences have been with more modern types of warfare, including the Korean War, the 1962 Sino-Indian border war, the 1969 Sino-Soviet border clash, and the 1979 Sino-Vietnamese border war.[35]

As a consequence of these trends, China's emergent military leadership is developing networks built around common unit affiliation as well as common educational experience, field performance, and other avenues of professionalization.[36] They generally denigrate the direct relevance of socialist ideology to military affairs while recognizing the need for civilian control over military forces.[37]

As in the civilian sphere, individual members of China's emerging generation of military leaders also possess far fewer political resources than their predecessors and hence are less able to serve as key power brokers or policy advocates than powerful military figures have done in the past. Equally important, on the organizational level, Chinese officers now command a military structure with little capacity to intervene *autonomously* in elite politics. Many changes in military structure, process, and personnel selection, most inaugurated under the reforms, have served to eliminate the ability of central or regional leaders to independently mobilize forces for political ends as part of a factional leadership struggle.

Most recently, Jiang Zemin has taken several actions that undermined further the ability of the PLA to intervene in politics. For example, he has promoted or moved every senior PLA officer who remains on active duty, and he has interviewed every senior officer prior to his promotion and promoted each one based primarily on their qualifications rather than on personal connections.[38] At the same time, Jiang has worked especially hard to improve his ties to the military leadership since 1990, having taken many actions that support professional military interests. In contrast, none of his remaining potential rivals enjoy close personal ties to military leaders that could be used to elicit support in a future struggle.[39]

Leadership changes since the Fifteenth Party Congress during fall 1997 confirm the general reform era trend toward a less political, more professional, and more corporate military leadership and the privileged position vis-à-vis the military enjoyed by Jiang Zemin over his senior civilian party colleagues. For example, although PLA representation in the Fifteenth Central Committee (CC) has remained roughly constant compared with the Fourteenth CC, a significant decrease took place in the number of CC seats held by PLA department heads, down from seven in the Fourteenth CC to only two in the Fifteenth CC. Moreover, none of the current senior PLA officer corps have extensive experience in Beijing political circles.[40]

In addition, the most powerful senior officers of the PLA (and formerly Deng Xiaoping's closest senior military supporters), Gens. Liu Huaqing and Zhang Zhen, stepped down at the Fifteenth Congress. They were replaced as the senior uniformed members of the party's powerful Central Military Commission (CMC) by two senior officers considered relatively close to Jiang: Gen. Chi Haotian and Gen. Zhang Wannian. Both officers were also named to the Politburo, and Zhang was selected to serve on the Chinese Communist Party (CCP) Secretariat.

With the retirement of Generals Liu and Zhang, no PLA leader today has the personal stature, power, or desire to challenge Jiang Zemin.[41] In fact, the military has no strong reasons to oppose Jiang. Indeed, he showed his continued strong support for military modernization goals by announcing at the Fifteenth Party Congress a plan to cut 500,000 troops from the 3-million-person strong Chinese army over the next several years. Jiang emphasized that in the future, a leaner, meaner PLA would stress quality over quantity, modernization over manpower, and professionalism over politics—all issues supported by the senior PLA leadership.

### Politics and the PLA

Despite all these developments, the Chinese military retains several important links with the past and has also developed some new features that together suggest its continued connection to politics and its continued, perhaps increased, interest in key policy issues.[42] Many members of the senior officer corps of the PLA enjoy strong personal links to networks of supporters within the organs of the PLA, especially at the regional and corps levels. Thus, despite their likely desire to avoid involvement in politics, their strong fear of chaos combined with these upward and downward career links could ultimately drag them into party leadership strife, either on a piecemeal basis or as a group.[43] Such personal links are probably augmented by other factional ties among active officers, based upon common affiliation in service arms and military academies.

Of equal concern is the impact of continued private business activities on the internal unity, discipline, and readiness of the Chinese military and the military's overall relationship to the civilian leadership. Although helping to cover increasing costs, the military's foray into the market threatens to exacerbate personal corruption, erode professional attitudes, encourage "localist" tendencies among grassroots units, widen the income gaps between more successful coastal units and less profitable inland units, and generally weaken the commitment to military over economic duties, thus endangering command and control.

Concern over such developments could affect civil-military relations and political stability in a variety of ways. First, it could eventually lead to military pressure on the civilian leadership to greatly increase government defense spending, permitting a reduction in the reliance on private money-making activities. Such pressure could prompt more widespread military involvement in politics, with possibly destabilizing consequences. Second, the military might succeed in controlling the most negative consequences of its economic involvement but still seek to influence domestic and foreign policy issues to protect or further their remaining business interests. This meddling could produce significant changes in Chinese external behavior or at the very least intensify existing, and rather serious, tensions between the military and the Ministry of Foreign Affairs over a variety of foreign policy issues. Finally, continued military involvement in the economy might produce a division between those officers who place a priority on professionalism and who believe business activities corrode the creation of a modern fighting force and those officers who gain greatly from such activities and view them as an essential foundation for continued military modernization, especially under conditions of insufficient public funding. This divide could lead to serious internal military conflict.

On a broader level, a significant number of conservative military officers are reportedly concerned that the stability, unity, and very essence of Chinese society and government are gravely threatened by a wide range of alleged social, political, and economic ills largely associated with the reforms. These include the emergence of an ideological and moral vacuum; the absence of a genuinely public-spirited government protective of the most impoverished segments of society; the steady disintegration of the public sector of the economy and its replacement by a rapacious and corrupt private sector; the general lack of discipline among most socio-economic classes; a fear of China's growing mass of uprooted, discontented peasantry; and the supposedly pernicious social and economic influence of foreign cultural and economic elements.

To cope with such supposedly grave threats to China's political and social order, proponents of the view that China has begun a moral decline (who are also found in civilian circles) enunciate a militarily and economically strong "populist authoritarian" form of central government designed to reinstill the values of a unified moral order, ensure the existence of a strong public sector in the economy, and significantly limit contacts with the "predatory" West. Continued, rapid growth could fuel such fears and concerns among more conservative military officers and lead to increased pressures by them on the military and civilian leadership.

Beyond the economic sources of military concern, a host of other issues could also serve to aggravate civil-military relations. Perhaps the most significant issues are "core" foreign policy concerns and tensions with the Ministry of Foreign Affairs, including those over Taiwan, the Spratly Islands, and relations with the United States; and the outbreak of a prolonged and severe civilian leadership struggle threatening the social order. Each of these issues could produce significant divisions within the military and lead to either overt or indirect military intervention in politics.

Specifically, a protracted power struggle among the civilian leadership could induce some of them to co-opt various groups within the military for partisan support, as has occurred in past political crises in China. In this instance, certain civilian leaders might stress highly conservative, nationalist themes to gain support from both mainstream and hard-line officers. In addition, protracted leadership struggles or escalating conflicts over economic or foreign policy issues among contending factions within the party leadership could prompt the military to intervene in leadership politics *on a unified basis* to ensure political stability, social order, and continued economic progress. Many knowledgeable Chinese and foreign observers argue that this form of military intervention is, on balance, the most likely, given the reduced ability and willingness of the military to become involved in civilian factional politics and the increased attention of a more professional officer corps to national unity and government stability.

Ultimately, however, the likelihood of military involvement will be linked primarily to the policy performance of the post–Deng Xiaoping leadership. The common political weaknesses of the civilian successors (and their likely fear of direct military intervention in politics) and the military's many concerns suggest that even a stable civilian leadership will probably encounter increasing pressure to placate the military on key domestic and foreign policy issues. This scenario will prove especially likely if senior retired military elders such as Liu Huaqing and Zhang Zhen remain active in the future. Even without the presence of such individuals, however, China's civilian successor leadership will likely face a growing need to listen closely to military views on a variety of matters and to generally incorporate senior military officers more fully into the policymaking process, both formally and informally. Such a development could eventually produce a collective civil-military leadership structure, despite the greater apolitical inclinations of the emerging professional officer corps.

Some media sources have asserted that the military had "taken control of" Taiwan policy during the crisis of late 1995 to early 1996. For example, reports appeared at that time that the military had seized control of the Taiwan Affairs Leading Small Group, established a special office within the CMC to handle the Taiwan crisis, forced through plans to attack Taiwan after the Taiwanese presidential election of March 23, 1996, and generally cowed the Politburo Standing Committee (PBSC) to support its "militant stance" toward Taiwan. I believe that either these statements are entirely false, or at the very least, that they significantly distort the relationship of the military to the party leadership. As suggested above, the military does not dictate Chinese policy in any area, even regarding sensitive territorial issues such as Taiwan. Both military and civilian leaders are fully aware that such direct and absolute military intervention in key policy areas would prove highly destabilizing to the regime as a whole, possibly resulting in a violent power struggle.

All credible evidence suggests that most policy toward Taiwan since at least 1992 has developed through a complex interaction between key senior civilian and military leaders, including Jiang Zemin, Wang Daohan, Li Peng, Gens. Liu Huaqing and Zhang Zhen, Gens. Zhang Wannian and Chi Haotian, Foreign Minister Qian Qichen, and prior to the Fifteenth Party Congress, PBSC member and NPC Standing Committee chairman Qiao Shi (who was an influential figure in the security apparatus). These individuals have largely shaped the views and decisions on Taiwan formally taken by the PBSC and the CMC. Although both bodies are formally responsible for decisions regarding Taiwan (the former has formal supreme oversight authority), neither entity wields genuine authority over policy through routine or regularized internal processes of decisionmaking in which all members participate as equal powers.

## NOTES

1. China's largely self-reliant development strategy emerged in the late 1950s, after the collapse of the Sino-Soviet alliance and the abrupt termination of assistance from the former Soviet Union.

2. At times, this diplomatic strategy also included, as an important corollary to the larger great power strategic game, extensive efforts to court lesser industrial

states such as Great Britain, Japan, France, and Germany, as well as secondary efforts to elicit support from newly emergent Asian and African states along China's periphery and beyond, through political or ideological appeals to Third World or socialist solidarity.

3. Much of the following analysis of China's changing security strategy is drawn from Swaine and Tellis, *Interpreting China's Grand Strategy.*

4. This recognition was facilitated, over time, by the gradual passing of those leaders, such as Mao Zedong, who were sympathetic to such policies for political or ideological reasons.

5. China's defense R&D base is deficient in many high-tech areas, including microelectronics, computers, avionics, sensors and seekers, electronic warfare, and advanced materials. See Bitzinger and Gill, "Gearing Up for High-Tech Warfare?" 17.

6. Operation Desert Storm confirmed the obsolescence of the Maoist notion of people's war. Those U.S. capabilities that most stunned the Chinese leadership included precision-guided munitions; stealth technology; the high volume of aircraft sorties; airborne command and control systems; satellite-based targeting; intelligence gathering; early warning and surveillance systems; coordinated large-scale naval, air, and land attacks; and the effective use of rapid deployment and special commando units. This list is taken from Shambaugh, "The Insecurity of Security," 3–15.

7. Much of the following discussion of China's military modernization program is drawn, with some modification, from Swaine, "Chinese Military Modernization," 320–338.

8. Allen, Krumel, and Pollack, *China's Air Force Enters the 21st Century.* Also see Arnett, "Military Technology."

9. Arnett, "Military Technology," 385.

10. Johnston, "Prospects for Chinese Nuclear Force Modernization," 17.

11. These threats or concerns include a militarily powerful United States; an economically powerful and increasingly independent Japan; a more militarily capable and economically emergent India; a host of rising second- and third-tier Asian powers (including South Korea, most of the ASEAN countries, and Taiwan); and the emergence of relatively unstable Islamic states on China's Central Asian borders.

12. It is important to note that Chinese rulers also recognized that to achieve such ambitious ends, the military modernization efforts of the Chinese state must be built on a prior foundation of indigenous scientific, technological, and economic capabilities. Hence, the strategy demanded that military modernization proceed at a pace that does not undermine the attainment of essential civilian development priorities; nor should it be allowed to proceed at a pace that unduly alarms periphery states or major powers and thus erodes China's generally benign threat environment.

13. In 1985, Deng Xiaoping announced a "strategic decision" to shift the guiding doctrine of China's military modernization from preparation for an early, large-scale, and nuclear war to preparation for a somewhat more peaceful environment where conflict would be limited to local, small-scale wars.

14. Many such conflicts pose the possibility of escalation and expansion in intensity, duration, and geographic area. According to Paul Godwin, a more generic definition of local or limited wars includes (1) small-scale conflicts restricted to contested border territory; (2) conflicts over territorial seas and islands; (3) surprise air attacks; (4) defenses against deliberately limited attacks into Chinese territory;

and (5) punitive counterattacks launched by Chinese into enemy territory to "oppose invasion, protect sovereignty, or to uphold justice and dispel threats." See Godwin, "Force Projection and China's Military Strategy," 4.

15. This list is derived from Shambaugh, "China's Military: Real or Paper Tiger?" 26–27; Swaine, "China," 203–205; and Mulvenon, "Appendix One."

16. Rapid reaction units (RRUs) are "specially trained for different geographical and climatic conditions, [and are] geared to strengthen mobility and operational coordination in preparation for small-scale warfare on and around China's border areas." Gill and Kim, *China's Arms Acquisitions from Abroad,* 64.

17. Such a naval force would be capable of engaging in what the Chinese term "offshore active defense" *(jinyangfangyu)*. According to Liu Huaqing, former commander of the PLAN, this concept means that "the PLAN should (eventually) exert effective control of the seas within the first island chain," which includes the Aleutians, the Kuriles, the Japanese archipelago, the Ryukyus, Taiwan, the Philippine archipelago, the Spratlys, the Paracels, and the Greater Sunda Islands. For the full text of Admiral Liu's remarks, see *Joint Publications,* 14.

18. Norris, Burrows, and Fieldhouse, *Nuclear Weapons Databook,* 372.

19. The following discussion of China's nuclear weapons program is taken primarily from Swaine, *The Role of the Chinese Military,* 38, and Swaine and Johnston, "China and Arms Control."

20. One knowledgeable PLA analyst has stated that, by the year 2000, the Chinese intend to increase their ICBM force to about thirty missiles; base them with fixed launchers in hardened silos; fuel them with solid-fueled propellants, and outfit as many as possible with multiple independent reentry vehicle (MIRV) warheads. See Shambaugh, "China's Military: Real or Paper Tiger?" 28.

21. More specifically, these goals include the possible need to (1) counter a future limited use of theater nuclear forces in a conventional attack; (2) deter an attack by highly accurate and powerful conventional stand-off weapons such as long-range cruise missiles or precision-guided munitions; (3) permit warning strikes to shake or undermine an enemy's determination to launch nuclear strikes, destroy its strategic intentions, and thus contain nuclear escalation; or (4) negate the neutralization of China's deterrent capability allegedly presented by TMDs or space-based ballistic-missile defenses (BMDs). I am indebted to Iain Johnson for this information.

22. These developments suggest that China's nuclear deterrence doctrine may be shifting from an emphasis on the maintenance of a minimal strategic force sufficient to inflict what is perceived to be unacceptable damage on a handful on enemy cities with a simple, undifferentiated countervalue second strike ("city busting") to the attainment of a limited yet more sophisticated range of strategic and substrategic capabilities to deter any level of nuclear conflict and, in a nuclear war, to contain escalatory pressures. The latter doctrine (often termed "limited deterrence") requires a nuclear force capable of hitting a range of countervalue and counterforce targets, including enemy strategic nuclear missiles, conventional military bases and troop concentrations, transport hubs and command and control centers, and so on. For further details, see Johnston, "China's New 'Old Thinking.'"

23. Detailed descriptions of these and other recent or imminent advances can be found in Swaine, *China: Domestic Change and Foreign Policy;* and Mulvenon, "Appendix One."

24. Arnett, "Military Technology," 380–381.

25. One source estimates that the total cost of China's purchase of Russian weapons and equipment during the period 1991–1994 was $4.5–6 billion. One should add to this the cost of the more recent Su-27 co-production agreement, which is estimated at $3 billion. The same source estimates that China has

purchased $2–3 billion worth of military equipment and technology from Israel since the early 1980s. See Gill and Kim, *China's Arms Acquisitions from Abroad,* 99.

26. It is estimated that Chinese defense production is currently at about 10 percent of capacity. See Frankenstein and Gill, "Current and Future Challenges of Chinese Defense Industries," 9.

27. This list is adapted from Frankenstein and Gill, "Current and Future Challenges," 7.

28. The following estimates are highly speculative and derive from my own analysis. They do not represent conclusions reached by RAND or the U.S. government. Moreover, these estimates do not assume that China would necessarily prevail in any effort to attain the capabilities listed.

29. The word "limited" here denotes the ability to carry out sea denial activities primarily against a small number of surface and subsurface assets in selected, limited areas over short periods of time.

30. Such targets would include all major metropolitan areas in Japan, Korea, Taiwan, the Philippines, Southeast Asia, and India and most major U.S. military installations in Asia.

31. Specific military systems relevant to such capabilities include (1) large amphibious landing craft, especially those capable of traversing wide, shallow mud flats as are found on the West coast of Taiwan; (2) medium-range fighter/interceptors; (3) short- and medium-range ballistic missiles; (4) conventional attack submarines; (5) improved $C^3I$ and carrier detection systems; and (6) long-range, stand-off, antiship weapons, including cruises missiles and anti-carrier torpedoes.

32. There is now a stable, functioning retirement system in the PLA based upon age, position, and rank. As a consequence, the average age of officers at every level of the PLA has declined significantly. See Mulvenon, *Professionalization.*

33. More than 79 percent of the 1994 officer corps has received some form of advanced education, and more than 55 percent had received professional military education. For further details, see Mulvenon, "Professionalization," x.

34. The percentage of officers whose career paths had involved both military and political work fell from 21 percent in 1989 to 8 percent in 1994. See ibid., x.

35. Equally striking, however, is the increase in the number of officers who have no combat experience at all (from 21 percent to 46 percent). (Ibid., xii–xiii.)

36. Ibid., x–xiii. None of the top twenty to twenty-five members of China's High Command (i.e., all of the regional commanders and heads of PLA central departments) have any experience as political officers. In general, the post–Deng Xiaoping military leadership derives primarily from ground force backgrounds and has served in interior provinces throughout most of their careers. I am indebted to David Shambaugh for this information.

37. It is important to point out that although most members of the senior officer corps probably place a higher stress on military modernization and professionalization, many undoubtedly still view the PLA as a weapon for party dominance and seek to maintain or advance their personal positions of power by defending continued party control.

38. Jiang has personally promoted forty PLA generals. Such promotions do not necessarily mean that these officers owe a sense of personal loyalty to Jiang.

39. I am indebted to David Shambaugh for this information.

40. Similarly, not a single senior party leader in the new Politburo has military experience.

41. Zhang Wannian and Chi Haotian reportedly have even less political ambition and personal clout than their two elder predecessors. Moreover, their presence

on the Politburo but not in the inner leadership core of the PBSC marks a continuation of Deng Xiaoping's effort to distance the PLA from involvement in elite politics while preserving its participation in critical policy arenas relevant to its professional interests.

42. The following discussion is drawn largely from Swaine, *China: Domestic Change and Foreign Policy.*

43. One factor that might serve to restrain such involvement, however, is the lack of strong personal connections between this generation of military leaders and those civilian party members who comprise the successor leadership. Such an absence of linkages means that few strong political incentives will remain that could draw individual PLA officers into elite strife.

# PART THREE

## Economic Reform and Social Stability

# ⊞ 8 ⊞

# The Challenge of Economic Reform and Social Stability

## *Nicholas R. Lardy*

In his speech to the Fifteenth National Congress of the Chinese Communist Party (CCP) in September 1997, Jiang Zemin laid out an ambitious program of economic reform that focused on the state-owned sector. He spoke of corporatizing medium and large state-owned enterprises (SOEs) while relaxing control over small enterprises. He explicitly recognized that in this process, personnel mobility and layoffs would be "hard to avoid" but that they would also be conducive to economic development. In this chapter I provide an analysis of the origins of the reform program, the challenges it is designed to address, and an initial assessment of its possible shortcomings.

The origins of Jiang Zemin's proposal are the enterprise reform program first endorsed by the Third Plenum of the Fourteenth Party Congress in the fall of 1993. The key features of this initiative were the development of diversified forms of ownership that would compete on equal terms in the marketplace and the introduction of modern corporate governance for state-owned firms. In the words of one specialist, this reform "is undoubtedly the most ambitious plan for China's reform since the launching of reform in 1978 and may well prove to be a watershed in China's modern economic history."[1]

## THE STATE-OWNED SECTOR

The actions at the Third Plenum of the Fourteenth Congress and at the Fifteenth Party Congress explicitly recognize that the state sector is the core of the challenge China's reformers face. Although the sector's relative contribution to output, particularly in manufacturing, has declined dramatically over time, for several reasons this decline overstates the extent to which the role of the state has diminished during the reform process. First, the decline in the role of the state has been far more modest in the service sector than in manufacturing. In construction, for example, state-owned firms in 1995 continued to be responsible for more than three-fifths of the value of all building projects in urban areas, a very small decline from their share in 1980.[2] Similarly, even though there has been a dramatic increase in the number of collective and private wholesale and retail establishments, in 1995 state-owned firms still were responsible for two-thirds of the combined value of wholesale and retail sales.[3] Telecommunications and long distance transport remain almost entirely within the domain of state ownership.

Second, even within manufacturing, focusing on the declining share of output produced in state-owned firms obscures the continued importance of the state-owned sector, both as a major source of employment and as the recipient of a disproportionately large share of investment resources. Employment in the state sector soared by 40 million, or more than 50 percent, between 1977 and 1996. State sector employment rose so briskly that the share of the urban sector labor force employed by the state declined only moderately, from 78 percent in 1978 to 70 percent by 1992 and then 65 percent by the end of 1995. And the decline since 1992 is somewhat overstated, since most of it is due to the reclassification of state-owned enterprises into what are called corporatized or shareholding firms.[4] As will be discussed later, in most cases the state remains the dominant shareholder in these firms after their conversion, and there appear to be only modest initial changes in corporate governance.

Similarly, the share of investment absorbed by state-owned industrial firms continues to be disproportionately high. The share of assets owned by state firms fell to 53.7 percent in 1995, compared to their 74.6 percent share a decade earlier. But this decline is only about one-half of the proportionate shrinkage in the share of industrial output produced in state-owned enterprises over the same period.[5] The inescapable implication is that the relative efficiency of state-owned firms in the use of capital has declined significantly over time.

Moreover, even though the share of output produced by state-owned firms has declined dramatically on average, there remain many important industries in which state-owned firms have yet to feel much competitive pressure from nonstate firms. In 1995 SOEs produced 91 percent of all electric power, 91 percent of all coal, 95 percent of all petroleum, 79 percent of all metallurgical products, and 77 percent of all chemicals.[6] Of course, the state continues to own the rail system, still the dominant mode of long distance transportation, most of the waterborne transport capacity, and all telecommunications operating companies.[7]

## Financial Performance of State Firms

Most measures suggest that the financial performance of SOEs has declined dramatically during the reform period. These measures include the rate of return on assets of state enterprises, the percent of state firms that are incurring financial losses, and the magnitude of fiscal subsidies provided to state-owned firms. Each of these measures provides an indicator based on annual financial data, sometimes called "financial flows." These data, since they are readily available, have received the most attention. Analysis of data derived from the balance sheets of state-owned firms provides more definitive support for the view that the financial performance of state firms has deteriorated over the course of reform.

This deterioration is reflected clearly in the changes in the ratio of financial liabilities to assets. In addition, in the reform era, state-owned enterprises have accumulated substantial financial liabilities that are not included in their balance sheets and thus not reflected in the official data on liability-to-asset ratios. Of these, unfunded pension liabilities are far and away the most significant and will be discussed in more detail below.

At the outset of reform, financial liabilities of state-owned industrial firms were equal to only 11 percent of the value of their assets (Figure 8.1). This figure, which is far below the average for industrial firms in market economies, is not surprising. It simply reflects the fact that during the planning era, state-owned firms remitted most of their profits and depreciation funds to the state treasury and, in return, received state budgetary grants to finance most of their fixed investment and to meet a significant portion of their working capital needs. These budgetary grants did not have to be repaid. Since enterprises had little need to borrow from banks, financial liabilities were quite modest.

After reforms began, these planning-era arrangements were scrapped. Starting in 1983, budget financing of working capital for state-owned firms was drastically curtailed, and in late 1984 the authorities announced that the budget would also no longer provide financing for fixed asset investment.[8] As a result, SOEs began to borrow more heavily from banks. By 1988 their liabilities, mostly bank loans, reached a value equal to almost half their assets. This ratio is roughly comparable to that typically found in market economies.

Rather than stabilizing, however, the ratio of liabilities to assets continued to rise after 1988. By 1993, the liabilities of state-owned industrial firms equaled approximately two-thirds of the value of their assets, and in 1994, the ratio reached four-fifths. By the end of 1995, the ratio for all state-owned firms reached an all-time high of 85 percent.[9]

The official data in Figure 8.1 significantly understate the liability-to-asset ratio for state firms, particularly in more recent years, because of both the understatement of financial liabilities and the overstatement of real assets. Liabilities are understated because they do not take into account interenterprise debt, which the Chinese refer to as "triangular debt"—unpaid bills that accumulate rapidly when the central authorities restrict the growth of bank credit. When firms are unable to borrow enough

**Figure 8.1   Liabilities of SOEs (in percentage of assets)**

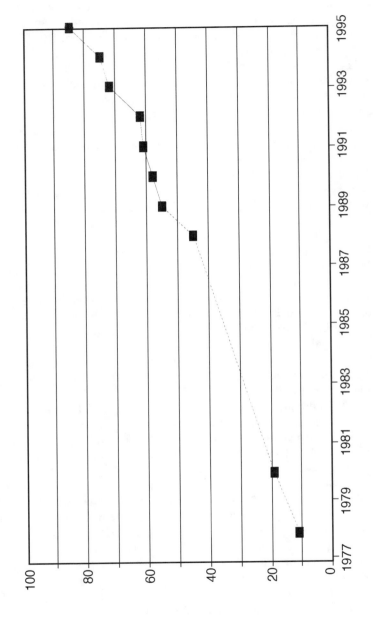

*Source:* Lardy, *China's Unfinished Economic Revolution*, 41.
*Note:* First three observations are for industrial SOEs only.

to pay for their inputs, for example, they frequently simply postpone paying their suppliers. To the extent the triangular debt phenomenon exists among state-owned firms, it does not affect the net liabilities of the sector as a whole since one firm's liability is another firm's asset. State firms, however, owe significant net indebtedness to nonstate firms, suggesting that it is easier for state-owned firms to refuse to pay nonstate firms than vice versa. At the end of 1994, this indebtedness amounted to RMB 440 billion yuan, about two-thirds of all interenterprise debt, and taking it into account increases the liability-to-asset ratio of state-owned firms from 75 percent to 83 percent.

Compounding the understatement of liabilities, data on enterprise assets are almost certainly overstated. First, Chinese firms use depreciation rates that are too low.[10] Thus, the depreciated value of plant and equipment, the single largest component of enterprise assets, is overstated. Second, many enterprises hold large inventories of finished goods that they value at full price. In many cases, however, the goods could only be sold at a significant discount, and in some cases the goods may not be salable at any price.[11] The failure to appraise inventories at their likely market value results in an overstatement of the value of enterprise assets.

All these factors—excluding net triangular debt to nonstate firms from liabilities, overvaluing plant and equipment, and carrying unsold inventories at their full price rather than market value—result in an understatement of the liability-to-asset ratio. Moreover, the degree of understatement probably has increased over time, both because triangular debt as a whole and net debt to the nonstate sector have increased and because inventories have grown rapidly in recent years.

These national figures obscure important regional variation. The most extremely indebted SOEs are located in China's industrial heartland—the northeast. In Liaoning, historically China's most industrialized province, at the end of 1992 the average liability-to-asset ratio for the province's 392 medium and large industrial enterprises was 190 percent, about three times the national average.[12] Because the average ratio was so far above the 100 percent critical level separating solvent from insolvent firms, it seems likely that virtually all of the medium and large state-owned firms in the province were insolvent. The situation in Heilongjiang Province also was unfavorable. In one of the province's fourteen districts the liability-to-asset ratio in 1994 was 86.1 percent, more than 11 percentage points greater than the national average. And nonperforming loans as a share of outstanding loans in the region at the end of October 1995 exceeded 55 percent, two and one-half times the national average.[13]

There are three implications of an average national liability-to-asset ratio that has risen from 11 percent to 85 percent. First, a significant portion of Chinese state-owned firms are insolvent—that is, the value of their liabilities exceeds the value of their assets. If they declared bankruptcy and liquidated, their creditors would not fully recover the funds due to them. Even in 1994, when the liability-to-asset ratio for state-owned industrial enterprises was 10 percentage points below that of 1995, liabilities exceeded assets for more than one-fourth of the enterprises, and liabilities were equal to assets in an additional one-fifth of all enterprises.[14] In short, even excluding net debts to nonstate firms, unfunded pension liabilities, and overstatement of assets, nearly half of all SOEs were at or beyond the brink of solvency. They remained in operation only because of generous access to additional bank loans.

Second, the continuous rise in the ratio of liabilities to assets suggests that many firms have negative value added: their output is worth less than the total cost of all of the labor and other inputs. Their borrowing over time rises relative to their assets because the funds are not used to finance fixed investment but to pay wages and taxes and to finance growing inventories of unsold goods.[15] This problem, which Ronald McKinnon identifies as value subtracting, was important in firms throughout Eastern Europe and the Soviet Union in the prereform era.[16] Thus, not only are a large number of firms insolvent, but many cannot even cover their operating costs from their income, which suggests that the program of restructuring of the state-owned sector will be enormously challenging.

Third, enterprises in China are so highly leveraged that an economic slowdown could easily create a liquidity problem for banks. An asset-to-liability ratio of 85 percent is the equivalent of a debt-to-equity ratio of well over 500 percent.[17] The average state-owned firm in 1995 was even more highly leveraged than Korean *chaebol,* which are notorious for their high debt-to-equity ratios of 300 to 400 percent.[18] The main shortcoming of such a high debt-to-equity ratio is that in an economic slowdown such as the one experienced in 1998, the earnings of an increasing share of these firms fall below the level necessary to amortize their heavy debts. In the first quarter of 1998, for example, the interest rate all banks were required to charge on one-year working capital loans, the most common loan made, was 8.64 percent.[19] But for state-owned industrial firms in the first quarter of 1998, the average rate of return on assets before interest and taxes was only 5 percent.[20] With financial liabilities equal to 85 percent of assets, on average, firms were capable of paying interest of only 5.9 percent on their financial liabilities. Stated another way, if all SOEs had devoted their entire pretax profits to interest payments, they could have met at most only two-thirds of their interest obligations.[21] As the growth rate continued to decline in the second and subsequent quarters of 1998, the share of SOEs unable to pay interest on their debts must have risen. In short, with such high leverage and low rates of return on real assets, a slowdown in economic growth has dramatically negative consequences for bank earnings and could lead to a liquidity crisis for banks.

## Corporatization as a Solution to the Crisis

Is the enterprise reform program endorsed by both the Third Plenum of the Fourteenth Party Congress in the fall of 1993 and by the full Fifteenth Party Congress in the fall of 1997 adequate to deal with the substantial challenge that enterprise reform presents? Only time will tell, but several shortcomings are already obvious.

First, the pace of conversion of SOEs to limited liability shareholding companies has been slow. By year-end 1996, 9,200 state-owned firms, only 3 percent of the total, had adopted the shareholding, or corporate, form of ownership set forth in the 1993 Company Law, which was passed shortly after the Third Plenum.[22] One obstacle to faster progress in corporatization is a provision in the Company Law mandating that the articles of association required to establish a firm under the corporate form of ownership identify the investor or investors in the company as well as the magnitude and form of their investment. Competing claimants, including government bureaus and ministries, frequently cannot reach a consensus regarding the identity of the firm's investors. This is a particularly difficult problem for firms with relatively large liabilities because, as a World Bank report stated: "Everybody wants the valuable assets, but nobody wants the liabilities."[23]

A second shortcoming of the current enterprise reform program is that little evidence points to significant changes in the governance of the relatively few firms that have converted to the limited liability shareholding form of ownership. There appear to be several reasons for this. Most important, many of the state-owned enterprises that have been "corporatized" have chosen to become wholly state-owned companies. Almost all of the 100 firms selected by the State Council in 1994 to spearhead the corporatization experiment, for example, have opted to convert to wholly state-owned companies.[24] This legal organizational form, which the Company Law permits, embodies the fewest changes from the rules governing state-owned enterprises.[25] For example, with only a single owner, there is no need for shareholder meetings. Moreover, the members of the board of directors of wholly state-owned limited liability companies are not elected but appointed. The powers of these boards are severely truncated, compared to the boards of limited liability companies that are not wholly state-owned. For example, they have no power to make or approve mergers, breakups, dissolutions, increases or decreases in a firm's capitalization, or the issuance of bonds. The authority to make these decisions is all reserved for "an organization authorized by the state."[26]

Another reason that there appears to be little change in the governance of corporatized firms is that their boards of directors are dominated by insiders—the senior managers of the firm. A World Bank study of enterprise reform reported: "In every case examined for this study, the majority of members of the boards of directors and the senior executives are one and the same. There is no real distinction."[27] The result is insider-dominated firms, a form of governance that has weaknesses that are readily apparent in Russia and some other transition economies. Among these weaknesses are "asset stripping, poor investment decisions, decapitalization through excessive wage increases, and increases in other private benefits."[28]

Insider domination has developed in part because of the small number of companies listed on the stock exchange. Through the end of 1996, less than 6 percent of those companies that had reorganized into shareholding companies were listed on the stock exchange.[29] In market economies, poor firm management and poor financial performance typically are reflected in a declining share price, a market signal that often leads to a takeover by stronger, more efficient firms. But when shareholding firms are not listed, capital markets are unable to provide this monitoring function. Poor managers and insider-dominated boards are less likely to be replaced.

Third, even when corporatized enterprises are publicly listed, individual shareholders "seem to have little, if any, influence on management."[30] This ineffectiveness is due in part to the small portion of the shares of listed companies actually available to the public. The majority shareholders almost always are traditional line ministries at the national level and industrial bureaus at the provincial and municipal levels.[31] In a few cases, they are newly established state asset management institutions. These institutional shareholders "are generally not organized in such a way to marshal sufficient information, experience and skill to assess effectively an enterprise's performance."[32] There are no institutional investors, such as pension funds, insurance companies, or mutual funds that might exercise influence on corporate governance on behalf of individual shareholders.

Beyond its slow pace and its failure to lead to significant changes in corporate governance, the enterprise reform program has other shortcomings. For one thing, state-owned firms have not relinquished their government functions once they became limited liability shareholding companies. Transformed firms continue to bear the responsibility for providing a broad range of social services that should be the responsibility of the government budget or the workers themselves. In addition, labor mobility and the role of the market in determining wages in the state-owned sector remain limited. This, in turn, reflects generally slow progress in divesting individual enterprises of the responsibility for providing unemployment insurance, old-age pensions, and health care to their workers.

Institutional constraints have also limited the ability of corporatized firms to develop a more balanced capital structure that depends less on debt and more on permanent equity financing. This failure is partly due to the fact that so few companies have been allowed to raise funds by listing their shares publicly. If more companies had been allowed to list, they would have been able to reduce their bank debt and thus their operating costs. In addition, the government has allocated insufficient resources to finance the write-offs of bad debt to facilitate mergers and takeovers of unprofitable firms and thus improve the capital structure of the 1,000 large state-owned enterprises that are to form the core of the new modern enterprise system. The state has allocated a total of 500 billion yuan for the enterprise reform program during the ninth five-year plan (1996–2000). But the majority of these funds, 280 billion yuan, will finance technical renovations of these firms, and another 160 billion yuan will cover worker redundancy payments. The amounts allocated to write off debts, 20 billion yuan in 1996 and an additional 30 billion in 1997, are grossly inadequate.[33] Direct debt reduction will be modest.

Even these limited resources are being provided in a way that appears to undermine incentives for improved enterprise performance. Firms in the reform program benefit from a reduction in their income tax rate from 33 to 15 percent; a dispensation to pay only 40 to 60 percent of this reduced tax obligation from their own funds while borrowing the rest from banks at a special subsidized interest rate; and an increase in their allowable annual depreciation rate from 3 to 5 percent.[34] In addition, firms that agree to merge with another firm are not required to pay interest on that firms' liabilities to banks for a period of two to three years.[35] But because there is no specified time frame for phasing out most of these new subsidies, the reforms represent a softening rather than a firming up of the budget constraints under which state-owned firms operate. A much larger initial write-off of accumulated nonperforming loans, combined with hard budget constraints in the future, would more likely lead to improved enterprise performance.

## IMPLICATIONS FOR BANKS

The increased obligations owed to banks by state-owned enterprises is reflected in the enormous buildup of total domestic credit relative to gross domestic product. Total loans outstanding by all types of financial institutions grew from RMB 190 billion in 1978 to RMB 7.5 trillion at the end of 1997. Loans outstanding as a percentage of gross domestic product almost doubled, from about 50 percent to 100 percent, over this period (Figure 8.2). The vast majority of these loans have been extended to state-owned firms. Many Chinese banks, unfortunately, have experienced a dramatic deterioration in the quality of their loan portfolios over the same period. The nonperforming loans of the four largest state banks rose in recent years, from 20 percent in 1994, to 22 percent in 1996, to 25 percent at the end of 1997.[36] Based on the very low rates of recovery on loans to enterprises that have gone through bankruptcy and liquidation, it appears that three of China's largest state-owned banks have negative net worth and thus are insolvent.[37]

Figure 8.2 also shows the buildup of bank credit in South Korea and Thailand, countries that began to experience banking and financial crises in mid-1997. The pace of expansion of domestic credit in China closely paralleled that in South Korea and Thailand from 1978 through 1992. Relative to gross domestic product, credit in China dropped in the austerity years (1993–1995), when Zhu Rongji brought inflation back under control. But in the past two years, credit expansion has resumed on a trajectory that is similar to that in Thailand and South Korea. These international comparisons raise several closely related questions. Why has China not already experienced a banking crisis? Is a crisis inevitable? If so, what form might it take?

There are five good reasons why China, in the short run, is unlikely to experience a crisis like that seen in several Southeast Asian countries and South Korea beginning in 1997. First, China's capital inflows predominantly take the form of foreign direct investment. Second, little of China's borrowing is short term. Third, Chinese currency is not convertible for capital account transactions. Fourth, in contrast to South Korea, Thailand, and several other countries in Southeast Asia that experienced currency crises beginning in 1997, China in the mid-1990s experienced record trade and current account surpluses. Finally, at the end of 1997, China had amassed $139.9 billion in foreign exchange reserves, enough to finance more than a full year of imports.[38] These advantages mean that a change in the sentiment of foreign lenders, speculators, or domestic firms that have outstanding, unhedged foreign currency liabilities is unlikely to precipitate a banking crisis.

Nevertheless, China is not immune to the adverse consequences of a weak financial system, characterized by a rapid buildup of nonperforming loans to SOEs that are financed largely by household deposits. The real consequence is the inescapable cost of the poor lending decisions that banks have made and are continuing to make. These costs are reflected in the long-term, continuous decline in the rate of return on real assets in state-owned industrial firms. The continued survival of value-subtracting state-owned enterprises is perhaps the most stark evidence of the ongoing waste of real resources. Households bear the cost of the poor lending decisions of banks, which is reflected in the very low rate of return households have earned on their savings deposits in banks during most of the reform

**Figure 8.2 Domestic Credit (as a percentage of GDP)**

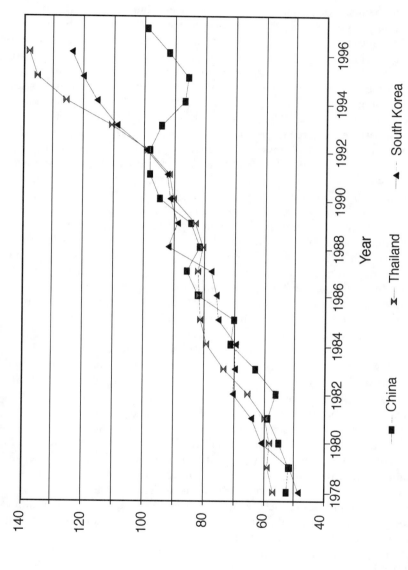

*Sources:* Lardy, *China's Unfinished Economic Revolution*, 78; International Monetary Fund, *International Financial Statistics*, November 1997.
*Note:* PRC data is through 1997.

period, and there is a very real risk that the large insolvent banks ultimately will default on their obligations to households.

The alternative to this threat of bank default is for the state to recapitalize the banks. Not only is this a costly process, but it presents competing problems. If government is unwilling to subject SOEs to hard budget constraints, recapitalization does not make sense because continued lending to money-losing state-owned enterprises would quickly consume any funds made available through a recapitalization program. At the same time, however, if the government does impose strict financial discipline on enterprises, a large number of bankruptcies and restructurings will result, with high political costs to the regime. Thus recapitalization is not a simple option.

Nonetheless, there are grounds for optimism. The Fifteenth Party Congress finally made a commitment to address problems of state-owned enterprises, and the Chinese government in fact addressed the problems of the banking and financial sector with some urgency in the immediate aftermath of the Congress. Newly elected Premier Zhu Rongji's repeated assertion that China would solve both the problems of money-losing SOEs and the problems of the fragile financial system within three years was particularly notable in this regard. If his program of financial reform—which includes recapitalizing and commercializing the banking system, subjecting enterprises to hard budget constraints, and increasing tax revenues by an amount sufficient to finance the recapitalization program—is carried out on the indicated timetable, China will emerge with a more efficient financial system and will be more likely to maintain a high rate of domestic savings. Both characteristics are essential for sustaining the high average rate of growth that China has achieved in the reform era.

However, if the leadership is unable to implement these fundamental reforms on a timely basis, the possibility of a financial crisis greatly increases. Most important, any growth slowdown, such as the one that emerged in 1998, is likely to expose the underlying weakness of the domestic financial system. Slower growth is cutting into the operating profits of many state-owned companies. Given their average high ratio of debt to equity, reduced profitability inevitably increases the number of firms unable to amortize their debts, further undermining the financial position of China's major banks. The regime has sought to counter the growth downturn by providing increased infrastructure outlays and a long-anticipated program of housing reform, but neither of these is a panacea. It is not clear that infrastructure spending can be ramped up fast enough to offset the softening of consumer demand. The initial plan to roll out housing reform in June 1998 was set back until the fall, meaning that it is unlikely to have any effect on the rate of economic growth in 1998.

Moreover, major currency depreciations and declining economies in Korea and Southeast Asia beginning in 1997 have cut the rate of growth of Chinese exports in the first seven months of 1998 by more than half compared to the prior year. Because of a decline in imports over the same period, China's trade balance has held up surprisingly well. But if export performance continues to soften or import growth picks up, the favorable trade balance could largely evaporate over the next twelve months. Because China has a large negative investment balance in its current account, a declining trade surplus creates the possibility of the emergence of a significant current account deficit.[39] A current account deficit, of course, can be financed by foreign capital inflows. But China's inflows of foreign direct investment, far and away its single largest source of capital inflows, were 1.3 percent less in the first half of 1998 than in the first half of 1997, portending the first year-over-year decline in foreign direct investment since 1990. The collapse of Chinese equity prices in foreign markets also has dramatically curtailed the ability of Chinese companies to raise money in Hong Kong and New York. In 1997, Chinese firms raised U.S.$7.5 billion on international markets. In the first half of 1998, investment slowed to a trickle of only a few hundred million U.S. dollars.

If a current account deficit emerges as foreign direct investment and equity investment decline, China will have to draw down its foreign exchange reserves, step up its external borrowing, or devalue its currency. The first of these alternatives could be used to postpone, but only temporarily, China's need to adjust to its changed international competitive position. Increased borrowing could serve the same function but likewise would not provide a permanent solution because it would become increasingly difficult for China to expand its borrowing, given its already large external debt. Devaluation, the last alternative, would pose difficulties for many Chinese banks and firms, given their large unhedged exposure to foreign currency–denominated debt.[40]

A banking crisis in China is most likely to arise when domestic savers lose confidence in the government's implicit guarantee of the value of their bank deposits. This loss of confidence could be triggered either by a growth slowdown that weakened the domestic banking system or by the prospect of a major devaluation in response to a large emerging current account deficit. If large numbers of households attempt to withdraw their savings, the insolvency problem of several of China's largest banks would become a liquidity problem, and the central bank would face two alternatives. First, it could supply funds to banks to meet the demand for withdrawals. This practice was not unheard of during the 1980s and 1990s, when the central bank extended loans to individual provincial branches of state banks to solve liquidity problems. If the central bank lends money to state-owned banks on a scale large enough to meet a demand for withdrawals throughout China, however, the resulting burgeoning increase in the money supply would be highly inflationary.

Thus the second, more likely, alternative is that the central bank would not serve as a lender of last resort. Banks would have no alternative but to sharply limit customer withdrawals of their savings. Again, this has occurred episodically in a few cities in recent years without dire consequences. If the practice became widespread, however, it would almost certainly further undermine confidence in the banking system and lead to a dramatic reduction in the flow of funds into savings deposits. Anticipating rising inflation, households likely would try to convert part of their increased holdings of currency into goods, again creating an inflationary spiral.

In short, a banking crisis in China is most likely to lead to an inflationary spiral, whether or not the central bank lends additional funds to state-owned banks in order to meet the demand for withdrawals by households. The flow of funds to the banking system would also decline, leading to a collapse of credit and a major economic contraction.

## CONCLUSION

The current stage of reform is far more difficult than earlier reforms. Economically, it is more complex because it requires closely coordinated reforms of state enterprises, the financial system, and tax administration. Politically, it is extremely challenging for two reasons. First, the required closure of insolvent firms and its consequences for the financial system are leading to the highest rates of unemployment China has experienced since the economic depression in the early 1960s, in the wake of the catastrophic Great Leap Forward.[41] In contrast to the reform of 1978 to 1996 in which almost everyone shared to some degree in the gains from growth, the current phase will reduce the real incomes of a significant portion of the population, at least temporarily. This is certain to stress the political system far beyond the range of experience of recent decades. Second, the restructuring of the banking system will require the state and the party to surrender substantial economic and political power. Eventually, the central authorities will have to allow both the emergence of private banks, either by the sale of shares of existing banks to individual investors or by licensing new private institutions, and an expansion of the role of foreign financial institutions. Until these changes occur, however, the prospects for financial reform and the emergence of a more efficient system for allocating capital will be limited.

## NOTES

1. Broadman, *Meeting the Challenge of Enterprise Reform*, xiv, 25.
2. State Statistical Bureau, *China Statistical Yearbook 1996*, 457. This figure probably overstates the role of state-owned construction firms, since increasingly they subcontract work to nonstate firms. This situation is probably not reflected in the official data.
3. State Statistical Bureau, *China Statistical Yearbook 1996*, 543.

4. Lardy, *China's Unfinished Economic Revolution*, 26–28.

5. The state share of industrial output fell from 61.9 percent in 1985 to 29.0 percent in 1995, a decline of more than half. The share of industrial assets owned by state firms declined by less than three-fifths. Lardy, *China's Unfinished Economic Revolution*, 28–30.

6. Ibid., 30.

7. At the end of 1995 private firms owned less than one-fifth and less than one-tenth of the haulage capacity of motorized vessels and barges, respectively. State Statistical Bureau, *China Statistical Yearbook 1996*, 515, 518.

8. State Council, "Notice," in National People's Congress, *A Classified Compendium of Laws*, vol. 2, 68–72. State Planning Commission, Ministry of Finance, and People's Construction Bank of China, "Interim Regulations," VI-79–VI-82.

9. Lardy, *China's Unfinished Economic Revolution*, 41.

10. The low depreciation rates assume long lives for fixed assets based more on physical wear and tear than obsolescence. World Bank, *China GNP per Capita*, 13.

11. Steinfeld, *Forging Reform in China*, chaps. 4 and 6.

12. Su and Lu, "State-Owned Enterprises' Financial Problems and Their Remedies."

13. Qiu Mingchen, "Concerning the Way to Advance the Transformation of the Method of Managing Credit Funds," *Jinrong shibao* (Financial news), May 18, 1996, 5.

14. The precise share in each of these two categories was 27.6 percent and 21.5 percent, respectively. A. Ming, "State-Owned Enterprises: How to Confront the Debt Ratio?" *Jinrong shibao* (Financial news), October 7, 1995, 1.

15. Dai Jianming, "Enterprises Cannot Rely on Loosening the Money Supply to Solve Their Problems," *Jinrong shibao* (Financial news), September 6, 1996, 1.

16. McKinnon, *Order*, 162–186.

17. In this calculation equity is defined as assets minus liabilities.

18. The top five *chaebol* at year-end 1996, prior to the onset of the Asian financial crisis, had debt:equity ratios that ranged from Samsung at 473 percent to Sunkyong at 262 percent. John Burton, "Seoul Fires Warning Shot over Chaebol," *Financial Times*, January 22, 1998, 6.

19. The rate changed to 7.92 percent on March 24, 1998.

20. China Economic Performance Monitoring Center, "Indicators for Performance of State-Owned Enterprises in First Quarter '98," *China Economic News*, no. 20, June 1, 1998, 13.

21. The lion's share of enterprise financial obligations are loans from banks. But they also have unpaid tax, wage, and pension payments obligations. To the extent that firms do not use their pretax profits to meet these obligations, they possibly could pay a higher share of their interest payments to banks.

22. "New Progress in Restructuring Economy," *Beijing Review*, June 2–8, 1997, 5.

23. World Bank, *China's Management of Enterprise Assets*, vii.

24. World Bank, *China's Management of Enterprise Assets*, 4. By the end of 1997, sixty-nine of seventy-three companies that had completed the transformation of their ownership had become wholly state-owned corporations. Sun Shangwei, "State Firms Reform Going Successfully," *China Daily*, December 16, 1997, 1.

25. Although state-owned companies are subject to provisions set forth in the Company Law, traditional state-owned enterprises are governed by the 1988 "State-Owned Enterprise Law of the People's Republic of China," in National People's Congress, *A Classified Compendium of Laws*, vol. 2, 1,029–1,034.

26. "The Company Law of the People's Republic of China," adopted at the Fifth Session of the Standing Committee of the Eighth National People's Congress

on December 29, 1993, in Foreign Broadcast Information Service, Article 66, China-94-017, 26–48.

27. World Bank, *China's Management of Enterprise Assets,* 40.

28. Ibid., 51. See also World Bank, *From Plan to Market,* 55.

29. At year-end 1996, a total of 514 companies were listed on either the Shanghai or the Shenzhen stock exchanges.

30. World Bank, *China's Management of Enterprise Assets,* 39.

31. At year-end 1996, of the companies listed on the Shanghai Stock exchange, the state held 43.9 percent of the shares, and the companies themselves held 27.3 percent.

32. World Bank, *China's Management of Enterprise Assets,* 40.

33. "State Council Outlines State Enterprise Reform Plan," China News Agency, December 1, 1996, in Foreign Broadcast Information Service, China-96-234. New China News Agency, "$3.65 b Goes into Special State Fund," *China Daily,* March 4, 1997, 2.

34. World Bank, *China's Management of Enterprise Assets,* 4.

35. New China News Agency, "Circular Issued on Debts of Merged Enterprises," June 21, 1995, in Foreign Broadcast Information Service, China, July 5, 1995, 48.

36. Lardy, *China's Unfinished Economic Revolution,* 119–122, 206.

37. Lardy, *China's Unfinished Economic Revolution,* 115–122.

38. For details on these five factors, see Lardy, *China's Unfinished Economic Revolution,* 197–199.

39. In 1997, for example, the investment balance was U.S.$16 billion. This arose because of net interest expenditures on outstanding foreign currency debt and profit remittances by foreigners who have invested in firms in China. Thus, although China had an all-time record trade surplus in 1997 of U.S.$46.2 billion, the current account balance was only U.S.$29.7 billion.

40. At year-end 1997, China reported its external debt to be U.S.$130.96 billion, of which U.S.$55.81 billion was owed by banks, other financial institutions, and enterprises. Sovereign debt was only U.S.$35.98 billion, with most of the balance borrowed by foreign-funded enterprises. "A Tight Grasp at Borrowing from Overseas," in *China Economic News,* no. 2, June 15, 1998, 7–8. The Bank for International Settlements and other independent sources, based on reporting by lending institutions, estimate that China's external debt is about one-fourth larger than the official figure. For example, J. P. Morgan estimates that China's total foreign debt at year-end 1997 was U.S.$161.5 billion. Zheng, "China Reaches for a Home-grown Path Forward," p. 8. Since sovereign debt is easily tracked and most foreign-funded firms have no incentive to understate their foreign currency obligations, most of the difference between the two figures is probably borrowing by Chinese financial institutions and enterprises that is not reported to the Chinese authorities.

41. Lardy, "The Chinese Economy Under Stress," 360–397.

# ⊞ 9 ⊞

# Perspectives on Social Stability After the Fifteenth Congress

## *Michel Bonnin*

---

The most important point decided at the Fifteenth National Congress of the Chinese Communist Party (CCP) was certainly the acceleration of the reform of state-owned enterprises (SOEs). The leaders seem convinced of the strategic necessity of this reform but at the same time are aware of the difficulties that will ensue in the realms of employment and social stability. Nevertheless, they look confident in their capacity to overcome those "temporary difficulties." In his report to the Congress, Jiang Zemin said: "Lay-offs and job mobility will cause temporary difficulties to a part of the workforce . . . but are conducive to economic development, conforming to the long-term interests of the working class."[1]

Since the Congress, however, Beijing leaders have expressed some wariness about this question, perhaps because the recent Asian economic crisis had some effect on the speed of growth and therefore on the capacity of labor absorption in coming years, and perhaps because many researchers and specialists have sounded the alarm on the question. For example, an inquiry on the situation of laid-off workers published by the State Bureau of Statistics in December asserted that "the problem of urban poverty is becoming increasingly conspicuous and social stability is under threat."[2]

"Stability" *(wending)* has been the supreme watchword of the regime and especially of Jiang since June 4, 1989. Only a very strong economic necessity will convince Chinese leaders to risk a stability they have so painstakingly succeeded in achieving, and it is quite possible that the stated aim of "basically solving the problem of state enterprises in three years" will be downgraded. Premier Li Peng declared on December 29, 1997: "We will take into consideration the ability of the people and enterprises to bear the burdens of reform. . . . We will quicken our steps if conditions are good and slow down if conditions are not ripe."[3] Even Zhu Rongji, who is behind the plan and who has since become the new premier, announced a national conference in May 1998 seeking ways to find reemployment for laid-off workers, hinting that this question could put his

153

SOE plan in jeopardy. He declared on February 15, 1998: "The key to achieving our target of helping our large and medium state-owned enterprises to turn round in three years is whether we can successfully settle laid-off workers."[4]

The wariness of China's leaders is not without reason. Even if SOE reform is not undertaken very forcefully (causing other problems), the question of employment in the years to come presents a risk to social stability in any case.

## THE THIRD WAVE . . . OF UNEMPLOYMENT

Since the beginning of the reforms, there have been three waves of unemployment. The first was in 1979, when a growing workforce in the cities was swollen by returning "educated youths," the second, less important, one arrived in 1989 when 10.5 million young city-dwellers went looking for jobs in the cities. The third one began in 1995, and official forecasts by the Labor Ministry predict difficulties for many years to come: During the Ninth Five-Year Plan, the labor force will increase by about 54 million (10.8 million per year), but according to the figures, only 38 million jobs will be available, leaving 16 million jobless in the year 2000.[5]

In fact, these figures already appear partly outdated. The acceleration of reform will bring into the open a larger part of the hidden unemployment than was planned, and recently the definition of "joblessness" has been widened. Bearing in mind the fact that official statistics are not always consistent in the People's Republic of China (PRC) and that unemployment statistics are "sensitive," the recent situation seems to be as follows. In towns and cities, in mid-1997, there were 5.56 million registered unemployed, translating to an official unemployment rate of 3 percent—quite low by world standards. But there were also 10 million laid-off workers (*xiagang zhigong:* literally, employees and workers who have stepped down). At the end of 1997, their number had increased to 11 million, and the forecast was for 10 million more by the year 2000, including 2 million in 1998.[6] This estimate is in line with the instructions of the National Working Conference on Reemployment held at the beginning of 1997: "Reduce staff and increase productivity, lay off and redistribute."[7] There also were 11.9 million "workers in difficulty" *(kunnan zhigong)* whose wages had not been paid for months (sometimes even more than a year) or had been significantly reduced because their enterprises were in financial trouble. Among them were 1.91 million pensioners and 2.96 million *tekun zhigong* (workers with special difficulties whose wages fell short of locally evaluated official minimum living expenses).

These figures—though certainly underestimated—are the highest ever and stand against a background of about 30 million surplus employees in the urban state sector and 130 million surplus workers in the countryside (according to different Chinese specialists, including officials of the Labor Ministry).[8] Moreover, the employment problem cannot be expected to resolve rapidly because the baby boom that took place from the 1950s to the 1970s means that the demand for employment will probably be in excess of supply at least until the year 2020.[9]

## LAID-OFF WORKERS AND WORKERS IN DIFFICULTY

In 1997, a few large-scale surveys were taken to gauge the situation and morale of laid-off workers. Even the official ones give a rather bleak image of their plight. About 60 percent of them are female, though they account for less than 40 percent of the urban *zhigong* (employees of state and collective work units). Laid-off workers are mainly middle-aged (30 to 45 or 50 years of age), a period in life that includes financial responsibility for children and sometimes also for parents, and about 60 percent of them have attained only primary *(chuzhong)* educational levels, posing considerable difficulty in finding new employment. Except for a very small minority who have found better-paying new employment in the private sector, most of the laid-off workers have suffered a significant drop in their income. According to one survey, 58 percent of them earn less than 200 yuan a month. In some provinces, like Heilongjiang and Jiangxi, the drop has been particularly large. Generally, when both parents in a family have been laid off, they are quite likely to rank among the urban poor or very poor.[10]

There are fewer surveys concerning "workers in difficulty" because this category is less easy to define. One survey shows, however, that the problem, though general, is particularly acute in some provinces: in Liaoning, in mid-1997, there were 1.72 million of them (22.2 percent of the urban *zhigong*); in Heilongjiang, 1.52 million (23.5 percent); in Jilin, 1.33 million (34.6 percent); and in Guizhou, 0.29 million (19.5 percent). In the northeast, some enterprises cannot even give a heating allowance to their staff, and people have no home heating during the winter. In some places, men sell their blood to survive, and women resort to prostitution. A Chongqing survey has shown a high percentage of *kunnan zhigong* with grave physical or mental illnesses and a high rate of mortality because they do not have the means to see a doctor.[11]

## POOR PERFORMANCE OF THE REEMPLOYMENT PROJECT

In principle, as Jiang Zemin said in his report to the Congress, these difficulties are temporary, and the restructuring of the economy should provide new employment opportunities for all the jobless. The government insists that in the new era, urban-dwellers should no longer rely only on the state to provide them with jobs. The media are full of examples of people who have found new employment by themselves and regularly blame the attitude of those jobless who have not obtained new employment.

Nevertheless, the authorities had to acknowledge the difficulties of finding new jobs. Thus, in April 1995, they launched a Reemployment Project (*zai jiuye gongcheng*) aimed mainly at providing unemployment insurance, job introduction, and job training. This project extends the measures already contained in Document 10 of the State Council from 1993, which sought to promote the "success" experience of the service center for reemployment in Shanghai.[12]

A survey carried out in early 1997 shows that the results were far from satisfactory. Only 4.5 percent of the laid-off workers thought that the project was very useful. There was great disappointment concerning the unemployment allowances that the central and local authorities were to pay using special funds. They amounted to only a small proportion of the average income of laid-off workers, which could be broken down as follows: 45 percent of the average worker's income came from a new job; subsistence allowance provided by their former enterprise, 27.2 percent; subsidies from relatives and friends, 13.3 percent; state unemployment insurance, 2.2 percent; local unemployment insurance, 1.8 percent; other, 10.4 percent.[13]

Many explanations exist for the poor performance of official efforts, one being a lack of funds. The fund for reemployment, which Li Peng promoted in his speech to the National People's Congress (NPC) in March 1997, has not been able to collect enough money, especially from local financial institutions, to meet needs. Even the model Shanghai service center was short of funds for that year.[14] Workers also complain about cadres, whom they frequently blame for the plight of their enterprises (and not without reason, according to a few inquiries made on the subject) and also for not being sympathetic to their fate. Cadres have even been accused of embezzling the money destined for the reemployment fund. The main problem, however, is probably that the economy simply does not create enough jobs for everybody, and it is particularly clear in regions like the northeast, where the whole economy is in decline. But in some cases, if employment was accorded first priority in decisionmaking, more jobs could certainly be found. For example, there are often instances of people who are told by labor bureau personnel to go and find a job by themselves in the street service sector but who get arrested by police for engaging in illegal business activities.[15]

## AN UPSURGE OF LABOR UNREST

This situation results in a deep feeling of grievance among those in different jobless categories. Some people are simply desperate, and many suicide cases caused by unemployment have been reported. But there is also wide-spread anger. Many of the unemployed feel that they have been deprived of their rights, and some have not hesitated to resort to illegal activities like theft or prostitution to earn a living.[16] At the same time, more and more people resort to collective actions like petitions, demonstrations, sit-ins, and traffic blockades to seek redress of their grievances. A few of these actions are well documented. What is particularly interesting is that in some cases their demands have included the right to demonstrate and even the right to form independent unions.[17]

## ANXIETY AND FRUSTRATION IN THE WORKING CLASS

PRC leadership is so preoccupied with the situation because the dissatisfaction is not limited to the unemployed themselves. In fact, the reforms are now causing general feelings of insecurity and a drop in status that threaten the traditional link between the party and the working class.

Millions of former state and collective units employees have already experienced a serious loss of privileges, and they are fated to experience many more. Though the *zhigong* have benefited from the general increase in the standard of living since the beginning of the reforms, they are now facing a very unfavorable situation in their bargaining position with the management (whether public or private) due to the mismatch between labor supply and demand. If they express dissatisfaction or demands, they are very often reminded that many people are waiting to take their jobs. Thus, the former so-called masters of the country (which they never really were, but still they had some status and certain privileges) are beginning to experience the fate of unprotected and exploited labor of a Third World country. Even in official surveys, examples abound of former state workers forced to work long hours in small private companies for very low wages that the boss pays irregularly.[18]

As a result, the *zhigong* seem to be more class-conscious than before. They consider management cadres to be "bosses" and deeply resent their corruption. The fact that the lay-offs almost always target employees, not the cadres who stay in their enterprises or receive other appointments when their enterprise is closed, also offends them. In fact, official figures show clearly that, as the number of *zhigong* has begun to decline, the ranks of the bureaucrats have become more and more numerous.[19]

Even in the "modern" shareholding companies, class struggle is obvious. In many companies, employees are forced to buy shares, or they will lose their jobs or at least part of their wages and benefits. But a significant portion of the shares are reserved for management, depriving the employees of any real decisionmaking power. There also is a clear conflict of interest between the management, who derive a substantial part of their income from the interest on shares (and therefore try to keep wages as low as possible), and the employees, who want to increase wages (their main source of income).[20]

## THE RISK OF SOCIAL AND POLITICAL INSTABILITY

### The Countryside Factor

The main source of instability in China today is certainly the employment situation of the urban employees and workers, but at least two other important factors must be taken into account: the question of the migrant workers from the countryside looking for jobs in the cities (*mingong*) and the peasant unrest that has broken out in many localities during the last few years. These issues are linked but not identical.

Though they have contributed to the development of the cities in the 1990s, the migrants also contribute to many problems and are regularly blamed for an upsurge in urban insecurity. They are blamed for the risk (perceived or real) that they pose to the difficult situation of employment in the cities.[21] In 1998, new measures were taken to prevent them from settling and working in urban areas, but the effects of these measures remain to be seen.[22] They might not force the migrants to go back to their villages, but they might be strong enough to increase the difficulties that migrants experience in their daily lives, some of which could increase instability. The most conspicuous problem is the fate of the millions of migrant children, who get no, or very little, education because they are not accepted in the city schools or only at a price too high for most parents.

The other related question is, what will happen to the employment pressure in the countryside if the estimated 70 million or more rural migrants come back and want their share of the fields? In the words of an official from the Ministry of Labor, "emigration of laborers is now a priority for the governments of inland regions in their efforts to reduce poverty."[23] If this possibility disappeared, the population burden of many poor regions could become unbearable. Peasant unrest is already a cause for concern for the party. It is triggered by various factors, the most important being government representatives' use of IOUs instead of cash to pay for crops and the heavy and arbitrary taxes imposed on farmers by local governments. Other infringements on peasant rights, like confiscation of land for projects that benefit only some local leaders, can also lead to violent action. Peasant unrest has become quite widespread: one source states that 10,000 "unruly incidents" took place in the countryside in 1997.[24] It must be remembered, however, that these incidents are scattered throughout the whole of China. The participants have no opportunity to establish any links with other dissatisfied people, nor even to air their grievances beyond their homes.

## A Divided Society

Social dissatisfaction and instability have numerous causes, and the decisions of the Fifteenth National Congress, as well as the prolonged financial crisis in East Asia increase the risks of social unrest. In fact, Chinese society is changing at such a pace that it is very difficult to predict where it will go. The obvious polarization could threaten the social fabric itself.[25]

The question is, could the social instability, which will inevitably increase, translate into some kind of political change? Observers such as Elizabeth Perry and Anita Chan have stressed the fact that the PRC does not consist of a united society on the one side and a united political system on the other.[26] Instead, Chinese society is very much divided and segmented into different socioeconomic categories with different and often conflicting interests. But it does not mean that a sizable proportion of these categories cannot unite against a common enemy and express common demands, given the right circumstances, which happened in 1989. If the employment situation and the economic situation as a whole deteriorated seriously in the coming years, there could again be common enemies and common demands from a significant portion of society.

In my view, the main obstacle resides on the other side—that of the political system. Until now, it has retained the capacity to prevent any protest from getting out of control and posing a serious challenge to its power. Since the beginning of the regime, social and political unrest has only been able to develop on a large scale when the leaders were divided and when one faction tried to use social dissatisfaction to defeat its enemies. This was true in 1956–1957 (Hundred Flowers Campaign), in 1966–1968 (Cultural Revolution), in 1978–1979 (Third Plenum and Democracy Wall), and in 1989 (Democracy Movement).[27]

Regarding the present situation, it seems that the regime has retained the essential means of social control, information control, and outright physical repression necessary to prevent a situation in which "a single spark (or even 10,000 sparks) can start a prairie fire," to use the famous Maoist image. Society remains as fragmented as ever, no "fire" being allowed to spread to other regions or sectors.[28] Since 1989, the leaders have made preparations to quell social unrest, the transformation of a large number of soldiers into armed police being one of the latest. All efforts from society to establish horizontal links and organize outside the sphere of the party-state are met with extreme severity and generally lead to very long prison terms.

Chinese authorities will do their best to minimize the social effects of the reforms, mainly by developing job training and improving the social security system, and will probably scale down the pace of layoffs and bankruptcies after the first thrust following the decision made during the Fifteenth Congress.[29] But if the socioeconomic situation deteriorates seriously, a split among the leadership is almost inevitable. In this case, one faction could decide to use the unrest to bring about political change, and something important could happen.

This is not, however, the most probable scenario. The anxiety about *luan* (disorder) is quite widespread in contemporary Chinese society as a whole and especially among the leaders, who have learned lessons from the collapse of the Communist regimes in the Union of Soviet Socialist Republics (USSR) and Eastern Europe. If the feeling of solidarity in the face of a very serious danger is strong enough among the leadership, it could dissuade them from calling society inside the political game. A protracted period of frequent but isolated social outbursts might ensue, as well as behind-the-scenes political infighting, but no important political change would result. Whichever of these two scenarios prevails, society should be less stable in the years to come than it has been since 1989.

## NOTES

1. *Renmin ribao,* September 13, 1997.

2. *South China Morning Post* (hereafter *SCMP*), December 15, 1997.

3. *SCMP*, February 5, 1998.

4. *SCMP*, February 16, 1998. In his closing address to the May conference, Zhu reiterated this point and insisted on its significance for "the future of our reforms, our development and our stability" (*Renmin ribao,* May 17, 1998).

5. Feng, "Unemployment in China," 10.

6. Qiao, "1997–1998 nian: Zhongguo zhigong zhuangkuang baogao," 313–314; and Li Boyong, labor minister, quoted in *SCMP,* February 10, 1998.

7. Li Boyong, quoted in *SCMP,* February 10, 1998.

8. Ibid.; and *Wen Wei Bo*, May 21, 1998.

9. Yang Yiyong et al., *Shiye chongjibo,* 313.

10. See, for example, Anonymous, "Xiagang zhigong"; and Jin Yi, "Dalu de dingshi zhadan."

11. Qiao, "1997–1998 nian: Zhongguo zhigong zhuangkuang baogao," 315.

12. Ibid., 316.

13. Anonymous, "Xiagang zhigong," 95.

14. Qiao, "1997–1998 nian: Zhongguo zhigong zhuangkuang baogao," 318.

15. Anonymous, "Xiagang zhigong," 96.

16. Ibid., 96, and Qiao, "1997–1998 nian: Zhongguo zhigong zhuangkuang baogao," 315. See also *SCMP,* December 10, 1997.

17. Jin Yi, "Dalu de dingshi zhadan"; and *China Labor Bulletin,* 1997, nos. 37 and 38. See also *SCMP*, December 11, 1997, December 16, 1997, January 6, 1998, and February 8, 1998; *Pingguo ribao* (Apple daily), January 19, 1998; *Mingbao*, July 18 and 19, 1997.

18. Qiao, "1997–1998 nian: Zhongguo zhigong zhuangkuang baogao," 319–320; Anonymous, "Xiagang zhigong," 95–96.

19. The ranks of the *zhigong* in the state sector have grown 45 percent between 1978 and 1997, whereas the category of "employees of Government agencies, Party agencies and Social organizations" has grown 158 percent. In 1997, the number of *zhigong* have decreased slightly in the state and collective sectors, whereas the "employees of Government agencies" have increased slightly. See *Zhongguo Tongji Nianjian 1997* and *Zhongguo Tongji Zhaiyao 1998*.

20. Qiao, "1997–1998 nian: Zhongguo zhigong zhuangkuang baogao," 324–329.

21. See opposing viewpoints on this question in Yang Yiyong, *Shiye chongjibo,* 319–320; and He, *Xiandaihua de xianjing,* 256.

22. For the measures taken in Shanghai and Peking, see *SCMP,* April 16 and 17, 1998.

23. *SCMP,* January 27, 1998.

24. *SCMP,* October 16, 1998.

25. At a time when many laid-off workers experienced great difficulties in their daily life, teachers in a Guangzhou primary school were stunned to learn that one of their pupils had received 57,000 yuan in "lucky money" for the Chinese New Year (*SCMP,* February 15, 1998).

26. Perry, "Labor's Battle for Political Space"; and Chan, "Revolution or Corporatism?"

27. Arguments on this point can be found in Béja and Bonnin, "La Chine ou la crise comme mode d'exercice du pouvoir."

28. On the inability of the autonomous Chinese Labor Movement of the 1990s to organize itself against the party-state (which does not mean that it does not have any significance in the long run), see Trini W. Y. Leung, "Worker Rebellions in the 90's."

29. See "Labor Unrest Forces Rethink on Reforms," *SCMP,* June 17, 1998.

# PART FOUR

⊞ ⊞ ⊞ ⊞

# Foreign Policy and
# Cross-Strait Relations

# ⊞ 10 ⊞

# The People's Republic of China's Quest for Great Power Status: A Long and Winding Road

## *Stuart Harris*

Foreign policy was not a central issue at the Fifteenth National Congress of the Chinese Communist Party (CCP), but what was decided there was important if only to reinforce existing policy trends. China's relatively recent but considerable pragmatism in international affairs was upheld with the reaffirmation of Deng Xiaoping Theory *(Deng Xiaoping lilun)*, extended by the endorsement of multilateralism, and facilitated by further moves away from ideology. Also significant was the strengthened position of Jiang Zemin, which paved the way for the China–United States summits in Washington, D.C., and Beijing of 1997 and 1998 and for his position on Taiwan Strait relations.[1] Little has changed, however, in the issues underlying China's quest for great power status.

There is no precision about what constitutes a "great power." Traditionally, the term had a substantially European connotation, implying some role in the management of what then constituted the international system. Today we might describe that sense of a great power more generally as having international interests and a capacity to project (usually military) power to protect or advance those interests. Even so, changes in the international system require a more nuanced approach, as debate about Japan's great power status illustrates. Although that debate usually revolves around questions of Japan's military power projection capability as well as its economic strength, in practice, Japan's difficulty in articulating a firm and consistent foreign policy is probably as important a qualification.

China already has many characteristics of a great power. It holds one of the five permanent seats on the UN Security Council, with veto power. It is one of five "legal" nuclear powers. It has an ancient and internationally respected culture. It has a large and growing economy, is a major international trader, and is an arms exporter. Its population size ensures that countries take into account its potential influence and that China must be considered in resolving any global problem.

Given all this, in many respects China might be said to already have many of the attributes of a great power. But although its Asian neighbors are increasingly respectful, not only does China not believe that it has the status to which its characteristics should entitle it, but many non-Chinese observers would agree.

Chinese observers generally accept that there are domestic and international reasons for this status demotion. The domestic reasons include its limited military capability; a low level of economic, social, and political development; an inadequate level of technological sophistication that limits its industrial, including defense industrial, capacity; and a continuing concern for its ability to feed and improve living conditions for a large and growing population. There are uncertainties about not just the social stability and political fragility of the Chinese nation but also its identity.

The international reasons include what China perceives as a generally unfriendly and often threatening international environment. In particular, China has felt subject to the unfriendly attention of a hegemonic and unipolar United States and, often, by extension, U.S. allies. Moreover, China was late in joining the international system. Therefore it was not involved in making the rules and formulating the norms of an international system that may not suit China's interests.

Now, China must collaborate with the international system—in the UN, in arms control, in world trade, on the environment, and over human rights. Yet in doing so, it "ratifies U.S. dominance and compromises its own freedom of action."[2] Although China would prefer not to have the United States as the security "balancer" in the region, it accepts that without that presence, it might face military challenges from Japan and an arms race among other Asian countries. China must open up internationally for economic and technological development, but the more it does so the more vulnerable it becomes. Although desirous of a stable international environment, China is strategically vulnerable to the United States, Japan, and Russia; possibly a unified Korea; and even, in the longer term, India.

Consequently, China is a dissatisfied great power. So what can it do, and what will it do, in the short term and in the long term? Answers to these questions are part of the major debate over China's direction. Andrew Nathan and Robert Ross believe that the long experience of vulnerability may give rise to the urge "to take a turn at being a great power."[3] The *Economist* believes that given China's recent history, it "is almost certainly ripe for a period of indignant reassertion."[4]

Realists in the West often assume China wants to achieve great power status by being increasingly assertive and aggressive. One well-publicized critique of the Chinese system argued that China is "an unsatisfied and ambitious power whose goal is to dominate Asia."[5] June Dreyer, like many others, believes China seeks to replace the United States as the hegemonic power in Asia—whatever that means.[6] Yet despite this regional emphasis, China's ambitions must be considered global as well as regional. For outside observers, the effect of China's international policies on the balance of regional and eventually world power is crucial. Western observers are also interested in China's adjustment to its status as a rising great power. Analysts commonly point to the rise of Germany versus Britain early in the twentieth century as illustrating the inevitability of conflict, overlooking the subsequent relatively smooth transfer of power from Britain to a rising United States.

Apart from questions about the validity or relevance of any or all influences on China of its history or culture, two important questions relate to China's capabilities and its intentions. The first and perhaps most important relates to capabilities: can China really become a hegemon? The second relates to intentions: is China's goal to dominate Asia, and what does that imply?

It is important first to address a prior question: whom do we mean when we talk of China? Can one leader, or even a small group, determine China's policy now and in the future the way Chiang Kai-shek, Mao Zedong, and to a lesser extent Deng Xiaoping are judged to have done in the past? Although the personal influence of individual leaders will not be negligible—see Jiang's enhanced authority since the Fifteenth Party Congress—in China's increasingly collective and institutionalized authoritarianism, foreign policy is less subject to personal influence and is unlikely to return to its radical and unpredictable past, being determined increasingly by the nature and interests of the state. Thus, relevant questions include how that collectivity defines those interests and sees them being advanced and how those decisions are made.

Although institutionalizing China's foreign policy facilitates continuity and consistency, overt competition among various groups for influence in particular contexts has increased. Particularly when policies are in the discussion and development stage, many statements by Chinese analysts will be part of the internal debate and should be assessed less from the perspective of what was said than why they were said.

## CAPABILITIES

The relationship between capabilities and intentions is obvious because some constraints will remain as permanent limits within which intentions have to be shaped. Intentions, however, also include the process of overcoming basic constraints on capabilities.

More so than questions about whether China can actually achieve dominant capabilities, there is debate about the pace with which China could achieve the capacity to become a regional hegemon, about the military power that it will be able to exert regionally, and about its likely ability to exercise global influence. In the regional context, given China's size, economic importance, and geographic location, it already has considerable strategic strength relative to bordering countries on the Asian landmass, including Indochina, Burma, and Central Asia. It has a strong strategic position on the Korean peninsula (where it is generally a stabilizing influence). If we ignore the relative nuclear capabilities, its stabilizing influence is also apparent, to a degree, along the China-Russia border.

Some analysts, however, believe China's military capability falls far short of a capacity to operate as a military hegemon in the mainly maritime region of the Asia-Pacific region, which is what hegemonic projection of Chinese power would require. Although China's strategists recognize this, and although some increase in China's naval capability has resulted, the navy struggles for influence in an overwhelmingly land-based military.[7] Robert Ross has observed that the Soviet Union, a similarly land-based power, had limited maritime power projection capabilities even at the peak of its military strength. In his view, the idea of China becoming a hegemon or having hegemonic capabilities in the next thirty years is not credible.[8]

Maritime superiority currently does not appear to be a high priority for China.[9] Its military preparations so far seem to fit only a sea-denial strategy. The PLA Navy (PLAN) is not equipped to be more than a coastal force.[10] Purchases of major up-to-date equipment items were limited until recently to four Russian-built Kilo-class destroyers. More recently, following the events surrounding the March 1996 crisis over Taiwan and China's desire to protect its position in the seas around Taiwan, China has contracted for the purchase of two advanced Russian destroyers and has increased its purchases of Russian SU-27 aircraft. But even with its indigenous construction of surface combatants and fast-attack craft and submarines (mostly falling short of up-to-date technologies), the PLAN's capabilities will still not achieve an effective sea-denial capability for a considerable time. Nor will the outstanding gaps be overcome simply through a continuation of China's economic growth. Gaps remain, particularly in the People's Liberation Army's (PLA's) air component and in its integrated logistical support, integrated combat systems, and industrial and technological support. In addition, the PLA must overcome deficiencies in basic maintenance skills and philosophies.

"China threat" arguments generally originate from the belief that China recently has substantially increased its military expenditures and from China's high-profile purchases of sophisticated military equipment from Russia. China's modernization processes have involved sizable increases (in real terms) in its military budget allocations, albeit from a low base. There have been many different estimates and assessments of its military modernization effort. The most widely accepted estimate of real growth, that of the Central Intelligence Agency, was that it averaged some 7 percent a year in the five years to 1994, a level that has probably not changed substantially since then.[11]

Estimates of China's military expenditures face transparency problems, in part intrinsic to China's budgetary processes, because the formal defense budget only covers current expenditures on pay, facilities, and operations costs. This problem may in due course be overcome.[12] In the meantime, estimates of the off-budget elements and of the extent of funds derived from the PLA's own commercial activities account for most of the differences among serious Western analysts. Recent research throws doubt on the belief that the PLA's commercial contributions to China's military modernization are "as much a cash cow as outside observers believe."[13] More alarmist estimates also often fail to allow for, among other things, inflation, and include other factors such as inappropriate adjustments according to purchasing power parity comparisons. They also commonly overlook a revenue constraint facing Beijing that is unlikely to be easily overcome. The revenue available to China's central government has been declining as a proportion of gross domestic product (GDP) and is now around 11 percent of total GDP. For most Western countries, the comparable figure is around 20 percent or more. Beijing's interest in resolving the problem of state-owned enterprises (SOEs) stems from the large drain they represent on budget outlays. Although at one time Beijing sought to pass these problems to the banks, this strategy is now putting pressure on the financial system because the banks' buildup of unprofitable loans is coming under increasing international scrutiny.

The following conclusions relate mostly to the decades immediately ahead. In the longer term, for China to catch up with such countries as the United States or even to surpass Japan would require massive changes in China's military organization and a significant shift in Chinese expenditure priorities.[14] In making such changes, China would provide substantial strategic warning to other regional countries well ahead of time. In any case, this process would be immensely expensive; even the United States is finding the prospective financial costs of the revolution in military affairs daunting.

Other constraints exist. In addition to its many ocean borders, a number of which are contested, China has fourteen land borders, some of which remain problematic, and most of the bordering states differ in cultures, religions, and political processes. The United States has two land borders, essentially uncontested. Whatever problems illegal immigration poses, the United States would be weaker and less able to exercise power globally with Russia rather than Canada on its northern border and India on its southern border instead of Mexico. Also, although China has reasonable resource endowments, it is becoming a major importer of food and energy resources. The economic interdependence this implies gives China a significant incentive to operate cooperatively in the international system, however much it may try to limit the vulnerability such interdependence provides.

China's global agenda bears significantly upon its concerns about its territorial integrity, particularly over Taiwan. China expends considerable effort in maintaining global support for its position on the "one-China" policy. Its need to maintain this support against Taiwan's continuing efforts to gain diplomatic recognition constrains its ability to influence international issues and to take sides in international disputes. Thus, it must be evenhanded in the Middle East, low-key in the UN-Iraq dispute, and cautious over the Balkans, as over Kuwait. Its growing economic strength will provide added countervailing influence, but until it has amicably resolved the reunification with Taiwan this constraint will not be overcome.

China's quest for great power status will also depend on its domestic political situation. Greg Austin has observed that China faces a challenge to maintain regime legitimacy and domestic political authority as a result of just those changes that it has to make to support achievement of that status.[15] With the inevitably decentralizing impact of economic development, the regime's traditional basis of control diminishes while the social tensions associated with rapid economic change increase.

Problems of domestic political instability remain. Large-scale peasant or worker protests have been reported in Hubei, Jiangxi, Sichuan, and Guangdong Provinces, and a wider range of problems, acknowledged by the leadership, is reported from time to time.[16] Although these reports should not be overemphasized, social and political problems of unemployment and the consequences of reform of SOEs are substantial and unlikely to improve quickly. Economic performance and social stability have become major legitimizing factors in China, but for those who have not benefited from economic growth, that legitimacy base does not exist. If social stability is thrown into doubt, stability is undermined more widely.

In the long run, China's capability to become a regional hegemon will compete with U.S. influence as well as those of other major powers in the region. China's ability to articulate and implement a firm and consistent foreign policy in a way that Japan cannot (and perhaps the United States, when the Congress and the administration are at odds) will give China an advantage in exercising a great power role. But in competition with the United States, China will have more constraints, despite its obvious existing and growing strength. Even if, improbably, the United States were to "withdraw" from exercising its hegemonic role sometime in the future, China could not undertake that role with anything like the ease of the United States.

## INTENTIONS

Many factors are cited as influencing China's intentions. They include China's desire to regain its historical "Middle Kingdom" status; its wish to revenge 150 years of humiliation by the West; and its belief in the superiority of Chinese culture over that of the Western "barbarians," linked perhaps to xenophobia. These factors are brought together in concerns about what is termed "Chinese nationalism." A recent National Defense University strategic assessment talked of nationalism as a basis of China's foreign policy.[17]

Questions of nationalism are complex and usually oversimplified. History has indicated that nationalism can be a powerful motivating factor—indeed, scholars consider it crucial in China's experience in this century. It may now be a potentially unifying factor, engendering loyalty to the idea of a Chinese nation and maintaining regime legitimacy. Signs of assertive nationalism have surfaced in such issues as the dispute between China and Japan over the Diaoyu or Senkaku Islands, in which Hong Kong and Taiwanese Chinese were vigorous participants. Some signs of economic nationalism against foreign investment are also encountered from time to time—both genuine and stimulated.

Yet in the international sphere, three qualifications are necessary. First, nationalism, a symbolic concept, may be viewed as an outcome of a shared culture that connects community interactions between fellow nationals in a way that would not occur with nonnationals. It can take various forms. The main distinctions relevant here are between ethnic nationalism, based on a presumed comparability of blood and race, and civic nationalism, in which individuals subscribe to the political, economic, and social system in which they live. Civic nationalism usually is considered equality-based, irrespective of ethnic, religious, or other differences, within all aspects of that system. Under threat, civic nationalism will produce a collective response. This need not, however, become an aggressive nationalism, nor one based on ethnicity. This equality-based civic nationalism is the stated objective of Chinese policy, although whether it holds in practice is unclear.

Second, there are normally multiple patterns of alignment. China is not monoethnic. To a degree, its authoritarianism supports an ethnic majority domination by the Han Chinese, but the "Han Chinese" concept oversimplifies the question of ethnic differences in China and their political significance.[18] Furthermore, even were China monoethnic, it would not necessarily guarantee unity: nationalism "is not the only character on the ideological scene."[19] People are not merely nationalists. They have other loyalties or drives: to religion, traditional institutions such as the family and clan, regional collectivities, or economic motivations and modernizing ideas, all relevant in China.

Third, nationalism is a construct that can be developed or used if leaders want to do so, but this development is not guaranteed to be successful or controllable. In practice, nationalism and government objectives in China or elsewhere commonly are at odds rather than consistent. Although nationalist concerns exist over Taiwan, albeit improbably over the South China Sea, the Chinese government knows from experience that nationalist groundswells can legitimize dissent from the governing regime. Hence their caution over People's Republic of China (PRC) nationals' involvement in the Senkakus dispute, which was in any case inconsistent with the regime's self-identification as a country that settles disputes peacefully by negotiation.

National identity and nationalism, although different and coming from different directions, are linked because the closer they are, the more predictable the future actions of the government.[20] There are real questions, however, regarding China's self-image. China faces a long historical problem of establishing an identity that, although based largely on territorial integrity, also embraces cultural and, to a degree, racial identity. In part, in China's view, this involves ensuring the return of Hong Kong, Macau, and Taiwan (however nominal) and avoiding concerns about its actions in Tibet, Xinjiang, and Inner Mongolia. Many argue that China will be aggressive and expansionist, hoping to recover territory previously part of the Chinese "empire." But although Richard Bernstein and Ross Munro believe China wants to dominate the region, they accept that China "does not covet its neighbors' territory—except for the unique case of Taiwan."[21]

The influence of Chinese history and perhaps culture will remain important, if only symbolically. How it affects intentions is not clear, however, other than establishing an assumption of China's entitlement to great power status, a continuing concern for its security, and an intention to achieve international respect and what it considers equality of treatment.

China's identity may have been clear when it was a revolutionary regime and to some extent a proselytizing one. At that time, it was also a Third World state and considered itself the leader of that sphere. To some degree, it maintains that claim, but with decreasing validity. Now, however, China has shifted from a radical ideology and in some ways has eschewed ideology altogether.[22] It has also moved from international isolation to active participation in the international system. Consequently, there is wide agreement that China is searching for its identity, if predominantly in the domestic sphere. There are also internal debates about to what extent integration with the international system means "Westernization" and the loss of China's national identity.

Domestically, China's identity of late has been based as much on its socialist identity as on its Chinese characteristics. China still considers itself to be at the primary stage of socialism. It accepts that reaching the final stage may take a very long time—"at least a century"—suggesting that the leadership wants to retain its socialist credentials while ignoring them in practice. Having moved from a centrally planned economy to an increasingly market-oriented one, however, and from ideology to substantial pragmatism, and having experienced rapid shifts in values and beliefs, its identity problem is unsurprising.

Were international players clear about China's national identity, defined by Robert Scalapino as how it perceives the essence of the nation in relation to others,[23] that identity might "provide a reasonable basis for expectations concerning that nation's future comportment."[24] At least it might tell us what the leaders would see as its interests, given that they articulate the national identity in a collective manner.

On the surface China could be considered to participate in the international system as a modernizing nation-state—something involving a significant change for it. Observers often emphasize its firm adherence to nation-state attributes: sovereignty, including, understandably in the light of its history, noninterference in its internal affairs; and the preservation of its independence, a concern reinforced in China's mind by its unhappy and relatively recent experience of dependence upon the Soviet Union.[25] That emphasis on sovereignty is often cited as singularly characteristic of China, yet it is hardly more so than that of the United States. In practice, however, China has accepted some constraints on sovereignty that globalization and participation in the international system require. These range from China's acceptance of the conditionality applied by the International Monetary Fund in its loans to China to recognizing a valid international interest in China's human rights.

China's leadership aspirations, regionally and perhaps more broadly, have certainly become more evident. Encouraged by the U.S. engagement policy, China seems to accept, on the one hand, that it would participate in international management with the United States, but on the other, it seems to want to build a power base in its region to counter Western pressures. Japan is similarly interested in a greater political as well as economic leadership role. Neither encompasses the other, however, in the elaboration of their ambitions.

The emergence of a softer Chinese diplomacy, China's constructive responses to the onset of the Asian economic crisis, its balanced reactions to the South Asian nuclear weapons tests, and its improved relationship with the United States since Tiananmen Square have raised its profile and potential influence, provided it can maintain them. This is particularly the case given the adverse consequences for most other Asian powers of the Asian economic crisis that began in 1997. By comparison (although a bit unfairly), perceptions of Japan's regional leadership capabilities have slipped in the light of its own economic difficulties and its domestic policy problems in addressing them. Nevertheless, China at best will match Japan's economic strength only in the long term, and Japan now has a more sympathetic relationship with the United States in part because of the rise of China. In the region, however, both face perception problems—Japan its history and China the uncertainties about future use of its growing power—that will not easily be overcome.

## HOW CHINA SEES ITS OBJECTIVES BEING ACHIEVED

China's recent emphasis on its interest in a peaceful international environment was stressed again by Jiang at the Fifteenth Party Congress, who also noted China's concern at undue international dependence. Particularly interesting in Jiang's report to the Congress was the weight given to Deng Xiaoping Theory, with its concern for independence and peaceful diplomacy and the continuity of Deng's "good neighbor" policy.

Deng's five principles—no yielding to outside pressure; no allying with big powers or blocs; no developing military blocs; no taking part in an arms race; and no military expansion—were rhetorical statements, but they were followed to a considerable extent by Deng when in power. He was responsible for China's opening to the world, for the normalization of relations with the United States and the resumption of relations with the Union of Soviet Socialist Republics (USSR), and for the elaboration of the ideas of "one country, two systems," with respect to Taiwan and Hong Kong.

Of course, China has fought many of its neighbors during recent decades, and Deng was responsible for the decision to teach the Vietnamese a lesson in the late 1970s. Force remained an accepted weapon in China's diplomatic armory, but China's use of force was normally for what it considered defensive purposes. Moreover, Deng was responsible for what was generally accepted as a constructive agreement with Britain on Hong Kong. China has since successfully negotiated border issues with its many neighbors, with considerable success in dampening down conflicts if not necessarily resolving its problems and making China more secure than it has been for over a century. On balance, Deng's philosophy brought Chinese foreign policy closer to the norms the international community claims to follow.

During the summit in October 1997 in Washington, D.C., Jiang said he wanted to view Sino-U.S. relations from a long-term strategic perspective, to seek common interests and see things from the other's viewpoint, to stick by the three communiqués, to handle differences with mutual respect and equality, and to settle the Taiwan issue properly.[26] Nothing from the Beijing summit in June 1998 suggested any departure from those views.

Jiang Zemin was pleased that the United States agreed to "build towards a strategic partnership," and this principle is now incorporated in the official Chinese discourse despite China's desire to broaden its exercise of international power and to make a shift from unipolarity to global multipolarity. Encouraging multipolarity is a means by which China believes it can advance its quest for great power status—hence its move toward closer relations with Russia, care in maintaining the Japan relationship, and the added motivation for increasing its links with Europe. Yet in seeking closer U.S. relations to match its increasing interdependence with the United States, China may have accepted that any substantial degree of multipolarity is not feasible for a considerable time.

All countries conceal to some extent their true intentions, but despite the occasional "boilerplate" presentation by an elderly military leader, a desire for a peaceful international environment is not surprising. It is in China's interest at this time to avoid international tensions and to cooperate internationally to develop its economic potential through modernization. But there are valid questions about the longer term, an issue to which I will return. Although China tries to reassure the world of its peaceful intent, skeptics say that its seemingly constructive attitude is window dressing, concealing China's real intentions. In the meantime, we must compare China's stated intentions with what China has done in practice, considering its reasons as well. This is a better guide to China, since our understanding of its policymaking processes is limited.

Given the history of international attitudes toward China and the compression of economic and social development into a period of around a quarter century, China's progress is substantial and largely consistent with its move toward integration into the global system. Starting from its reentry into UN membership, China has joined most of the international organizations and now participates in most of the international regimes and institutions.

Realists would argue, particularly regarding membership in international economic organizations, that China belongs because they confer financial, technological, and scientific inputs on its economic modernization, but that China does not support the legitimacy of these organizations. Once it joins, and its great power status is more assured, it will want to shape the regimes that the institutions represent more to its liking. This has, of course, been the pattern of traditional great powers and is perhaps not all that unreasonable. In practice, however, this self-interest has not been apparent thus far, so the realist argument begs the question of China's intentions. It assumes that China's intentions differ so substantially from the intentions of those already in the system that they could not be achieved within the generality of norms and values of the international system in the political as well as the economic field. These include support for the UN, arms control, peaceful dispute settlement, support for cooperative regimes, and the like.

Moreover, for those comfortable with the status quo, the wish to maintain it is understandable. In fact, however, that status quo has been far from static, as the United States and other major powers (and Australia, where feasible) continually seek to adapt and adjust these regimes to ensure that international rules and norms and their implementation cohere with their national interests. Indeed, not only does the West often confuse "its own policy preferences with international norms,"[27] but the failures on the part of many members to adhere to these norms are conveniently overlooked.[28] For example, China can be criticized for managing to have its contribution to the UN reduced to less than 1 percent of total contributions despite having one-fifth of the veto power, but the United States, with rather more influence, remains unwilling to pay its outstanding dues.[29]

A realist view that China's relatively conforming behavior is a temporary phase is not inconsistent with the idea that countries can learn. It implies that any such learning is simply adaptive learning—how regimes adapt to China's own needs and the requirements of the international environment without changing their worldview.

An alternative view is that countries are capable of learning cognitively and not just adaptively and actually can change their view of the world. The process of learning is complex, and observers hold different opinions and concepts on the subject, mostly because of the behavior of the Soviet Union.[30] The evidence in practice is strong that a process of learning has occurred at the level of individuals, institutions, and government involved in China's foreign policy process.

This process is most evident in China's experience with the international economic system. The fact that military power has diminished as the basis for international influence, relative to economic power and what Joseph Nye called "soft power," has particular interest in the context of China. In the economic field, China underwent a major learning process subsequent to its economic opening in the late 1970s. The idea of global interdependence, increasingly apparent in the discourse of China's leaders from the mid-1980s, is contrary to what had been Chinese political culture for many centuries and the worldview that this reflected. This change in the discourse did not come from a decision at the top reflecting adaptive learning but from a basic shift in understanding, attributable in part to the global socialization roles played by international institutions and in part to an extensive internal debate in China that moved Chinese thinking toward a new worldview.[31]

In this process, Chinese policy thinkers and leaders abandoned many deeply rooted assumptions about the nature of the international economic environment. They saw the old and new world orders as historical categories in a relative sense and the new international order as in conformity with the objective needs of the development of modern productive forces. Acknowledging this higher stage of economic development that needed more than national markets to survive, these leaders came to accept and internalize the reality of one world market with capitalism as the prevailing force and with the need for economic cooperation globally and regionally. Among the specific changes in thinking, following intensive study, was a conclusion that trade, rather than being exploitative as Karl Marx had indicated, could be mutually beneficial.[32]

Not all of the changes in China's approach have come from a sophisticated understanding of global interdependence, nor have all those with influence accepted the new views any more than such people have elsewhere. But the rapid shift in China's participation in international economic organizations cannot be ignored. Moreover, China seems willing to accept the costs as well as the benefits of global interdependence, as in its participation in the Asia-Pacific Economic Cooperation (APEC), although like other countries it sometimes argues about the costs, as in its efforts to join the World Trade Organization. Nevertheless, where it has been accepted within such institutional arrangements, its role has been constructive, and any changes it has sought have been gradual and nondisruptive.[33]

In security issues, China has tended to move more cautiously. Among the Chinese academics and think tanks, however, there is extensive discussion of the "new" approach to security, emphasizing interdependence, common interests, and a widening of the definition of security.[34] In the regional context, China initially regarded multilateral security discussions as devices potentially designed to constrain China. Like the United States, China preferred bilateral approaches, but it did, somewhat reluctantly, join the multilateral ASEAN Regional Forum (ARF), and now accepts that such dialogue encourages the United States and Japan as well as China in regional cooperative behavior. Shortly thereafter, at the Fifteenth Party Congress, China formally endorsed multilateralism for the first time and stressed the need for China to participate actively in multilateral forums.

At the global level, China has increasingly participated in UN activities, its contributions including a peacekeeping contingent serving efficiently under an Australian UN commander in Cambodia. It provided Chinese participants for the UN inspection teams in Iraq. China has also moved substantially toward accepting much Western thinking on arms control, despite its traditional security paranoia and its exclusion from rule making for many of these arrangements. It was a signatory to the Comprehensive (Nuclear) Test Ban Treaty (and, unlike the United States and Russia, has not pursued subcritical testing exercises, thought by many to breach the spirit, if not the letter, of the treaty). It has accepted for some time that nonproliferation of weapons of mass destruction is in China's interest. A signatory to the Nuclear Non-Proliferation Treaty, despite its imbalance for developing countries, it supported making the treaty permanent. It was an original signatory to the Chemical Weapons Convention and is a party to the Biological Weapons Convention. It has supported U.S.

efforts on North Korea and has joined the so-called Zangger Committee, which groups equipment suppliers who have signed the Nuclear Nonproliferation Treaty to prevent the spread of nuclear weapons and prepares lists of equipment that should not be exported without safeguards.

Although it has accepted certain commitments under the Missile Technology Control Regime, China still differs with the United States, notably over exports of missiles and parts. Given the ambiguities over those issues, however, judgments are difficult. More clearly, despite improvements in many areas of human rights in China, it has not met numerous obligations it has accepted under international agreements to which it is a signatory. There are also important questions about how far Beijing's writ can run in administering its adherence to its international commitments, even when it enters into such agreements in good faith.

In putting China's international behavior under the microscope, it is possible to find what one seeks—either that the glass is half empty or is half full. A major problem is the criteria against which we judge its activity internationally. Samuel Kim, James Feinerman, David Lampton, and others who have written on the subject tend to compare performance against the specifics of agreements—and often find gaps in performance.[35] It might be more reasonable to compare China's behavior with that of other great powers: British flouting of UN sanctions against South Africa, French bombing of the Greenpeace vessel in New Zealand, U.S. mining of harbors in Central America, and the Russian attack on Chechnya, all considered what great powers "have to do." Relative to these criteria, the judgment on China might be less critical, but in a sense potentially more worrying.

Finally, given the importance of learning in influencing international policies and defining national interests, it becomes important who makes foreign policy and what are the major influences. It is generally accepted that the PLA is one of these important influences.[36] Here, however, I limit myself to asking what differences would arise were the PLA to determine the path of China's quest for great power status. It is often suggested that China would be more assertive and aggressive on many issues, but even assuming (improbably) that a PLA-driven China was monolithic in its views, this is not a certain outcome. Moreover, there are reasons for thinking the influence of the presumably softer-line Ministry of Foreign Affairs has increased significantly.

If we assume that the PLA seeks hard-line solutions, then it has been remarkably unsuccessful. Certainly, on some smaller issues such as joint exercises in the ARF confidence-building processes or joining the land mine convention, the PLA has prevailed, at least temporarily. Yet military modernization has achieved limited priority in budget outcomes. On Taiwan issues, the PLA's influence is assumed to be strong. Yet Jiang's relatively conciliatory "eight points" remain in place, and recent moves suggest an even softer line, whatever the rhetoric over particular activities of the Nationalists on Taiwan. The Chinese position on the South China Sea in discussions with the Association of Southeast Asian Nations (ASEAN) has been moderate, illustrated in the joint China-ASEAN communiqué of December 1997.[37] Moreover, in the arms control arena generally, much of the progress in China's participation is contrary to what were understood to have been PLA views in the past.

## CONCLUSION

This chapter has been concerned with long-term aspects of China's quest for great power status and the implications of the Fifteenth Party Congress for these. The overall impact of the Congress was to reinforce the existing trends in China's international relations policies, which have tended to integrate China more closely into the international system. Although this trend is positive, for the longer term some key issues remain.

- China is already a great power, and what we are considering is the degree to which its present status reflects its potential. It has aspirations for an enhanced role in international management, and no doubt aspires to a preeminent position in the region such that it will be able to protect and assert its interests in competition with other states, particularly the United States. If so, it is undoubtedly a less than satisfied power, but its great power capability will remain incomplete for a considerable period.
- China's size and the growth of its economy, which will in any case almost certainly increase in size substantially, even if unevenly, already give it certain advantages, as does its capacity to articulate a relatively consistent foreign policy.
- Nonetheless, China's many domestic constraints will limit its ability to play a dominant great power role. It has a long way to go for reality to match the full range of its possible aspirations as a great power. Lee Kuan Yew's suggestion that it may take as much as fifty years for China to match Europe or Japan, let alone the United States, offers a useful perspective.[38]
- In the meantime, the capabilities of other major regional powers will grow in influence. China will continue to suffer indefinite limits on its ability to exercise the kind of dominance in Asia that the United States currently can and will exercise for some considerable time. Those limits will include its interest in ensuring that other regional great powers do not combine in opposition to it.
- As well as its large number of land borders, which are often problematic, these limits will include the major constraints on its maritime power projection capability.

- China's global influence has, in one sense, been increased by its acquisition of Hong Kong. Specifically, the reversion places constraints on Western pressure. But Hong Kong also limits China's freedom of action for face, as well as economic, reasons. In particular, however, China will be constrained in its capacity to exercise global influence while the need to retain global support for its Taiwan position remains.
- At the same time, in the new international context where military power is less important relative to other sources of influence, China increasingly will be able to exercise economic and political influence. Its ability to provide the bases of popular culture, societal attraction, technological innovation, and lifestyle that add up to soft power will, however, take longer to develop.
- In what will be a relatively long short term, China's intentions will reflect its interest in avoiding international tension. There is evidence, however, that it is behaving cooperatively not just because international cooperative behavior is in China's national interest but also in part because of a changed understanding of the way the world works.
- In the long term, China's participation in the international system will depend in part upon how far its cognitive learning proceeds. It will also depend upon how the rest of the world responds by accommodating equitably to what China feels it is entitled to in the exercise of its great power status, while accepting that there will be differences in their respective assessments.
- The dangers for the region are twofold. First, because cognitive learning can take different directions, adverse global responses can lead to negative learning and increase China's influence over those antagonistic to international cooperation. Second, history would suggest that the inevitable accretion of power will lead to the usual response—an arrogant assertion of that power. This view will not necessarily be countered by the imperfect record of behavior of existing great powers in complying with international rules and norms.

In foreign policy terms, the Fifteenth Party Congress kept the Chinese polity on the largely constructive path set out for it by Deng Xiaoping. China, however, still is at the beginning of a long and winding road in its quest for great power status.

## NOTES

The comments of Brian Job, Jim Richardson, and Ramesh Thakur are gratefully acknowledged.

1. Jiang Zemin's Report at the Fifteenth National Congress of the Communist Party of China, Beijing, September 1997.

2. Nathan and Ross, *The Great Wall*, xiii.

3. Ibid., 34.

4. *The Economist,* January 3, 1998, 18.

5. Bernstein and Munro, *The Coming Conflict with China.*

6. June Dreyer, cited in Hawkins, "For All the Tea in China," 16–17.

7. Austin, *China's Ocean Frontier,* 284.

8. Ross, "Assessing the China Challenge"; see also Ross, "Beijing as a Conservative Power."

9. Yung, *People's War at Sea,* 48.

10. Yung, *People's War at Sea;* see also Wilhelm, *China and Security;* Swaine 1998.

11. USIS Asia-Pacific wireless file, February 27, 1995.

12. It does not cover research and development and weapons procurement, much of which is in the budgets of state enterprises in the defense industry. There seems to be a move to cover more of the procurement of domestically built weaponry out of the official defense budgets.

13. Cheung, "China's Entrepreneurial Army"; see also Mulvenon, *Chinese Military Commerce, 1997.*

14. China does have the advantage of nuclear capability, which Japan does not, although it is widely believed it could achieve this in a short period of time. Its navy, however, was judged in the early 1990s as a very advanced and sizable fleet, compared with a very large but low-quality Chinese fleet (*Jane's Defence Weekly,* April 11, 1992:662–664; see also Commonwealth of Australia, *Asia's Global Power,"* 90–91). Little change in relativities has occurred as both continue to modernize.

15. Austin, "Strategic Implications."

16. See, for example, Xie and Hua, "China: Worsening Social Order"; see also Pei, "Is China Democratizing?" 79–81.

17. National Defense University, *Strategic Assessment,* chap. 4, 4.

18. Gladney, "Ethnic Identity in China."

19. Gellner, *Encounters with Nationalism,* viii.

20. Leaders and elites largely determine national identity; nationalism tends to come up from or be stimulated at the popular level.

21. Bernstein and Munro, *The Coming Conflict with China,* 208.

22. At the Fifteenth Party Congress, Jiang put state-to-state relations ahead of party-to-party relations, involving a substantial downgrading of ideology (*Jiang Zemin's Report*).

23. Scalapino, "China's Multiple Identities," 215–216.

24. Dittmer and Kim, "In Search of a Theory of National Identity," 31.

25. China's reluctance to develop too close relations with other countries is elaborated in Harding, "China's Cooperative Behavior."

26. The *three communiqués* refers to the three cornerstone documents—the Shanghai Communiqué of 1972, the Normalization Communiqué of 1978, and the August 17 Communiqué of 1982—that have provided the basic framework for China-U.S. relations since Nixon's path-breaking trip to the PRC in 1972.

27. Lampton, "A Growing China," 130.

28. Moreover, the United States has not signed many of these international arrangements reflecting accepted international norms—ranging from the law of the sea to many human rights conventions.

29. Lampton, "A Growing China," 133.

30. See, for example, Tetlock, "Learning in U.S. and Soviet Foreign Policy."

31. Kim, "China's International Organisational Behavior," 433–444.

32. See, for example, Ma, "Recent Changes."

33. Jacobsen and Oksenberg, *China's Participation in the IMF;* Harris, "China's Role in the WTO and APEC."

34. A useful summary of the main points of the argument can be found in "China: Roundup Comparing New Security Concepts," and "Army Paper on 'New Security Concept.'"

35. Kim, "China's International Organisational Behavior"; Feinerman, "Chinese Participation"; Lampton, "A Growing China."

36. This is discussed at length in Chapter 6.

37. China and ASEAN agreed to resolve disputes through peaceful means without resorting to the threat or use of force and to settle disputes in the South China Sea through friendly consultation and negotiations "in accordance with universally recognised international law" (Text of Joint Statement; see also *Far Eastern Economic Review,* January 8, 1998, 32).

38. Lee Kuan Yew, 1998. In *Taipei Chung-kuo Shih Pao* (FBIS-EAS-98-017) January 5.

# ⊞ 11 ⊞

# Cross-Strait Relations

## Kenneth Lieberthal

Relations across the Taiwan Strait constitute one of the most important issues in East Asia, one of the few issues for which miscalculation can bring truly tragic consequences. It is also an issue in which both history and contemporary politics weigh heavily, making resolution a delicate and complex matter. Indeed, given the current realities it makes more sense to think of long-term management of this sensitive issue than of a near-term resolution to it.

### HISTORICAL BASES

The outline of the issue can be drawn simply. Japan acquired Taiwan as one of the spoils of the Sino-Japanese War of 1894–1895 and retained control of the island until 1945. With Japan's defeat in World War II, Tokyo relinquished Taiwan to the Republic of China (ROC), then the ruling government on the mainland. The government of the ROC fled to Taiwan as it lost the civil war on the mainland, and it has remained in power on Taiwan to this day. Since its founding in 1949, however, the People's Republic of China (PRC) has claimed sovereignty over Taiwan. Until the late 1980s, leaders of both the PRC and the ROC agreed that Taiwan was a part of China but disagreed over which of them was the legitimate government of China. Since the late 1980s, the ROC government has relinquished any ambition to govern the mainland portion of China and has developed a democratic system of government on Taiwan but formally maintains that the island of Taiwan is part of China. The PRC insists that this fundamental "one China" posture never change.[1]

The U.S. role in this situation has deep roots. During the early stages of the Cold War, the United States reacted to the June 1950 North Korean invasion of South Korea in part by using U.S. naval power to prevent a PRC attack on Taiwan to oust the Nationalist government there and complete the Communist victory in the Chinese civil war. After the Korean War ended in 1953, Washington signed a security treaty with the ROC on

Taiwan in 1954 that remained in effect until 1979. As part of the normalization of diplomatic relations with the PRC in 1979, however, the United States abrogated this security treaty, and the Taiwan Relations Act (TRA) took its place. Although the primary purpose of the TRA was to establish a legal framework for ongoing U.S. interaction with Taiwan, it also included language designed to maintain an American role in Taiwan's security, including a provision for the continuing sale of defensive arms to Taiwan.[2]

Beijing and Washington signed a communiqué on August 17, 1982, setting forth the principles that would govern future U.S. arms sales to Taiwan.[3] These principles are broadly drawn and have been subject to vigorous debate over their precise meaning since 1982. In fact, a strict application of these principles could, under certain circumstances, conflict with the pertinent provisions of the TRA.[4]

The United States thus has become a significant actor in the cross-Strait issue, even without ever directly seeking to mediate relations between the two sides. Both sides regard the U.S. posture as of potentially critical significance in structuring both the psychological and the actual military balance across the Strait. In effect, therefore, the cross-Strait issue is a three-sided issue, even though the PRC regards it as a strictly domestic Chinese matter.

As Taiwan has democratized over the past decade, the political clout of the "one China" stance on the island has diminished for several reasons. Taiwan's population is overwhelmingly Taiwanese, with mainlanders (those who crossed over from the mainland at the conclusion of the civil war) a small minority of less than 10 percent. In addition, Taiwanese lived under the rule of Japan from 1895 to 1945, but under the aegis of the mainland for only a few years in the late 1940s before the seat of the ROC government moved to Taipei. Furthermore, by the late 1990s, Taiwan had developed a culture quite different from that on the mainland—highly educated, heavily middle class, Western-oriented, and democratic. The combination of lifestyle developments and political democratization has made the issue of maintaining Taiwan's distinctive identity a politically potent issue in Taiwan politics.

The mainland has watched these developments with an unease that, since 1995, has at times bordered on alarm.[5] Although Beijing repeatedly has signaled its patience in managing the Taiwan issue and its preference for reaching a peaceful settlement of the issue, it has also made clear its absolute intolerance of any notion of de jure independence for Taiwan. Should Beijing become convinced that Taiwan will seek de jure independence, most knowledgeable observers agree that the PRC likely would use military force to prevent this development. Indeed, some feel that if there is no significant progress toward agreement across the Taiwan Strait within some period of time (say, within a decade), the PRC may resort to military means to force the issue.

The Kuomintang (KMT) government on Taiwan has developed a carefully crafted set of policies regarding the mainland. It envisions three phases: exchanges and reciprocity in the short term, mutual trust and cooperation in the medium term, and consultation and unification in the long term.[6] This approach has been designed to postpone any serious discussion of reunification until the mainland has become, like Taiwan, relatively well off economically and democratic politically. Meanwhile, during the protracted period before these conditions take root on the mainland, these policies seek to expand Taiwan's diplomatic recognition and activities. At times, KMT leaders have spoken openly of Taiwan's own sovereignty, meaning, apparently, that it is up to the people of Taiwan to decide Taiwan's political future.

Since appearing on the political scene in the late 1980s, the opposition Democratic Progressive Party (DPP) has become a major force in Taiwan's politics and may become the dominant political party in the coming years. Various factions in the DPP have articulated differing approaches to cross-Strait relations,[7] but in sharp contrast to the KMT, to date all have opposed even the distant prospect of unification of Taiwan with the Chinese mainland. The prospect of a DPP victory in the presidential election in the year 2000 therefore causes great unease among decisionmakers in Beijing.

The United States is deeply concerned about the continuing well-being of the people of Taiwan, with whom it has long historical ties. Washington likewise attaches great importance to managing its relations with the PRC successfully, recognizing that the PRC is the world's most populous country, has one of the world's largest economies and militaries, and is of central importance to the Asia region. Washington thus wishes to see the two sides of the Taiwan Strait develop their ties in a manner that minimizes the chances of future conflict while preserving the democratic system and quality of life of the people on Taiwan. Any agreement *freely* reached between Beijing and Taipei would be acceptable to Washington. The United States would be deeply disturbed, though, by actions on either side that unilaterally sought to break out of the framework that has existed for years, precipitating a crisis. Washington is also mindful of the fact that Taiwan has fared well historically and relations across the Strait have proceeded more smoothly when the United States is enjoying relatively good relations with the PRC.[8]

As this overview suggests, the cross-Strait issue looks very different when viewed from Beijing, Taipei, and Washington, respectively. More specifically, the issue takes on the following coloration in each capital.[9]

Beijing views the Taiwan issue as part of the century-long goal of achieving national unity after the dismemberment of a weak China in the late eighteenth and early nineteenth centuries. It can accept a variety of approaches to tie Taiwan to the mainland, and its approach to the reversion of Hong Kong, if anything, has given further legitimacy to its real flexibility.

The one outcome Beijing finds totally unacceptable is Taiwan's sovereign independence from the PRC. Beijing views U.S. arms sales to Taiwan as an act strengthening Taiwan's resolve not to negotiate unification with the PRC. Thus, Beijing wants the United States to restrain its weapons sales to Taiwan and to pressure Taiwan into negotiations with the mainland. Beijing is divided in its tactical assessments about the prospects for negotiating with Taiwan under Lee Teng-hui versus some future president. Thus, analysts in the PRC hold various views of the best way to keep Taiwan from moving toward de jure independence and to prepare for eventual unification.

Taiwan argues that the ROC is a legitimate government that has never been under Beijing's control. The ROC has never paid taxes to the PRC, nor has it ever permitted the PRC to exercise authority over the people of Taiwan. The ROC also argues that Japan relinquished control over Taiwan to the Republic of China, which still exists on Taiwan. As noted above, although the ROC government on Taiwan formally espouses a "one China" policy, it no longer aspires to reestablish its rule over the Chinese mainland. Rather, it articulates a concept of "China" as a cultural sphere comprising two equal sovereign entities, the PRC and the ROC. Accordingly, the ROC government on Taiwan wants the international community to recognize its accomplishments and to accept its legitimacy, even as it develops economic and cultural ties with the PRC and even if it indicates that at some future point, when the conditions are right, it might consider some sort of unification (via a confederation or some similar structure) with the PRC. Because it views U.S. support as extremely important for its well-being, Taiwan has made every possible effort to ensure ongoing U.S. arms sales and political support.

Washington wants the cross-Strait relationship to develop in a fashion that maintains peace, sustains a high quality of life for the people of Taiwan, and enables the United States to develop a wide ranging, constructive strategic partnership with Beijing. Seeming inconsistencies in U.S. policy toward this situation often stem from different priorities in the executive branch versus those on Capitol Hill.[10] Fundamentally, the United States opposes both provocative actions that raise tensions in the area and the use of military pressure or outright military force to resolve this issue. Washington recognizes that military conflict across the Taiwan Strait could involve the United States, seriously challenging U.S. relations with the PRC and perhaps poisoning the well of U.S. ties with Taiwan. It is in the best interests of the United States for the PRC and Taiwan to find a way to manage the cross-Strait relationship that avoids crisis in the region.

In addition to the perspectives of each of the parties, it is important to factor in several realities when considering how best to manage cross-Strait relations for the foreseeable future. First, political power in Taiwan is subject to democratic checks and is fragmented. There are substantial divisions within both the KMT and the DPP, as well as among additional splinter parties such as the New Party. Although public opinion polls establish that a substantial majority of the population would oppose rash steps toward independence, most politicians currently accept the conventional wisdom that at this point, striking a deal permanently tying Taiwan to the mainland would be political suicide.[11] In practical terms, it is not possible as of 1999 for any political leader in Taiwan to reach an agreement for eventual unification with the PRC that could obtain the necessary legislative endorsements to give it a solid legal foundation. A precondition for political accord with the PRC is a process of developing a political consensus in favor of such an accord on the island. This process inevitably will take years and will require, in all likelihood, that one political party both control the Executive Yuan and obtain a strong majority in the Legislative Yuan. Thus, the PRC has no realistic chance of achieving active control over Taiwan in the foreseeable future. The best Beijing can hope to do is to eliminate the possibility that Taiwan will assert de jure independence.

Second, Taiwan cannot assert de jure independence without provoking a PRC military response, with potentially tragic consequences for everyone involved in the region. PRC military exercises in 1995 and 1996 effectively laid down a marker, making clear that Beijing was willing to pay a very high political price internationally, if necessary, to prevent Taiwan from going independent.

Finally, there is no realistic possibility in the near future that the United States will place more restrictive limits on its arms sales to Taiwan, a policy choice that reflects both principles and politics. The United States carefully limits its arms sales to Taiwan to defensive weapons. The TRA requires that such sales be made with the sole criterion of maintaining Taiwan's security, given the military situation it faces across the Taiwan Strait.[12] Advances in PRC military capabilities, especially in missile technology, require ongoing modernization of Taiwan's military capabilities in turn. Although the August 1982 Sino-American communiqué called for a reduction in arms sales as tensions in the region diminished, the PRC military exercises of 1995 and 1996 and continuing development of pertinent PRC military capabilities arguably constitute evidence of increasing tension within the framework of this communiqué.[13] In addition, Taiwan enjoys sufficient political support on Capitol Hill that it would be very difficult for the White House to impose new limits on arms transfers to Taipei.

Within this context, conflicting perspectives, differing interests, and simple mistrust create the possibility that miscalculation of one sort or another could be a fateful step toward tragedy.[14] None of the sides involved has full understanding of—or full trust in—the other parties and their likely responses in various scenarios. Beijing and Taipei fear even incremental steps by one another that seem to decrease the possibility that they will achieve their individual long-term objectives. As Beijing and Taipei each act to secure their interests by boxing in the other side, the potential for sudden crisis and substantial miscalculation will continue to exist. This is true even though at present, neither side will deliberately precipitate a crisis.

It is important, therefore, not to simply drift along with the status quo because it holds very serious potential dangers. Yet any realistic outcome must satisfy, at a minimum, both the keen sense of identity among the people of Taiwan and the core commitment of the government in Beijing to overcome the dismemberment of China that it views as a consequence of past imperialist aggression.

## FUNDAMENTALS OF A SOLUTION

Any feasible future arrangement regarding cross-Strait issues must reconcile current tensions over sovereignty, identity, and subordination. It is necessary to find a formula that provides reassurance that the "one China" principle will not be violated, that allows each existing government to share in the sovereignty of that "one China," and that does not impose a "center-provincial" structure on relations between the mainland and Taiwan.[15] At this point, it is neither possible nor wise to attempt to specify in detail an agreement that can, in fact, only be worked out through negotiations between the two sides. But it may be helpful to suggest seven basic elements that in one form or another may appear in any framework permitting both Beijing and Taipei to look to the future with confidence. These basic elements are as follows.

Interim arrangements. The parties may establish an interim arrangement to govern the cross-Strait situation for a period of roughly five decades (that is, two generations), concluding on a date when formal talks toward political unification of the country will begin. Both sides know that each will undergo considerable evolution over the course of the coming fifty years, and problems that now seem intractable may then prove quite manageable. Only the voluntary consent of both sides could move the date for commencing talks on unification forward.

Not quite one China. The parties may agree that for this interim period Taiwan and the PRC both exist within "one China" but that the relations between them are neither between exclusive sovereign entities nor between a central government and a province. Rather, the relations are those between "the two sides of the Taiwan Strait," neither of which will challenge the fundamental unity of the country. In other words, both sides agree not to challenge the concept of "one China" by claiming a sovereignty that excludes the other, but the specific hierarchy of relations between them remains for future negotiations to work out.

Not quite independent. Taiwan may explicitly agree that it is a part of China and will not claim de jure independence. This is merely a subset of the second principle, but it is so core to achieving a stable situation with the PRC that it warrants separate articulation.

Prohibitions on force. The PRC may explicitly agree not to use force against Taiwan. Beijing has asserted repeatedly that it cannot forswear the use of force (although it prefers a peaceful solution) as long as Taiwan holds out the possibility that it will seek sovereign independence. If Taiwan accepts the third principle, Beijing should be able to reciprocate by renouncing the use of force against Taiwan. The PRC should agree to various confidence-building measures to lend credibility to this pledge.

Autonomy. The parties may agree that during the interim period, each side will retain autonomy in its own domestic affairs and foreign policy, constrained only by the above noted commitments. This stipulation on domestic affairs should not be difficult to implement, given the long history of autonomous management of domestic affairs on both Taiwan and the mainland. The foreign policy side will require delicate negotiations to reach pertinent agreements. The Hong Kong Special Autonomous Region (SAR) has membership in many international organizations, but Beijing dictates its foreign policy. Taiwan is in a different category and, realistically, must retain greater autonomy.

It should be possible to work an agreement wherein Taiwan has an active, rewarding diplomatic presence internationally and participates substantively and consistently in many international organizations and multilateral activities. Beijing's key concern will be whether Taiwan is using these opportunities to prepare for a bid for de jure independence. It should be possible to construct a framework that reduces this prospect and thus relieves Beijing's anxieties over this issue.

Negotiations. The parties may agree to undertake regular talks at a high political level to reduce areas of conflict and enhance mutual confidence. These talks should address, among other issues, Taiwan arms purchases, possibly linked to PRC force deployments; opening up of markets on both sides of the Taiwan Strait to goods and services from the other side, including related measures to facilitate trade and investment; and establishment of a full array of direct contacts between the populations on both sides of the Taiwan Strait.

Fundamentally, cross-Strait relations will improve only as mutual trust is increased and mutual interests are enhanced. As it is in the interests of Taiwan, Beijing, and Washington that this comes to pass, the initial set of agreements noted above must be followed up with these initiatives to firm up a foundation for peace.

Terminology. The parties may agree to reduce tension further by changing the name of the People's Republic of China to "China" and changing the name of the Republic of China to "Taiwan, China" (or some similar locution). There may be merit in trying to develop some terminology, such as *da zhongguo,* to refer to the two parts of China together. If nothing else, these name changes would provide further distance between the present situation and the civil war of the 1940s and thus perhaps improve the atmosphere for development of cross-Strait relations.

However appealing or feasible, agreements are not self-executing. To increase the political strength of these agreements, they should be embodied in domestic legislation (or possibly constitutional provisions) in each country. In addition, some creative thinking about how to monitor implementation of the above agreements is necessary, especially because they are intended to govern for a prolonged period of time. Some sorts of bilateral bodies may have to be formed.

## CONCLUSION

Many of the foregoing elements are controversial. I put them forward, however, in an effort to focus discussion on the fundamental issues that must be resolved to ensure peace and prosperity in the future for the two sides of the Taiwan Strait. We see here a situation in which both sides have demonstrated that they have complementary economic needs and share a desire to increase mutually beneficial contacts. Yet the future offers danger and uncertainty, with very high stakes for all concerned. The current state of tension injures the interests of both sides and limits the ability of both sides to work together to address such common issues as the current Asian financial crisis.

All sides must seek solutions in their own interest that fully account for present realities and sensitivities while providing for long-term security, prosperity, and dignity. As already noted, politics in Taiwan probably do not currently permit conclusion of the various agreements outlined in the above seven points, and yet failure to reach such agreements leaves the stability of this region in some peril. Renewing the process of active negotiations in the short term can begin to build the trust and momentum that over a period of three to five years may permit both sides to grapple with the fundamental issues.

# NOTES

1. For an overview of this history, see Tucker, *Taiwan, Hong Kong, and the United States.*

2. For a detailed analysis of the politics of the TRA, see Hao, *Dilemma and Decision.* The text of the 1954 U.S.-ROC mutual defense treaty is available in MacFarquhar, *Sino-American Relations.* The text of the Taiwan Relations Act and the documentation surrounding the normalization of Sino-American Relations are available in: Harding, *A Fragile Relationship,* and in Dumbaugh, *Taiwan.*

3. Text in Harding, *A Fragile Relationship,* and in Dumbaugh, *Taiwan.*

4. Specifically, the TRA says that the United States will make available any weapons necessary for Taiwan to maintain its self-defense capability. The communiqué, by contrast, declares that the United States "does not seek to carry out a long-term policy of arms sales to Taiwan" and "intends to reduce gradually its sales of arms to Taiwan, leading over a period of time to a final resolution" (Article 6 of the communiqué). President Ronald Reagan declared in a statement accompanying the communiqué that the policy set forth therein "is fully consistent with the Taiwan Relations Act" (text in Harding, *A Fragile Relationship,* 386). In U.S. Senate hearings directly after the communiqué was issued, the Congress made clear (with administration support) that it did not and could not amount to an official revision of the TRA: U.S. Senate, Hearings Before the Subcommittee on Separation of Powers of the Committee of the Judiciary: Second Session on the Taiwan Communiqué and Separation of Powers.

5. President Lee Teng-hui's June 1995 visit to the United States marked an important turning point in the PRC's evaluation of the situation. Before then, Beijing felt a "soft" policy of conciliation would eventually produce reunification. Lee's 1995 visit convinced many in Beijing that Lee sought to move Taiwan to full independence, and Beijing reacted very harshly; see Sutter, *China Policy.*

6. "Guidelines for National Unification," adopted by the National Unification Council on February 23, 1991, and by the Executive Yuan on March 14, 1991.

7. See, for example, the *Minzhujinbudang Zhongguo zhengce yantao hui, huiyi shouce* (DPP China Policy Forum, forum handbook). This handbook presents materials from the February 13–15, 1998, DPP forum on policy toward China.

8. See the testimony by U.S. Department of State, East Asian and Pacific Bureau Deputy Assistant Secretary Susan Shirk before the House International Relations Committee, May 20, 1998.

9. The following three paragraphs are based on both documentary sources and personal discussions with pertinent officials in all three capitals.

10. The early stages of this are detailed in Hao, *Dilemma and Decision,* and in Sutter, *Executive-Legislative Consultations.*

11. A summary of polls published by the Mainland Affairs Council in December 1997 shows that as of November 1997, only 9.5 percent of respondents wanted "independence as soon as possible," whereas a total of 80 percent wanted either "the status quo now, decision later" or some stance that was more pro-mainland than that.

12. Harding, *A Fragile Relationship.*

13. Ibid.

14. The worst case would look like the following: Taiwan leaders take initiatives that the PRC views as effectively bidding for independence. The PRC responds with military activities, such as a blockade. U.S. forces challenge the PRC military in the region, drawing from U.S. military assets based in Japan. Blood is

spilled, inflaming passions in all capitals. The first major steps toward a new Cold War in Asia are thus taken.

15. Some people living on Taiwan reject a "one China" framework altogether. Should Taiwan ever act decisively along that line, confrontation and tragedy become almost inevitable.

# ⊞ 12 ⊞

# Making Sense of Beijing's Policy Toward Taiwan: The Prospect of Cross-Strait Relations During the Jiang Zemin Era

## *Yun-han Chu*

---

On the eve of the lunar New Year in 1998, Beijing once again launched a major propaganda campaign for the opening of political talks with Taipei.[1] At a seminar in the Great Hall of the People to commemorate the third anniversary of Jiang Zemin's eight-point proposal on reunification with Taiwan,[2] Vice Premier Qian Qichen, the foreign minister, and the deputy leader of the Taiwan Affairs Leading Small Group (TALSG) called on Taiwan to respond to Jiang's offer to end cross-Strait hostility and to open discussions under the "one-China" principle. "The key to a stable and healthy development of cross-Strait relations," said Qian, "lies in the process of political discussions."[3] Qian's message also made it clear that Beijing was not interested in resuming functional talks but only in talks designed for negotiating political issues.

This well-orchestrated event was part of Beijing's latest round of peace overtures, which began to take shape in the second half of 1997. Beijing had rolled out its propaganda machinery as early as the drafting stage of the Fifteenth National Party Congress documents. Wang Daohan, chairman of the semiofficial Association for Relations Across the Taiwan Strait (ARATS), member of the TALSG, and Jiang's political mentor, offered the first clear signal that Beijing had softened its conditions for talks with Taiwan.

In an interview by Hong Kong–based media, Wang emphasized that the two sides "could discuss any topic under the 'one-China' principle."[4] Jiang Zemin, in his report to the Party Congress, repeated the same message. He reiterated his appeal that, as a first step, the two sides of the Taiwan Strait should hold negotiations and reach an agreement on "officially ending the state of hostility between the two sides under [the] one-China principle."[5] As a follow-up to Jiang's renewed appeal, Qian Qichen issued a statement less than three weeks before Jiang launched his first state visit to the United States, calling on Taipei to hold preparatory talks to lay the groundwork for the opening of political talks.[6]

Upon Jiang's return, Beijing offered the clearest gesture of its readiness to resume the cross-Strait talks between the ARATS and the Straits Exchange Foundation (SEF) of Taiwan since the disintegration of semi-official talks in June 1995. The ARATS issued an invitation to Chiao Jen-ho, SEF secretary general, seeking his participation in a seminar to be held in Xiamen during late November 1997, with the implicit understanding that Chiao would be able to meet with his counterpart, Tang Shubei, Beijing's top negotiator and executive vice chairman of ARATS.[7] Thus, in a way, Qian's most recent commentary on Jiang's peace proposal represents nothing more than another Beijing attempt to woo Taipei into political talks.

Even so, the commentaries offered by Qian and scores of senior officials on January 26, 1998, did carry a strong signal that Beijing has lowered the threshold for the opening of political talks with Taipei. Qian dropped hints that although negotiations must take place under the "one China" principle, "one China" did not necessarily mean the People's Republic of China (PRC). Qian said, "As far as cross-Strait relations are concerned, the one-China principle means there is only one China, Taiwan is a part of China, and the sovereignty and the territorial integrity of China cannot be divided." As a footnote to Qian's remark, Tang Shubei added, "We do not think cross-Strait negotiations require the precondition that Taiwan must first recognize the People's Republic of China government as the central government." In recent memory, these have been the most conciliatory words from Beijing's senior cadres on the sensitive issue of the one-China principle.[8] All this courtship points to one possibility: the Beijing leadership has reached a new consensus on its policy toward Taiwan—to give Jiang's eight-point proposal another boost.

Why did Beijing decide to push vigorously for the opening of political talks with Taipei in the second half of 1997, after shutting off all channels of communication for more than two years following the 1995–1996 Strait crisis? Why did Beijing decide to take back its stern preconditions for the resumption of cross-Strait talks, such as demanding that Taipei drop the campaign for UN membership and terminate its so-called head-of-state diplomacy? The recent policy adjustment raises three sets of issues with regard to Beijing's overall strategy toward Taiwan. First, in the short-run strategic calculus, what does Beijing hope to accomplish by opening political talks with Taipei, in particular by negotiating and possibly signing an agreement "officially ending the state of hostility"? What changes in its internal and external policy environments prompted Beijing leadership to rediscover the instrumental value of pushing for political talks with Taipei?

Second, in the medium- to long-run strategic calculus, what does Jiang Zemin hope to accomplish toward "peaceful reunification" during his tenure? What kind of strategic thinking was behind his eight-point proposal? And third, why has Jiang's eight-point proposal remained so prominent, surviving the missile crises and other setbacks? What has and has not changed since its introduction in January 1995? Are the reasons why Jiang's eight-point proposal is promoted today the same as they were when it was first promulgated?

In this chapter I address these three sets of question through an analysis of the policy apparatus responsible for the formulation and implementation of Taiwan policy. For a systematic understanding of Beijing's policy toward Taiwan in the post–Deng Xiaoping era, one must identify and define the leadership, structure and processes in the domain of Taiwan policy. The emerging policy apparatus in many important ways resembles the PRC's national security policy arena as defined by Michael Swaine,[9] but its bureaucratic span is far less elaborate, the unity and stability of the inner core is comparatively higher, and the task of consensus-building is less messy and time-consuming.

## THE TAIWAN AFFAIRS POLICY APPARATUS IN THE POST-DENG ERA

With the passing of influential elders such as Li Xiannian, Wang Zhen, and Chen Yun and the rapid deterioration of Deng's health in 1994, the collective leadership of the "third generation" was finally fully in charge, and the transition to the post-Deng and post-elder era was, for all practical purposes, complete. Having positioned himself for a smooth power succession, Jiang Zemin, the Chinese Communist Party (CCP) secretary general and first among equals in the six-member Politburo Standing Committee, took over the presidency after the Fourteenth Party Congress and forced his rivals, Yang Shangkun and Yang Baibing, out of the Central Military Commission (CMC).

### The TALSG

In tandem with this turnover at the CCP's highest echelon, the policy apparatus responsible for Taiwan affairs also underwent a major reorganization. In April 1993, Jiang Zemin replaced Yang Shangkun as the leader of TALSG, whose membership was also thoroughly restructured.[10] First, the organization of the TALSG was streamlined; its membership was reduced from twelve to six and retained only two of the previous members, Wang

Zhaoguo and Jia Chunwang. To reduce redundancy and simplify the task of policy coordination, the CCP Taiwan Affairs Office and the State Council Taiwan Affairs Office were merged into one. The reappointed TALSG consisted of the following six official members:[11]

- Jiang Zemin, the leader of the TALSG
- Qian Qichen, the deputy leader of the TALSG, serving concurrently as the deputy leader of the Foreign Affairs Leading Small Group (FALSG)
- Wang Zhaoguo, the head of the CCP United Front Work Department and the head of the CCP/State Council Taiwan Affairs Office (CTAO)
- Jia Chunwang, the head of the Ministry of State Security
- Xiong Guangkai, the head of second department (military intelligence) of the general staff department of the Central Military Commission[12]
- Wang Daohan, the chairman of ARATS and Jiang's political mentor, as well as his most trusted policy adviser

This new structure suggests four changes in the parameters of the Taiwan affairs policy apparatus during the transition to the post-Deng, post-elder era. First, the decisionmaking process became more regularized and formalized. With Jiang's personal involvement, the TALSG became the true inner circle where all important matters dealing with Taiwan were discussed and policy proposals formulated. In the past, the TALSG had been merely a mechanism for coordinating policy among responsible party organs and state agencies. Previous TALSG leaders, who were typically not senior cadres of the highest caliber,[13] did not take active leadership roles—since the early 1980s, the ultimate power in Taiwan affairs had rested with Deng, not by statute or formal executive position but simply because of his prestige and connections in the system. After the 1994 Fourth Plenary Session, however, the process became more formalized. There were no more elders wielding power behind the curtain, and Jiang had to come forward and take over the helm of the TALSG himself to exercise active leadership in the Taiwan policy domain.

Second, the decisionmaking function of the TALSG became better delineated and more focused. The scope of membership no longer covers all the branch systems (*xitong*) involved in the implementation of the Taiwan policy (Figure 12.1). With the downsizing of the inner circle, only key members representing systems that carry out "essential" political, military, and intelligence functions in the Taiwan policy domain were officially included (Figure 12.1).[14] These are the foreign affairs system (represented by Qian Qichen); the party united front work system[15] (represented by Wang Zhaoguo), responsible for directly dealing with the authorities and the people of Taiwan; the People's Liberation Army (PLA) system (represented by

**Figure 12.1 PRC's Taiwan Affairs Policy Apparatus**

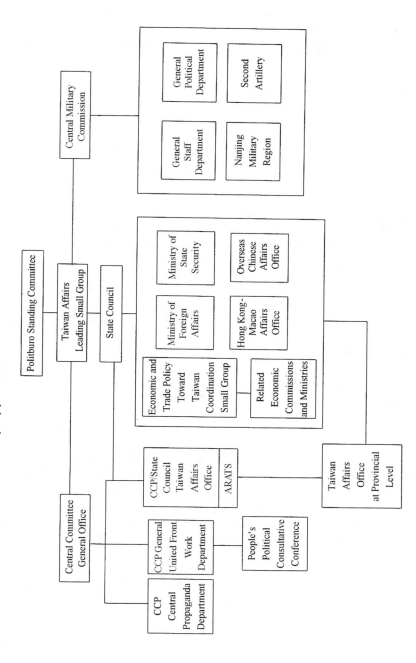

Xiong Guangkai); and the intelligence and counterespionage system (represented by Jia Chunwang). Wang Daohan's role was unique because he served as Jiang's personal representative as well as top adviser. Wang's membership in the TALSG enabled him to handle the most sensitive high-level contacts, both in the open and behind closed doors, with Taiwan and important third-party countries such as the United States and Japan, on behalf of Jiang Zemin. His membership also enabled him to organize a think tank group outside the normal bureaucratic system (Figure 12.2), and to look after Jiang's personal political interests in the formulation and implementation of Taiwan policy.

Ostensibly missing were the propaganda system and the financial and economic system. The propaganda system was not officially present possibly because it performs a supportive role. The financial and economic system was not directly involved in this high-level decisionmaking mechanism because issues dealing with cross-Strait economic ties are mostly of a technical, rather than a political, nature. In addition, the task of accelerating cross-Strait trade and investment flows had been delegated largely to the local governments, which have aggressively promoted their local interests when seeking Taiwanese investment. As the TALSG concentrates itself on political decisions, the technical task of coordinating policy among economic ministries and between central and local authorities in dealing with cross-Strait economic issues was transferred to a specialized coordinating mechanism under the State Council, the Economic and Trade Policy Toward Taiwan Coordination Small Group, headed by vice premier Li Langqing.[16]

Third, this new leadership structure suggests that the trend of replacing the more ideological, personalistic, and top-down pattern of decision-making typical of the Maoist era with a more pragmatic, bureaucratic, and consensus-oriented pattern of the reform era has finally penetrated the domain of Taiwan policy.[17] In stark contrast with the 1980s, when the Taiwan policy domain was best characterized by a "Deng-in-command" model, in the post-Deng era, top leaders including Jiang Zemin himself all have come from a technocratic or professional military background. Few of them claim much hands-on experience in dealing with Taiwan affairs. Unlike the elders, whose revolutionary credentials alone gave them decision-making fiat, Jiang and his colleagues would have to rely more on the policy analyses and recommendations provided by a wide range of research institutes and departments (Figure 12.2).[18]

Although it is possible that the different systems would try to advance their own policy priorities and protect their own organizational interests, to be effective and credible they must back up their policy recommendations with quality information, robust scenario analysis, and well-articulated strategic reasoning. Members of the TALSG operate in a more circumscribed policy environment, with less room for personal policy predilections.

**Figure 12.2  Research Arms Under the TALSG**

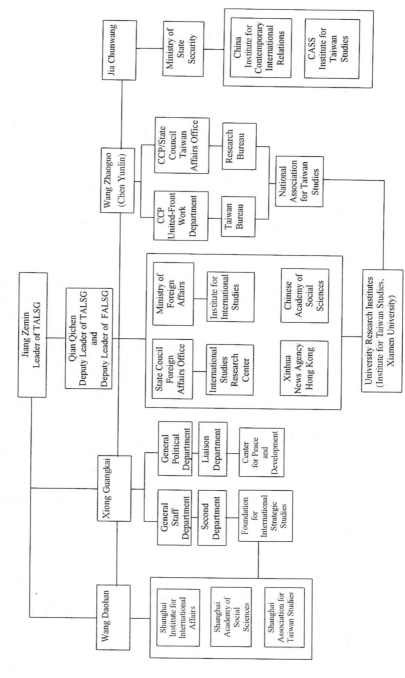

Effective leadership regarding Taiwan issues can only be built with effective policies, meaning that they must accord with both higher-level national strategic priorities and changing situations and environments.

Fourth, in the absence of a paramount leader, Jiang ultimately had to play a game of coalition politics in advancing his own policy agenda. Fortunately for him, the subset of senior party and military leaders that were represented in the TALSG was more congenial than the third generation collective leadership itself, namely the Politburo Standing Committee. Besides Jiang and Wang, there were only two weighty members in the TALSG, Qian Qichen and Xiong Guangkai, who reported directly to the two most influential members of the Politburo Standing Committee.[19] Thus, as long as Jiang can bring Li Peng, Qian Qichen's immediate boss in both the State Council and the FALSG, into the fold, as well as Xiong's superior Liu Huaqing, he can push TALSG's policy proposals through the Politburo Standing Committee as well as the Politburo under most circumstances.

### Jiang Zemin's Leadership Role

Although the outlook, intentions, and organizational interests of the foreign affairs system and the PLA system do not necessarily converge with Jiang's own, most Beijing watchers agree that Li Peng and Liu Huaqing are Jiang's political allies at the highest reaches of the policy process and that their political interests were more compatible with his than were Qiao Shi's or Li Ruihuang's. It is reasonable to assume that these few top civilian and military leaders generally interact with each other in a collaborative and consultative fashion. Therefore, unlike the domestic policy domain, which has been fraught with wide-ranging, cross-level, complex, and fragile bargaining, the fragmentation of authority was not as serious in the Taiwan policy domain.[20] It goes without saying that the new structure of the TALSG was itself a product of coalitional politics engineered by Jiang himself, and it evidently helped strengthen his steering power and simplify the task of consensus-building.

After the Fifteenth Party Congress and the Ninth National People's Congress (NPC), Jiang Zemin enjoyed an even firmer grip on Taiwan policy. Qiao Shi, Jiang's only potential rival on the Standing Committee of the Politburo, stepped down. Also, with the retirement of Liu Huaqing, the PLA was no longer represented on the Standing Committee, marking the resurgence of the party's supremacy over the military. Furthermore, the partial reorganization of the TALSG in April 1998 attests to Jiang's unequivocal leadership in the Taiwan policy domain. The reappointment of the TALSG members carried a strong element of continuity. All the existing members of the TALSG stayed on except for Jia Chunwang, who left the minister of state security post and became the head of Public Security Ministry after Zhu Rongji reshuffled the State Council in March 1998.

Three new members were admitted to the TALSG: Chen Yunlin, who succeeded Wang Zhaoguo as the director of the CCP/State Council Taiwan Affairs Office around early 1997; Zeng Qinghong, Jiang's general chief of staff and most trustworthy troubleshooter; and Xu Yongyao, who replaced Jia Chunwang as the head of the Ministry of State Security.[21] The appointment of Chen Yunlin and Xu Yongyao to the TALSG was clearly based on their official portfolios. The appointment of Zeng Qinghong suggested that Jiang Zemin wanted to buttress the political credential of his most trustworthy protégé in this highly sensitive as well as prominent policy domain long before the senior wise man, Wang Daohan, fully retired.

Two important conclusions emerge from the above analysis of the current leadership, structure, and process in the Taiwan policy domain. First, in the post-Deng era, Jiang succeeded in carving out Taiwan affairs as one of his domains of responsibility. Although the ultimate decisionmaking power still lies within the Politburo, as the leader of the TALSG Jiang nevertheless enjoys effective control over agenda setting in this highly salient policy domain. He is more than just "the first among equals" when it comes to Taiwan affairs. Most of the new policy proposals came from his personal initiatives.

Second, under Jiang's leadership, the PRC's policy toward Taiwan became more comprehensible as well as predictable. For one thing, the policy process was relatively free of lengthy deadlocks and messy compromise, a problem typically associated with a diffuse and fragmented pattern of authority at the top. For another, policy proposals coming out of the TALSG tend to carry a strong element of pragmatism and realism in part due to the growing significance of think tanks in the policy formulation process.[22]

The consensus over Taiwan policy has grown out of a common commitment to some higher-level national strategic priorities—most importantly, Beijing's fundamental interest in maintaining a peaceful and stable environment for the sake of economic reform and in preventing the West from forming an anti-China containment policy.[23] It is also fostered by a shared assessment of the constraints and opportunities present in the international environment, in the United States-PRC-Taiwan triangular relations, and in Taiwan's changing political and economic conditions. In a nutshell, the three frames of reference listed above offer a credible account of Beijing's policy toward Taiwan: Jiang's personal political calculation, the requirement for a close coordination with the higher-level national strategic priorities, and the inducement of the external policy constraints and opportunities.

## MAKING SENSE OF BEIJING'S LATEST PEACE OVERTURE

At first glance, Beijing's renewed peace offer amounts to nothing more than a return to its basic approach to the Taiwan issue: that political negotiation is the route to peaceful reunification, as laid down by Deng Xiaoping in the beginning of the reform era.[24] From a long-term perspective, all the united front work and diplomatic, military, and economic measures targeted at Taiwan formed two sides of the same strategic coin: to preserve the prospects for peaceful reunification and to cajole Taipei to the negotiating table.

Beijing justified the saber-rattling strategy it employed during the summer of 1995 and March 1996 on the ground that the prospects for peaceful reunification were threatened by what the PRC had perceived as Taipei's "creeping independence" strategy, culminating in Lee Teng-hui's trip to Cornell. But as soon as the crisis situation dissipated, leaders wanted to restore the momentum of peace overtures; the only consideration was the best time for launching a new round of peace overtures. Entering the second half of 1997, Beijing believed the overall policy environment seemed ripe for a revival of the peace process. Beijing had regained the upper hand in its diplomatic contest with Taipei; the July 1997 Hong Kong handover had gone smoothly; the difficult issue of personnel reshuffling at the highest echelon had largely been settled on the eve of the Fifteenth Party Congress; and the preparations for Jiang's first state visit to the United States were well under way. All these developments would supposedly strengthen Beijing's leverage at the negotiating table.

We can get more political and strategic mileage out of Beijing's recent policy adjustment, however, than the above analysis entails. Following the analytical framework outlined earlier, I believe that there are some sophisticated strategic calculations behind the timeliness of Beijing's latest peace overture.

First, Beijing's recent accommodation is a double-edged strategy. Beijing will earn political points whether Taipei does or does not come to the negotiating table. If Taipei agrees to the opening of political talks, starting with some preparatory meetings, Beijing eventually will put the one-China principle on the table and force Taipei to clarify its position, hoping that its elevated great power status and favorable international trends will help it put the genie back in the one-China bottle again. If the talks collapse, Beijing's diplomatic and propaganda machinery will prosecute Taiwan in the international arena for its "crime of dividing the nation" and for its "reckless separatist tendencies." If Taipei refuses the opening of political talks on Beijing's terms, Beijing could conveniently blame Taipei for the protracted stalemate and for the volatile situation over the Strait, a situation all countries in the Asia-Pacific community disdain. Beijing would also find it convenient to paint Taiwan's democratization in a separatist light and to characterize Taipei's efforts to rejoin the international community as "rocking the boat." Overall, from Beijing's standpoint, the odds of getting a "no response" answer from Taipei that continues deadlock are far greater than the resumption of talks, at least during Lee Teng-hui's remaining tenure.

Second, Beijing's recent peace overtures are a fine-tuned public relations plot designed to induce Washington, in particular the Clinton administration, to accept the following strategic equation. The firmer the U.S. commitment to the three communiqués, the more conciliatory Beijing's approach to the Taiwan issue, and the firmer Beijing can lock Taipei into the one-China principle through political negotiation, the less likely that PRC-U.S. relations will be held hostage to the Taiwan issue. Therefore, the argument goes, it is in the best interests of the United States to urge Taipei to come to the negotiating table under the one-China principle; otherwise, as the volatile situation continues to drift, both sides face a growing risk of military conflict in the Strait. The Beijing leadership is determined to build up its leverage in this triangular strategic interaction because it recognizes increasingly that without U.S. cooperation, it cannot defuse the ticking bomb of Taiwan independence through political means alone. To drive home the point, in the second half of 1997, Beijing synchronized each wave of political overtures toward Taipei perfectly with each juncture of the first Clinton-Jiang summit, from the warming-up stage to the touchdown of Jiang's return flight.

Third, Beijing's strategists also hope that a new wave of peace overtures will shift the weight of the cross-Strait policy debate inside Taiwan, even if only marginally. In the short run, Beijing hopes that the peace overtures will drive a wedge between President Lee and the Taiwanese business community, which has been increasingly impatient with the stalemate and critical of Lee's "Go slow, don't rush" (*jieji yongren*) policy. Over the medium term, Beijing hopes that its softer approach will foster some new thinking among the Kuomintang's (KMT's) next generation leadership and the pragmatist elements within the Democratic Progressive Party (DPP) camp. Beijing believes the island's political landscape is clearly on the verge of another major shift after the KMT's debacle in the November 1997 local elections and at a time when all the prospective candidates for the 2000 presidential race are positioning themselves on the pressing cross-Strait issues.

Last, but not least, Beijing's renewed peace offer suggests that Jiang Zemin has not entirely given up the hope that he can engineer some kind of breakthrough in the area of cross-Strait relations—for example, by prying open the "three links" or setting in motion the process of political negotiation, during his next five-year tenure. Although this is no longer imperative for his power consolidation after the Fifteenth Party Congress,

Jiang probably still wants to give it a shot for his place in history. After all, the promulgation of the eight-point proposal is an indelible hallmark of Jiang's leadership. It would be a major setback if he and his political allies were to allow this so-called historic policy guideline to lose its political momentum so quickly and prematurely.

Therefore, although (or perhaps because) his handling of cross-Strait relations had been challenged by the military and his rivals in the Politburo in the aftermath of Lee's Cornell trip, Jiang Zemin is motivated to restore and reaffirm the guiding authority of his eight-point proposal.[25] More importantly, the staying power of Jiang's eight-point proposal suggests that the implicit bottom-line position in this post-Deng policy guideline came very close to Jiang's best offer for a negotiated peace for many years to come, given his domestic political constraints. To determine the prognosis for cross-Strait relations during Jiang's next five-year tenure, I must first describe the political genesis of Jiang's eight-point proposal.

## THE POLITICS OF JIANG'S EIGHT-POINT PROPOSAL

Taiwan policy has always been one of the most exclusive and prominent policy domains for CCP paramount leaders. During the Maoist era, the power of setting the guidelines for Taiwan issues rested firmly in Mao's hands. Not even Premier Zhou Enlai was in a position to make final decisions on important matters. During the reform era, Deng Xiaoping decided all important issues regarding Taiwan and Hong Kong. Even Hu Yaobang and Zhao Ziyang had no chance to weigh in.[26] Therefore, for symbolic reasons alone, Jiang Zemin would not permit any other member of the Politburo Standing Committee to assume leadership over this highly salient, but not necessarily highly rewarding, policy domain.

As the designated pivot of the third generation collective leadership, Jiang must have felt strongly that he must carry this torch himself. For the same reason, he was apparently motivated to put his personal mark on Taiwan policy. Much like the issuance of the historic "On Twelve Important Relations" (*lun shierda guanxi*), a new policy guideline on the Taiwan issue would make a strong political statement about Jiang's era. This was probably the reason Jiang decided to act on Wang Daohan's recommendation to draft a new policy document on the Taiwan issue after the first Koo-Wang talks in 1993.[27]

An even more compelling reason for Jiang's new policy initiatives toward Taiwan was the looming challenge of cross-Strait relations themselves. Profound changes had taken place in the PRC's surrounding environment following the Tiananmen crackdown. First, in the international system, the icy clarity of the Cold War was replaced by the confusion of the so-called new world order. The emerging structural configuration of the Asia-Pacific security order had created room for Taiwan's diplomatic maneuvers. Second, after the collapse of the Soviet Union, the PRC was increasingly viewed by its neighbor countries as the major power aspirant, whose long-term strategic interests would potentially conflict with those of a defending hegemon, the United States, and a regional rival, Japan. Third, the transformative potential of the new world order invited the people of Taiwan to explore an alternative path of nation building (for a time, anyway), while Taiwan's fast-paced democratization brought about a realignment of state-society relations and a thorough indigenization of the KMT's power structure. These concurrent developments precipitated a fundamental shift in Taiwan's overall orientation toward cross-Strait relations as well as its international status.

During Taiwan's democratic transition, two trends particularly disturbed Beijing. The first was the rising support for Taiwanese independence and the corresponding decline of Chinese identity among the Taiwanese populace. This trend paralleled the phenomenal growth in the DPP's electoral strength since the late 1980s. The second disturbing trend was the narrowing of ideological distance between the incumbent KMT mainstream faction and the DPP. The Beijing leadership believed that these two power blocs had not only formed a tacit alliance to oust the KMT non-mainstream faction but also gradually converged over a range of policy domains, from constitutional reform to cross-Strait relations to foreign policy. For instance, both the mainstream faction and the DPP favored popular presidential elections. Both emphasized the need to slow the trend of cross-Strait economic integration and to continue the ban on the direct trade, sea, and air links with mainland China. Against this backdrop, Beijing grew increasingly alarmed by a series of bold foreign policy initiatives undertaken by Taipei, starting with the pursuit of "dual recognition" in 1989 and culminating with an all-out drive for UN membership beginning in early 1993.[28] These moves amounted to a concerted effort to establish a separate international identity and marked a clear departure from Taipei's long-standing one-China principle.[29]

These trends had serious consequences for Beijing's Taiwan policy. They dampened the prospects for peaceful reunification over the long term and created a series of diplomatic crises over the short run. Especially during the early 1990s, Taipei effectively used its ascending economic and political status in the Asia-Pacific region to drive home the point that Beijing could not impose international isolation on Taiwan or block the gradual improvement in the island's external relations. Taipei effectively exploited the boycott of the West against Beijing in the aftermath of the Tiananmen crackdown and the eagerness of the French and U.S. governments to salvage their distressed defense industries, winning approval for the purchase of both Mirage fighter jets from France and F-16s from the United States in 1992. Taipei was admitted concurrently with Beijing and Hong Kong to the first ministerial-level regional economic consultation body—the Asia-Pacific Economic Cooperation (APEC) in 1991.[30] And in the winter of 1993–1994, Lee Teng-hui successfully conducted his "holiday diplomacy," paying unofficial visits to the Philippines, Indonesia, and Thailand. All these developments pointed to one possibility: the Taiwan issue was going to pose a major challenge to Jiang Zemin's untried leadership.

Around the time that Jiang took over the helm of the TALSG, cross-Strait relations were showing ample signs of strain, despite the upward trend of cross-Strait economic interdependence. The first Wang-Koo talks in Singapore in April 1993 did not bring about a political thaw across the Strait as Beijing had hoped. The low-level negotiation over functional issues between the SEF and ARATS stagnated. Throughout 1994, Taipei had persistently rejected Beijing's proposals to hold the second set of Koo-Wang talks. The cross-Strait stalemate made Beijing increasingly anxious as Taiwan continued to push for international recognition and to consolidate its democratic transition.

At the same time, the diplomatic contest between Taipei and Beijing intensified after Taipei launched its UN membership drive in early 1993. Beijing perceived this move as a stepping-stone for formal independence. It responded first by issuing the "White Paper on the Taiwan Problem and China's Unification" in mid-1993, wherein it rejected all the proposals Taipei raised for participating in the international community, including "one China, two seats."[31] Also, the PRC mobilized all diplomatic resources at its disposal to block Taiwan's attempt to reopen the debate on Chinese representation in the UN General Assembly and pressured all major powers to reiterate their observance of the one-China principle. Furthermore, to send a strong warning signal, the PLA conducted its most extensive military exercises in forty years in autumn 1994. Two unrelated incidents made the situation even worse. President Lee was highly critical of mainland Chinese leadership regarding the tragic boat accident on Thousand-Island Lake, and the Beijing leadership was deeply upset by the statements Lee Teng-hui made in his interview by a Japanese author, Ryotaro Shiba, in April 1994.[32] A crisis in the Strait was clearly in the making.

From Jiang's standpoint, the precarious situation required a new policy initiative. The old strategy, which placed much hope on the reopening of CCP-KMT negotiations, was overtaken by these events. Deng Xiaoping's "one country, two systems" formula provided little guidance on how to deal with the rising tide of Taiwanese independence. Jiang had to find ways to prevent cross-Strait relations from developing into a major crisis. His policy advisers determined that to jump-start the peace process and to lure the new KMT leadership back to the negotiating table, Beijing must offer some new policy incentives by promulgating a major policy proposal. To complicate matters, a policy proposal of this nature required the collective endorsement of the Politburo. Thus, Jiang could take the initiative but could not bear the full responsibility. The process of formulating such a policy document was under way as early as in the second half of 1993, within a writing group comprising some leading Taiwan experts from all the major research institutes, including some PLA institutes. The draft document was then circulated among members of the TALSG and, subsequently, among members of the Politburo for comment. Reportedly, Wang Daohan and Wang Zhaoguo were intimately involved in the revision process before its final approval around fall 1994.

Jiang's eight-point proposal for peaceful reunification was significant in a number of ways. First, with the official approval of the Politburo, the policy document enjoyed a solid political backing among the collective leadership of the third generation and became *the* unequivocal policy guideline on Taiwan affairs for the post-Deng era. Second, the document revealed an important strategic adjustment in Beijing's current approach toward Taiwan. Although it maintained the "one country, two systems" formula, the new guideline placed more emphasis on concrete proposals, for stepwise rapprochement between Taiwan and mainland China during the stage preceding reunification, such as a cross-Strait summit and signed agreements to end the state of hostility. These characteristics suggested that the third generation leadership discounted the possibility of speedy reunification in favor of reaching a bilateral accord on a transitional framework, which hopefully would hold the long-term prospect of peaceful reunification, facilitate bilateral economic exchange, stabilize the status quo, and preempt the independence option. In this way, Jiang could pass the "Hong Kong first, Taiwan next" hot potato to the next generation while preserving a stable and peaceful environment for China's economic reform.

Third, the proposal suggested that Jiang was ready for a political bargain. The document revealed that as long as Taipei was willing to come to the negotiating table under the "one China" principle, Beijing stood ready to address Taipei's three conditions for lifting the ban on "three links." Namely, the PRC must renounce the use of force against Taiwan, recognize Taiwan as a political entity on an equal footing, and allow Taiwan reasonable space for international participation. To sweeten the offer, the document implied that "one China" did not necessarily mean "the PRC," because throughout the proposal the term "PRC" never appeared. Fourth, the document reflected Beijing's new reading of Taiwan's internal politics, acknowledging Taiwan's democratization and the resultant Taiwanization of the power structure. It recognized Taiwan's emerging political pluralism and attempted to reach out to all political parties and social forces. Moreover, it suggested that despite a growing suspicion of Taipei's hidden agenda among Beijing leadership, Jiang still pinned high hopes on Lee Teng-hui, who continued to enjoy a firm grip on Taiwan's mainland policy.

The promulgation of Jiang Zemin's eight-point policy proposal gave Taipei a chance to review its strategic options. Taipei regarded Jiang's eight-point proposal as part of his larger scheme to consolidate his power as China entered the post-Deng era. It reasoned that although Jiang's ostensible objective was to end the stalemate with low-level cross-Strait talks and thereby reinvigorate cross-Strait relations, Jiang's unspoken objective was to defuse the Taiwan issue and thus prevent a potentially crippling crisis for Jiang's untried leadership during the sensitive period of power succession. This reading reconfirmed long-held assumptions about the predicament of the CCP leadership and about the policy inclinations of Jiang Zemin. Taipei did not want to throw cold water on him, however, because Taiwan increasingly regarded him as an element of moderation within the CCP leadership ranks.

Thus, in return, Lee Teng-hui offered a lukewarm six-point response to Jiang's peace overture in April 1995 but continued to follow a two-pronged strategy, meaning that any significant improvement on Taiwan-mainland relations had to be accompanied by a parallel measure to strengthen Taipei's international position.[33] It redoubled its lobbying efforts on Capital Hill to pressure the White House to grant President Lee Teng-hui a visitor visa for his summer trip to his alma mater while boosting the cross-Strait relations by making a series of goodwill gestures: not only agreeing to hold the second Koo-Wang talks in Beijing but agreeing to hold the talks annually and to expand the agenda to include political issues. Taipei's reading of Jiang's political predicament probably was right on the mark, but its calculation that Jiang would be lured into accepting Taipei's rules of the game was perhaps too far off the mark.

The White House decision on Lee's visa took Beijing by surprise. It touched off Beijing's worst fear—that the United States was pursuing an undeclared policy agenda of containing China and playing up the Taiwan card. To ward off any possible domino effect of Lee's visit to the United States, Jiang Zemin had little choice but to allow the hard-liners to set the policy tone for the moment. Beijing launched a week of missile tests off Taiwan's northern coast in late July to remind the United States, Japan, and Taipei of the dire consequences of sponsoring (or pursuing) the cause of Taiwanese independence. On the eve of the KMT Congress to nominate the president in late August, the PLA launched the second round of missile tests near a Taiwan-controlled offshore island. With a clear aim of disrupting President Lee's reelection bid, Beijing decided to extend the military threats well on to election day.

## THE PROSPECTS FOR CROSS-STRAIT RELATIONS

It is still too early to make a full assessment of the consequences of the March 1996 Strait crisis. There are reasons to believe, however, that lessons from those events will help to stabilize cross-Strait relations, at least for the short and medium term. The closer encounter helped all sides—including the United States and Japan—reach a better sense of each others' bottom-line positions and update their risk assessments concerning any unilateral attempts to change the status quo.

Jiang Zemin apparently emerged from the Strait crisis unscathed. During the crisis, he went along with the PLA and allowed the hawkish option to run its full course. He also accommodated a more assertive PLA in managing cross-Strait relations. But in the aftermath of the crisis, it became quite clear that the saber-rattling strategy had its limits and produced many undesirable side effects. It might have dampened the momentum of the Taiwan independence movement and have thrown a wet blanket on the popular aspiration for some extravagant diplomatic ventures, like the UN membership drive. At the same time, however, it pushed the United States and Japan into a stronger military alliance and forced them to take a clearer position on extending security commitments to Taiwan.

One of the lessons that Jiang drew from the ill-fated attempt to cajole Taipei to the negotiating table in 1995 was that unless the United States was interested in playing a more active role in status quo management, Taipei could reject Beijing's peace overture at virtually no cost. To regain control over the tempo of cross-Strait relations, Jiang had to play up the U.S. card. Clinton's decision to rebuild the political foundation of U.S.-China relations, based on the concept of a forward-looking strategic partnership, gave Jiang Zemin a golden opportunity to revive the political momentum of peace overtures toward Taiwan.

Beijing has been quite successful in persuading the Clinton administration to view Taipei's diplomatic venture through a separatist lens and to perceive the need to restrain Taiwanese aspirations for independence. In exchange for the PRC's cooperation in other issue realms, the U.S. government has very forcefully urged the two sides to resume the dialogue, emphasizing that Taipei should take the initiative. Jiang also personally pressured Clinton to take an unambiguous stand on the issue of Taiwan's international status. During his first state visit to the United States in October 1997, Jiang secured the Clinton administration's pledge to uphold the "three nos"—no support for Taiwanese independence; no support for two Chinas or "one China, one Taiwan"; and no support for Taiwan's membership in international organizations that require statehood. Furthermore, during Clinton's China trip, to reciprocate Jiang's bold move to broadcast their joint press conference live in Beijing,

Clinton decided to publicly announce the "three nos" at a seminar held in Shanghai.

The implications of Clinton's "three nos" policy are twofold. Clinton's statement reaffirms Jiang's political credibility in managing Washington-Beijing-Taipei triangular relations. At the same time, however, it reinforces Beijing's resolve to insist on its terms for the resumption of cross-Strait discussions. The statement has made it increasingly unlikely that Jiang will offer Taipei more political concessions than what the eight-point proposal presented or implied. As a result, in Beijing's latest round of peace overtures, Qian Qichen and Tang Shubei did not step outside the policy parameters set by Jiang's eight-point proposal. They only clarified these existing peace offers in less ambiguous terms.

Taipei did not find Jiang's eight-point policy proposal very appealing when it was first offered. Nor will it this time. One reason Taipei is not very enthusiastic about direct political negotiations, much less striking a lasting political accord soon, is that there is simply no domestic consensus over Taiwan's bottom-line position at the negotiating table. Obviously, the DPP will fight to the end if a cross-Strait accord, even an interim agreement, precludes the independence option. For proponents and sympathizers of Taiwan independence, as long as there is hope for their first choice in the future, there is no hurry to settle for second or third best now.

It is unlikely that Jiang will sign any political accord without a provision precluding Taiwanese independence. As long as the two sides of the Taiwan Strait cannot reach agreement over any aspects of the more fundamental issues, the political standoff is likely to continue, leaving cross-Strait relations vulnerable to unexpected political events on either side of the Strait.

## NOTES

1. This chapter is based on numerous meetings and interviews that I have conducted with PRC officials and scholars since 1995. For the sake of political prudence, I will keep all sources anonymous.

2. Jiang Zemin unveiled his historic proposal, entitled "Continue to Promote the Reunification of China," on January 30, 1995, the eve of the lunar New Year.

3. *South China Morning Post,* January 27, 1998.

4. *United Daily News,* May 30, 1998.

5. Xinhua News Agency, September 12, 1997.

6. Xinhua News Agency, September 30, 1997.

7. The SEF declined the invitation but offered a counterproposal, sending its chairman, C. F. Koo, to pay an informal visit to Beijing, which was indirectly rejected by ARATS.

8. In a private meeting with some visitors from Taiwan, Wang Daohan reportedly offered an even more flexible interpretation of the one-China principle. It was

said that he characterized the one-China principle as a commitment to an ongoing process of constructing a new and unified China. *Wenghui Bao* of Hong Kong later ran a report to correct this characterization.

9. See Swaine, *Chinese Political and Bureaucratic Calculations and Behavior Regarding Taiwan.*

10. In Chinese, the TALSG is called *Duitai gongzuo lingdao xiaozu.*

11. Refer to Yang Kai-huang, "An Explanation and Evaluation of PRC's Taiwan Policy"; and Tsai, "The Decision-making Apparatus."

12. Xiong was later promoted to the deputy chief of general staff.

13. Before Jiang, Liao Chenzhi (the former head of the CCP United Front Department and the State Council Overseas Chinese Affairs Office), Deng Yingchao (the widow of Zhou Enlai), and Yang Shangkun (the nominal head of state) had by turns served that post. See Yang Kai-huang, "An Explanation and Evaluation of PRC's Taiwan Policy."

14. Of course, it is quite possible that some systems were not entitled to an official membership but were invited to sit in the regular meetings of the TALSG.

15. The CCP/State Council Taiwan Affairs Office is supervised by both the Central Committee General Office and the State Council. Its primary function is to carry out united front work against Taiwan. At the same time, it is responsible for the coordination among State Council agencies.

16. In Chinese, it is called *Duitai jingmao gongzuo xietiao xiaozu.*

17. For this general trend, see Hamrin and Zhao, *Decision-making in Deng's China.*

18. For an analysis of the role of various research institutes and departments in the overall Taiwan affairs policy apparatus, see Tsai, "The Decision-making Apparatus."

19. Li Ruihuan is Wang Zhaoguo's superior in the united front work system. As far as Taiwan policy is concerned, however, Wang reports to Jiang rather than Li Ruihuan.

20. For the model of fragmentation of authority, see Lieberthal and Lampton, *Bureaucracy, Politics and Decision Making;* and Lieberthal, *Governing China.*

21. Based on the report of the *United Daily News,* April 20, 1998.

22. One can always question the quality of the policy analysis conducted by these Taiwanese affairs think tanks. My personal observation is that they are getting better over time as far as monitoring Taiwan's internal political dynamics. The reasons are quite simple. First, most of the leading analysts have taken field trips to Taiwan. Second, most of them are in frequent contact with scholars and specialists from Taiwan. Third, they have easy access to Taiwan's leading newspaper and political commentaries, which provide a rich source of information. Some PLA-related research institutes even regularly browse through Taiwan-based Web sites.

23. For an analysis of the PRC's national security strategic guideline, see You, "China's Foreign Policy."

24. Deng laid down the basic guideline of peaceful reunification at a CCP high-level meeting held December 8–22, 1978. See *Selected Works of Deng Xiaoping (1975–1982).*

25. For an excellent analysis of the 1995–1996 Strait crisis, see Swaine, *Chinese Political and Bureaucratic Calculations and Behavior Regarding Taiwan.*

26. For decisionmaking policy toward Hong Kong, see Ram, "Decisionmaking."

27. On this point, also refer to Sheng, "China Eyes Taiwan."

28. Dual recognition means a foreign government simultaneously extending diplomatic recognition to the PRC and the ROC governments. Taipei made its first

attempt on July 20, 1989, when the ROC government established formal diplomatic ties with Grenada, in spite of the fact that St. George's had maintained formal ties with Beijing since 1985 and officially recognized the government of the PRC as the "sole legal government of China." See Chu, *The Security Challenge for Taiwan*.

29. Around the early 1990s, the incumbent native elite adopted the view that adherence to the one-China principle endangered the ROC's sovereign status in the international community. This principle has entrapped Taiwan in diplomatic isolation since the early 1970s. Also, this principle provides Taiwan with little multilateral guarantee against PRC's forced retrocession, while giving the PRC all the pretexts it needs to refuse foreign intervention in the case of military confrontation.

30. Following the Asian Development Bank precedent, Taiwan was admitted with Taipei's de facto acceptance of the designation "Taipei, China." That formula honors the principle of one China while acknowledging the reality of two Chinese regimes and consequently two governments.

31. Jiang Zemin did not inject much personal input into this sternly phrased document, which had taken shape during Yang Shangkun's tenure.

32. On the impact of the interview on the perception of Beijing leadership, see Sheng, "China Eyes Taiwan."

33. This is deemed politically prudent because it can dispel the suspicion of the DPP and alleviate the fear of a substantial portion of the population that favors the preservation of status quo. It is also deemed strategically necessary because only with a stronger multilateral backing for Taiwan's political autonomy will Taiwan have the confidence to engage mainland China in closer economic cooperation and possibly direct political negotiations. It also helped clear away any false impression that the international community might have about the possibility that the two sides were moving quickly toward a political rapprochement.

# PART FIVE

# Looking Forward:
# The Challenges of
# Regionalism, Nationalism,
# and Globalization

# ⊞ 13 ⊞

# Institutionalizing de Facto Federalism in Post-Deng China

## *Zheng Yongnian*

In early 1997, Deng Xiaoping, China's last strongman, passed away. In September of that year, the Chinese Communist Party (CCP) held its Fifteenth National Congress and consolidated Jiang Zemin's power position as the core of the third generation of leadership. In March 1998, the Ninth People's Congress elected Zhu Rongji as China's premier. All these events symbolized the beginning of a post-Deng era. Chinese far away from Beijing watched these events and raised the age-old question: Can China be governed by a *Zhongnanhai* (China's White House) without Deng Xiaoping?

Since reforms began in the late 1970s, this question has been asked repeatedly in academic circles both inside and outside China. The issue was raised largely because of China's rapid development; the economy has grown about 10 percent per year since 1980. A related question of immediate significance is whether the established institutions of central-local relations can accommodate such drastic economic development and the consequent sociopolitical changes. It is no wonder that much research has concerned changes in central-local economic relations (e.g., fiscal decentralization) and their sociopolitical impacts.[1]

Although some have predicted that China will soon become a great power, many others have foreseen that the old institutions of central-local relations will collapse and that China as a nation-state will disintegrate.[2] Under what circumstances could this collapse take place? For all those who have predicted it, the answer is rather simple and lies in the contradiction between economy and politics. The Chinese model of reform in the post-Mao era has been regarded as "economic reform without political reform."[3] For Susan Shirk, who espouses this model, the very success of Chinese reform to date has been due to this characteristic.[4] But for others, this model of reform will contribute to the collapse of central authorities. For Lucian Pye, without political reform, China has encountered enormous difficulties in building a modern nation-state. Pye has argued that China is a "civilization pretending to be a nation-state," which, if left to follow its current course, could fragment into separate political entities.

Without modern institutions for central-local relations, central power over localities remains rather symbolic, and "sovereignty calls for theatrical representation."[5] According to James Miles, China will split apart, as it has repeatedly from the dim beginning of time through the warlord period of the twentieth century. The very nature of authoritarian regimes creates a myriad of destructive emotions that will spill over, just as they have in some of the former Eastern bloc countries and the Soviet Union.[6] Similarly, Jack Goldstone has argued that without political reform, the Communist regime has shown four major vulnerabilities similar to those associated with the collapse of earlier Chinese regimes, including a split within the ranks of the party leadership, a rift between the party leaders and China's other elites, a decline in the party's direct control of Chinese society, and discontent among the foot soldiers of the revolution (i.e., peasants and workers).[7] Certainly, if central authority collapsed, China might be united no more.

It is important to see how China's rapid economic development has affected its central-local relations. Equally important, however, is how political factors have affected central-local relations. China's political reform has lagged far behind its economic reform, and the model of "economic reform without political reform" makes sense only in relative terms. A neglect of central-local political reform often leads to various misperceptions of central power over the provinces. There are no good reasons to predict the collapse of central authorities, however. We need an approach capable of explaining not only how rapid local economic growth has been achieved but also why the central state still stands as powerfully as it does.

Much has been said about how the old institutions of central-local relations have been weakened. In this chapter I paint a rather different picture—that the central-local relationship has been strengthened due to institutional changes introduced during the reform era—and I identify some key institutional factors likely to shape central-local relations in the post-Deng era. But first, I offer a caveat. The strengthening of central-local relations does not mean that the central state has become more powerful than the provinces or vice versa. It means only that various institutional factors have come into being to bring the center and the provinces together.

## THE DEFINITION OF INSTITUTIONS

Institutions matter in mediating the interplay between the center and the provinces. There is no widely agreed-upon definition of institutions, but the concept is used here to include both formal organizations, informal rules, and procedures that stipulate implicitly and explicitly the ways in which the center and the provinces *should* cooperate and compete with each other. These rules prescribe acceptable forms of behavior and proscribe unacceptable kinds of behavior.[8]

In terms of central-local relations, three institutional features can be identified in the reform era: de facto federalism, reciprocity, and cultural norms. This section provides a brief explanation of each feature, and the following section examines how they worked under Deng Xiaoping.

Implicit in post-Mao economic decentralization (e.g., the contract system, tax-division system, and one-level-downward appointment system) is the first feature: de facto federalism, a relationship between a unitary system and a feudal system. De facto federalism can be defined as follows:

> A relatively institutionalized pattern which involves an explicit or implicit bargain between the center and the provinces, one element in the bargain being that the provinces receive certain institutionalized or ad hoc benefits in return for guarantees by provincial officials that they will behave in certain ways on behalf of the center.

The rise of de facto federalism in post-Mao China comes mainly from two factors: the nature of state power and the institutional withdrawal of state power. Given the fact that great diversities have always existed among Chinese provinces, the reach of state power has its own limitations.[9] Even under Mao's totalitarianism, the Chinese economy and regime were not well integrated, and the structure of decisionmaking was fragmented.[10] Indeed, great local autonomy was preserved, even strengthened, by the two waves of economic decentralization Mao initiated during the Great Leap Forward and the Cultural Revolution. In addition, the institutional withdrawal of state power rendered the provinces rather independent in managing local affairs. Post-Mao decentralization can be understood not as devolving central power or returning power to the provinces, but as withdrawing national institutions from the provinces or reducing the reach of state power. It is a process of localizing state power, as evidenced by property rights localization, a fiscal contract system, a tax-division system, and the one-level-downward appointment system.

Under this scheme of central-local relations, the provinces are allowed to plan economic development and implement different policies to provide economic incentives in their jurisdictions. De facto federalism recognizes the active role of the center in rebuilding central-local relations. The center devolves decisionmaking power to the provinces, but the provinces have to behave in a manner that is still to a great extent dictated by the center. Moreover, federalism also recognizes that the provinces have their own interests and can take policy initiatives, even make policies independently, but the policies they make need to be legitimated by the center, at least formally.

A second institutional feature is reciprocity, which is implicit in de facto federalism. My concept of reciprocity derives from Robert Axelrod and Robert Keohane's idea that reciprocity fosters interdependence and co-operation among egoists.[11] In many respects, reciprocity is similar to what is called "clientelism." It exists in different degrees in different forms of politics such as clientelist politics, factional politics, and bureaucratic interest group politics.[12] Importantly, reciprocity between the center and the provinces is not symmetrical; exchanges are not equivalent. Unlike anarchy, in which it is always rational for an egoistic player to defect due to absence of a mechanism for enforcing promises, the center in a de facto federalist system has less (but not *no*) difficulty in monitoring the provinces because the center and the provinces coexist in the same hierarchical system.

A third institutional feature is cultural norms. These can affect behavior by providing individuals, in Ann Swidler's term, a "tool kit" of habits, skills, and styles from which people construct strategies of action. In other words, cultural norms shape behavior by offering ways to organize action rather than by specifying the ends of action. They create habits of interpretation and repertoires of practice grounded in experience.[13] According to Peter Katzenstein, "What matters is not only the compliance of political actors with social standards that shape their interests and behavior but the competence of actors to (re)interpret their identities and thus to (re)define their interests and behavior."[14]

Given that the center and the provinces have interacted for centuries, the shadow of the past necessarily affects the way the two actors define their interests and construct their strategies for dealing with each other. Indeed, as Axelrod has shown, reciprocity leads to cooperation through repeated games. The Prisoner's Dilemma holds that both players benefit more from successful outcomes than from mutual defection but that each player achieves the most successful outcome by defecting, provided that his or her partner cooperates. Nevertheless, when an indefinite sequence of such games is played, cooperation may become rational for the players. According to Axelrod, the rationality of cooperation depends not only on the immediate payoff facing the players but also on the "shadow of the future."[15] For this reason, I consider cultural norms as institutions mediating central-local relations.

## HOW INSTITUTIONS WORKED UNDER DENG XIAOPING

Deng Xiaoping once argued that without political reform, economic reform would not take place, and the fruits resulting from economic reform could not be protected. Economic success in China still puzzles China scholars for varying reasons. First, economic reform has been implemented without concomitant political reform. Second, the center still retains overwhelming political discretion and, theoretically, has the authority to reverse the reform process. Third, China has not developed a consistent commercial law (e.g., property and contract law) or an independent court system for adjudication. The list goes on.

So how has economic success been achieved? The answer, I believe, lies in a unique institutional feature of central-local relations: de facto federalism, under which both economic and political power is decentralized from the central state to local governments rather than individual enterprises and society.

In analyzing the transition from a planned economy to a market one and from authoritarianism to democracy, the discussion of state-enterprise relations has stressed economic decentralization, whereas the discussion of state-society relations has stressed political decentralization. Economists appreciate this type of economic decentralization because it enhances an important value: economic efficiency. If economic decisionmaking authority is decentralized to local units, each unit can adapt its economic policies to the preferences of its local residents.[16] Economists thus emphasize decentralizing economic decisionmaking authority from state organizations to individual enterprises. Economic efficiency can be maximized by competition among individual enterprises.

Logically, economic reforms in Communist countries should aim at marketization and privatization. To reform their economies, the leadership must introduce changes in property relations. A legally recognized private sector must come into being. Individual enterprises must be given broad decisionmaking authority with regard to production, sales, price setting, and wages. Although it is necessary to decentralize decisionmaking power to local governments at early stages of reforms, such economic reforms are incomplete until individual enterprises gain full authority. Decentralization only transforms a planned economy to a mixed market economy. The ultimate goal of economic reforms is a laissez-faire economy in which the state does not intervene.

Similarly, the literature on political transition in Communist countries has focused on political decentralization vis-à-vis state-society relations. Political transition means democratization and the decentralization of power from the state to society. The logic of political reforms is as follows. The Communist state must "modify the decision-making mechanism by including a broader portion of the society in the political process, and it must modify the ideology to accommodate new economic measures. This leads to redefining and extending rights and tolerating spaces for free expression and collective action for individuals and groups in society."[17]

The importance of this type of de facto federalism, which has been prevalent in Deng's China, has not been appreciated. As an institution of central-local relations, de facto federalism has had a significant impact on China's economic performance and political development.

With the rise of this kind of federalism, the center decentralizes economic decisionmaking authority to provinces and lower levels of government. Instead of privatization, property rights are decentralized to the provincial governments rather than to individual enterprises or individual entrepreneurs. Provincial governments become de facto owners of state enterprises. Thus, even though the center gradually withdraws from the economic affairs of individual enterprises, provincial governments become highly interventionist. In other words, de facto federalism creates an institutional setting and legitimacy for provincial governments to intervene in economic activities within their jurisdictions. Consequently, local interventionist states, whose actions I call local developmentalism, come into being. But de facto federalism does not deny the development of markets. Rather, this development is highly encouraged because intense competition exists between different jurisdictions and between enterprises with different forms of ownership. Local protectionism exists at early stages of economic reforms, but with the deepening of decentralization, it is constrained.[18]

With the rise of de facto political federalism, even though the political spaces for free expression and collective action for individuals and social groups are extended and the Communist regime turns to consultative authoritarianism, political participation is still very limited. The focus here is power shifts not between the state and society, but between the center and the provinces. The center is unwilling to decentralize political power to society. Instead, it believes that political participation should be constrained and that mass mobilization cannot help the transition to an efficient government.

For the center, the initial goal of political decentralization to local states was to strengthen local government organizations and make them more efficient in responding to social demands and changing social and economic circumstances. With the deepening of economic reforms, great changes occur in the power basis of local governments, and central-local relations become highly interdependent. Although the center still holds great power over the provinces, without the cooperation of provincial governments, the center cannot accomplish much. Furthermore, with economic reforms, the decentralization of power gains momentum and is increasingly not merely at the discretion of the center. At some point, decentralization becomes irreversible. As a result, while the provinces develop and strengthen their own power bases, the center also adjusts its relations with the provinces. The center recognizes the de facto independent power of the provinces at the same time as it develops its own independent power to constrain provincial behavior.

Mutual adjustment in the relations between the center and the provinces leads to changes in state structure. Governmental political participation, or "areal democracy," occurs.[19] Provincial governments have the authority not only to deal with local businesses but also to influence decisionmaking at the national level. Democracy in terms of state-society relations may emerge to varying degrees in different regions, but political participation is very limited and depends on local factors such as the levels of economic development, local political cultures, the attitude of local leadership toward democracy, and the measures of political reforms introduced by local leadership.

The significance of de facto political federalism for economic reforms lies in the fact that economic decentralization does not in itself generate a momentum toward marketization and has to be implemented by an authoritarian regime. Decentralizing political decisionmaking power to the provinces indeed strengthens provincial power in initiating economic reforms and creates a counterpower to central bureaucracies that often serve as a major impediment to economic reforms in Communist countries. Further, this federalism itself is an important aspect of democracy. Powerful local governments can serve as a serious constraint on the center and protect local societies from the center's arbitrary exercise of power, even though local governments are often reluctant to share political power with society.

With the rise of de facto federalism, reciprocity becomes a natural approach to central-local relations. In a well-developed federal system, the division of central-local power is rather highly legalized and institutionalized. Formal rules, organizations, and institutions mediate central-local relations. By contrast, in China's federalism, central-local power is not divided in a clear-cut way; the relations between the two, to a large degree, are not institutionalized; and informal rules and institutions must play a more important role in the interaction between the center and the provinces. De facto federalism strengthens the interdependence between the center and the provinces, but without formal institutions coming into being, reciprocity becomes a norm in resolving central-local conflicts.

How has reciprocity mediated central-local relations? The most powerful explanation so far has been given by Susan Shirk,[20] who states that we can study Chinese politics much as we would other non-Communist regimes and that central-local relations thus can be understood in the context of China's institutions.[21] The CCP has ultimate authority over the provinces, but top leaders (including the Communist Party general secretary, Politburo members, or Politburo standing committee members) are chosen by an elite selectorate, which consists of the members of the Central Committee, the revolutionary elders, and top military leaders. The operational procedure by which party, government, and military officials in the selectorate are appointed by top CCP leaders but also have the authority to choose top CCP leaders creates a relationship of "reciprocal accountability." Thus, assuming that a rational provincial official will seek to be promoted in the Chinese political hierarchy, central authorities could "play to the provinces" to gain political support from provincial officials by providing them political incentives through the appointment system or the central *nomenklatura*. However, provincial officials could also "play to the center" because they form the majority of the selectorate and their votes are an important source of a given top leader's political legitimacy.[22]

Shirk's model is rather logical and parsimonious. Many other institutional elements have been excluded from the model, however, and reciprocity has been defined rather narrowly as a process of mutual selection. The preferences of individual leaders are seen to result from their rationality. As rational politicians responding to career incentives, policymakers competing for the top positions must play to the selectorate and especially to the largest blocks with it, that is, provincial officials. The model explains how the center and the provinces play to each other to achieve reciprocal accountability. But given the fact that reciprocity is asymmetrical, the model is unable to explain why the center as a rational actor does not maximize its power versus the provinces. In other words, the model does not provide a sound explanation of consistent decentralization that, to a large extent, has weakened central power. Certainly, as a power maximizer, the center would not have had such a reform strategy that would lead to the decline of its power. It seems to Shirk that the center has to behave as it does. Her only major reason is that numbers matter because the largest block in the selectorate are provincial officials. But this is not a satisfactory answer. Numbers change. An example is the Central Committee of the Fourteenth Congress of the CCP of 1994, where the largest block was no longer provincial officials. Even with such a change, reciprocity between the center and the provinces still continues.

Next, one strength of a rational approach is its ability to explain changes.[23] Egoistic politicians interact with one another in a given institutional setting and attempt to maximize their own power and interests, creating tension among themselves and introducing change to the institution per se. Unfortunately, as she admits, Shirk's model cannot explain those changes because she defines institutions too narrowly and her analysis is too institutionally deterministic.[24]

I have added two institutional elements to Shirk's analysis in an attempt to provide a more satisfactory explanation of reciprocity between the center and the provinces. One is de facto federalism, and the other is ideational—that is, cultural norms. First, Shirk's "reciprocal accountability" needs to be explained in the context of federalism rather than a narrowly defined "selectorate." As discussed above, intergovernmental decentralization means, to a large extent, that the center withdraws its institutional power from the provinces, and provincial governments become independent players in dealing with provincial affairs. Without provincial cooperation, the center will not be able to govern the country. The fact that the provinces are governed by provincial governments plays an essential role in establishing reciprocity between the center and the provinces.

Second, ideational factors also play an important role in mediating asymmetrical central-local relations. Rationality or "interest" explanations have their limitations. Albert Hirschman argued that leaders in developing countries not only have "interest" but also have "passions."[25] Indeed, the "passion" of Chinese leaders for development has played an important role in safeguarding consistent intergovernmental decentralization. Decentralization becomes irreversible not because it is impossible to reverse the process but because the center does not want to do so. As one observer noted in the context of fiscal centralization, it is difficult to differentiate between the case of the center choosing not to exercise its prerogatives and the center being unable to do so."[26] Also, when top leadership "select" the members of the selectorate, the standard of selection—the tendency to promote rapid economic development—becomes a, if not *the*, most important political standard for the top leadership in selecting provincial leaders. This means that the members of the selectorate will not necessarily say "yes" to the top leadership and its policies.

Ideational factors not only constrain arbitrary behavior of leaders in conducting reciprocity between the center and the provinces but also prevent the provinces from deviating greatly from the center. Cultural norms affect provincial leaders' behavior in two ways. First, leaders pursue not only power and material interests but also symbolic interests such as prestige, reputation, and moral authority (or popular recognition). Second, as discussed above, culture gives individuals a "tool kit" to construct their strategy of action. It defines the context of both material interests and symbolic interests and thus constrains the way provincial leaders define their "interests" by informing them of "right" and "wrong" behavior or "good" and "bad" interests.

Both the center and the provinces have learned what is bad or good and what is wrong or right over the long history of their interaction. What we now know as China was divided into several states many times during its long history, but the division of the nation seems abnormal to most Chinese. Reflecting on the 1989 Tiananmen crisis, W. J. F. Jenner predicted the death of the Communist state and argued that the collapse of the regime would not be due to the problems of Communist dictatorship but to the tyranny of history.[27] The reverse argument, however, could be made: that the unity of China is due to the mercy of history.

A unique mindset has been formulated over the long history of center-province relationships: that unity is good and right and division is bad and wrong. Consequently, although power struggles or other conflicts between the center and the provinces often resulted in a divided nation, history did not end there. In other parts of the world such as Europe and South Asia, the collapse of an empire often resulted in the creation of several permanent sovereign territories or states. By contrast, the collapse of an existing Chinese empire was only the beginning of the struggle for a new and united empire. Scholars have long puzzled over what made China so different from Europe or South Asia and what held Chinese societies together for so many centuries, but according to recent studies, one major factor is cultural or state identity.[28] Without doubt, the strong state identity has had a major impact on provincial officials' dealing with the center. As one commentator pointed out, "one sign of the strong tradition of centralization is the way in which the warlords asserted provincial sovereignty. . . . The warlords fought each other in order to unify the country; the territorial divisions came about only because they disagreed over who should do the unifying."[29]

That strong state identity also exists among provincial government officials today. A survey among provincial officials in 1994 showed that 84 percent of interviewees believed that increasing income disparities among provinces would result in social instability, and 16 percent argued that the country would break up if the issue could not be resolved. Furthermore, when asked whether the center or the provinces should take major responsibility to solve the problem, nearly 70 percent answered "both," whereas 22 percent argued that the center should be responsible.[30] With a strong state identity, provincial officials would not be overwhelmingly local interest–oriented and would tolerate the center's arbitrary behavior if they believed that such behavior comported with "national interest," that is, national unity.

## INSTITUTIONALIZING DE FACTO FEDERALISM IN THE POST-DENG ERA

Institutional factors change. So does de facto federalism. In the post-Deng era, central-provincial relationships will be institutionalized to a great degree but will still be characterized by de facto federalism rather than federalism. That China has entered the post-Deng era has been symbolized by the passing of the second generation of leadership and the establishment of the third generation. The exit of the old guard also signals the end of the old base of political legitimacy. The political legitimacy of the old guard was based on their revolutionary experience, and their behavior toward provincial officials, who hardly could challenge central power, was rather arbitrary. With the generational changes in leadership, new leaders have begun to search for a new base of political legitimacy, as shown at the Fifteenth Congress of the CCP.[31]

Without the old guard, new leaders tend to rely increasingly on institutional factors to mediate the relations between the center and the provinces. The old guard withdrew central institutional power from the provinces, but the new leadership has made efforts to penetrate into the provinces. This does not mean, however, that there will be a wholesale recentralization movement. As discussed above, de facto federalism renders decentralization irreversible. What the center does is build *selective* national institutions in the provinces. As a matter of fact, selective centralization has become the new leadership's major strategy to strengthen central power.

Selective centralization is exemplified by two major reforms: taxation reform and central banking system reform. In 1994, the central government began to implement a new, federal-style taxation system. Before 1994, the center lacked its own institutions to collect taxes. All taxes from the provinces were collected by provincial governments first and then were divided between the center and the provinces through bargaining. Provincial governments were regarded as only part of the central authority or an extension of central power, rather than institutions with their own power base.

The new taxation system has had a major impact on the old system and changed the interaction between the center and the provinces. First of all, under the new taxation system, taxes were divided into three categories: central, local, and shared. Central taxes would go to the central coffers, local taxes would go to local budgets, and shared taxes were to be divided between the center and the provinces according to previously established agreements. Second, under the new system, tax administration is centralized. Instead of authorizing local tax offices to collect virtually all taxes, the center now collects taxes with its own institutions independent from the provinces. In other words, the center has established its own revenue collection agency—the national tax service.

Nevertheless, the new system also recognizes independent provincial power—that is, provincial authorities can collect several types of taxes without central interference. In other words, there are now two parallel and independent systems for tax administration: a national system for central taxes and a local one for local taxes. Shared taxes are collected by the central government first, then divided between the center and the provinces. This is the way that a federal taxation system works.

These institutional changes shifted fiscal power from the provinces to the center to a great degree. Total government revenue has increased quite dramatically. Annual revenue increases were about 20 to 30 billion yuan before 1993, but they totaled 85 billion yuan in 1994 and 122 billion yuan in 1996. Central collection as a proportion of total tax collection has increased from less than 30 percent to around 50 percent. If the locally collected revenues that local governments are obligated to remit to the central coffer are included, the central government's share reaches about two-thirds of total government revenue. Because the center collects and redistributes most revenues, the fiscal dependence of the provinces on the central government has increased substantially. Before 1994, the central government tended to rely heavily on such coastal provinces as Shanghai, Shandong, Zhejiang, Jiangsu, and Guangdong for revenue contribution. But now this trend has been reversed.[32]

Similar efforts have been made to reform China s central banking system. In terms of central-local relations, China's central banking system was previously quite decentralized. The central bank, the People's Bank, established branches in every province and assumed that all provincial branches would take orders from the center. But in reality, local branches were often exposed to political influence from local governments because their personnel were hired and their welfare was provided by local governments. This frequently led local branches to ignore orders from the central bank and subordinate themselves to local influences. Indeed, local branches of the central bank often became an effective instrument for local governments to promote local economic growth. Nonetheless, rapid local growth was achieved at the expense of the stability of the national economy.[33]

At the end of the 1980s, the central government introduced changes into the central banking system and decided that all directors of local branches should be appointed by the central bank rather than by provincial governments. The central government expected that all local branches could act in accordance with central directives and be independent from local political influence. Nevertheless, the change did not bring about the expected results. Local branches had developed their own independent institutional interests, and they preferred to use their resources to develop local economies because they could benefit greatly from local growth. This dissonance eventually led to the crisis of macroeconomic management in the mid-1990s.

Thus, after Zhu Rongji became China's new premier and a new government was established in March 1998, the central government declared a most daring measure to reform China's financial system. All provincial branches of the central bank would be eliminated, and a dozen or so cross-provincial or regional branches would be established in the years to come. The reform attempted to follow the U.S. model of federal-state relations by limiting the institutional ability of provincial governments to intervene in the central banking system.[34]

Compared with its position on economic reforms, however, the center has been hesitant to decentralize political power to the provinces, even though institutional reforms have devolved certain aspects of power to the provinces, as exemplified by the 1984 *nomenklatura* system reform.[35] Initially, the central leadership's priority was not the division of power between the center and the provinces but how to "play to the provinces" or, in Shirk's term, to promote local economic growth. The political legitimacy of the old guard could hardly be challenged, but rapid local economic growth strengthened provincial powers, especially in the coastal provinces. For the new leadership, the issue now is how central power over the provinces can be legitimated by sharing national power with the provinces, if not dividing power between the center and the provinces.

One major approach to power sharing is the recruitment of more provincial leaders into important national power institutions. The power of provincial leaders was reflected in the composition of the Eleventh, Twelfth, and Thirteenth Central Committees (the selectorate), where they formed the largest bloc. After the crackdown on the 1989 pro-democracy movement, the central government attempted to recentralize its power: in the Central Committee selected at the Fourteenth National Congress (1992), the leaders from various central bureaucracies formed the largest block (46.1 percent), and the power of local leaders declined (22.8 percent). But when the Fifteenth National Congress selected members of the Central Committee in 1997, the power of local leaders was strengthened (29 percent), whereas that of central bureaucracies experienced a relative decline (44.6 percent).[36]

More importantly, a leadership transition in terms of geographic distribution has occurred. During Mao's time, the majority of the party elites came from central China, especially Hunan, Jiangxi, and Hubei. Since 1978, party elites in the Central Committee increasingly hail from the eastern coastal areas, where rapid economic growth has been achieved. For example, Hebei, Jiangsu, Shandong, and Zhejiang provided nearly 45 percent of the Fourteenth Central Committee (1992), whereas cadres from Hunan, Jiangxi, and Hubei composed only about 9 percent of the party leadership.[37] According to one study, beginning with the Deng era, the political mobility of provincial leaders has been determined to a great degree by their economic performance. The worse the economic performance record, the more likely the provincial leader will be demoted. Provincial revenue contributions during the leaders' tenures have also played a role in determining the political mobility of provincial leaders.[38]

The passing of the old guard will also introduce changes into the pattern of reciprocity between top leaders and the selectorate. The institutionalization of reciprocity has become possible, meaning that the power of the selectorate is protected by institutions rather than the goodwill of the old guard. This development is exemplified in the changing process by which the selectorate selects top leaders. During the Thirteenth Party Congress in 1987, Zhao Ziyang introduced a system called "differential elections" into the selection of top leaders. Because the number of candidates exceeds the top positions available, "differential election" means limited competition among top leaders, which in turn gives the selectorate a say in choosing top leaders.

During the Thirteenth Party Congress, the center changed its election rules slightly in an attempt to reduce the power of the selectorate. A pre-election election was added. But even so, Chongqing mayor Xiao Yang, who was initially chosen as a candidate for the Politburo, was not selected in the final differential election. During the Fifteenth Party Congress, the center again slightly changed the election rules. Before the final election, elections were carried out separately by different candidate groups because it is easier for the center to monitor small-scale elections. The evolution of this election process implies that once the differential election system has been introduced, the center cannot eliminate it to centralize its power, though it is able to modify election rules to secure its leadership.

## CONCLUSION

It has been argued that federalism is the best and only true way to institutionalize central-local relations.[39] I believe, however, that even with the institutionalization of central-local relations in various aspects, central-local relations will remain de facto federalist rather than federalist.

To legitimize federalism is not an easy task because it stands in contradiction to the ideology of the CCP. The history of warlordism early this century links the concepts of chaos and federalism together.[40] Thus, for many, federalism will result in a divided China, or a divided China will become federalist. Given that federalism has been discussed in the context of Hong Kong, Taiwan, Tibet, Xinjiang, and other territorial issues, the ideological legitimacy of federalism becomes more complicated. Although these territorial factors have pulled China toward federalism, the ideological barrier has not been not easy to overcome. Indeed, for many within the CCP, federalism has been seen as an ideology that will divide China. As long as federalism cannot be legitimized ideologically, a transition from de facto to de jure federalism is unlikely to take place.

Practically speaking, the timing is not "right" for the legitimization of federalism per se. Compared to de facto federalism, the advantages of federalism are obvious. Although the institutionalization of the former is favorable for political stability since it reduces the tension between two actors, the institutionalization may also render the system rigid. Great diversities among the provinces exist, and achieving equality of rights among them (implicit in federalism) is not likely. Rich provinces prefer a weak center, whereas poor provinces prefer a strong one. The recent call for recentralization by poor provinces lacks any other good reason.

Without doubt, top leaders fear that federalism will lead a China with great diversity to disintegration. Also, because the leadership's priority is to promote economic development rather than to divide power between the center and the provinces and among provinces, the center must continuously adjust its relationship with the provinces and mediate the relations among the provinces in accordance with changing circumstances. The legitimization of federalism will render such continuous adjustment less likely. By contrast, de facto federalism has the advantage of flexibility.

The center needs the creative ambiguity implicit in de facto federalism. It requires, for the time being, not a clear-cut division between the center and the provinces but ambiguity between them. As long as the center maintains its relative power over the provinces, it will be able to adjust central-local relations. Nevertheless, in the long run, selective institutionalization of de facto federalism will lay an institutional foundation for China's de jure federalism.

## NOTES

The author would like to thank Nicholas R. Lardy, Edward Friedman, Pi-chao Chen, I. Yuan, Ryosei Kokubun, and others for their comments on this chapter. Special thanks go to Hung-mao Tien and Yun-han Chu for their help in revising the chapter.

1. The literature on central-local relations in post-Mao China continues to grow. An incomplete list would include the following: Goodman, *China's Provinces in Reform;* Goodman and Segal, *China Deconstructs;* Breslin, *China in the 1980s;* Jia and Lin, *Changing Central-Local Relations in China;* Huang, *Inflation and Investment Controls in China;* Shi, *Central-Local Relations in the People's Republic of China;* and Schroeder, *Regional Power in China.* The volume of works in Chinese is also enormous. For example, see Wang and Hu, *Zhongguo guojia nengli baogao;* Wu and Zheng, *Lun zhongyang difang guanxi;* Xin, *Daguo zhuhou.* For reviews of the study of central-local relations, see Chung, "Studies of Central-Provincial Relations in the People's Republic of China"; and Chung, "The Expanding Space of Provincial Politics and Development."

2. Jenner states, "The state, people and culture known in English as China are in a profound general crisis. . . . The very future of China as a unitary state is in question." See Jenner, *The Tyranny of History,* 1. Goldstone concurs: "We can expect a terminal crisis within the next 10 to 15 years." See Goldstone, "The Coming Chinese Collapse," 52. Finally, Bachman adds: "the dissolution of the People's Republic of China (PRC), not so much due to the late twentieth century equivalent of warlordism but by the growing irrelevance of the central leadership and the deliberate ignorance of the center's directives by some, if not all regions of the country. . . . A weak confederative Chinese state de facto is in the making." See Bachman, "China in 1993," 30.

3. See, for example, Shirk, *The Political Logic of Economic Reform in China.*

4. Ibid.

5. Pye, "China: Erratic State, Frustrated Society," 60. According to Pye, "although government in the People's Republic involves more concerted policy efforts, it is one of the great illusions of the day that Chinese authorities are as omnipotent as they pretend to be. In a host of fields, from tax collecting to controlling economic activities in Guangdong, Fujian and other dynamic provinces, central

authorities know that feigned compliance still reigns and that it is best not to attempt the impossible by demanding precise obedience. Sovereignty, after all, calls
for theatrical representation" (59–60).

6. Miles, *Legacy of Tiananmen.*

7. Goldstone, "The Coming Chinese Collapse," 41–46.

8. See March and Olsen, "The New Institutionalism."

9. For a discussion of the limits of state power, see Shue, *The Reach of the State.*

10. Donnithorne, *China's Economic System;* Lyons, *Economic Integration and Planning in Maoist China;* and Lieberthal and Oksenberg, *Policy Making in China.*

11. See Axelrod, *The Evolution of Cooperation*; Keohane, *After Hegemony* and "Reciprocity in International Relations."

12. On clientelist politics, see Walder, *Communist Neo-Traditionalism,* and Oi, *State and Peasant in Contemporary China*; on factional politics, see Nathan, "A Factionalism Model for CCP Politics," and Pye, *The Dynamics of Chinese Politics;* and on bureaucratic interest group politics, see Lampton, "Chinese Politics," and Lieberthal and Oksenberg, *Policy Making in China.*

13. Swidler, "Culture in Action."

14. Katzenstein, *Cultural Norms and National Security,* 19.

15. Axelrod, *The Evolution of Cooperation.*

16. For example, Bennett, *Decentralization, Local Governments, and Markets.*

17. Hasegawa, "The Connection Between Political and Economic Reform."

18. Zheng, *Institutional Change.* Scholars also call the Chinese style of decentralization "federalism, Chinese style" and show how it has promoted China's
rapid economic growth. See Montinola, Qian, and Weingast, "Federalism, Chinese
Style."

19. For a discussion of the concept of "areal democracy," see Maass, *Area and Power.*

20. Shirk, *The Political Logic of Economic Reform.*

21. Shirk says: "My starting point is the unusual idea that we can study policy-making in communist countries much as we would in non-communist countries: by looking at the patterns of competition among politicians who operate in an
institutionalized political setting. Scholars who study policy-making in democracies look at the way electoral, legislative, and executive powers and procedures
create political incentives for politicians and set the ground rules for collective decision-making. Different sets of institutional arrangements generate distinctive political incentives and decision-making rules and thereby lead to predictable policy
outcomes." Ibid., 7.

22. Ibid., esp. pt. 2.

23. For an excellent discussion, see Barry, *Sociologists, Economists and Democracy.*

24. "We are still a long way from a genuine model of communist political institutions and policy-making. In studying the Chinese reform, I often found myself unable to explain changes in policies by the institutional context and fell back
on ad hoc explanations instead." Shirk, *The Political Logic of Economic Reform,*
339.

25. Hirschman, "The Rise and Decline of Developing Economics."

26. Yang, "Reform and Restructuring of Central-Local Relations," 74.

27. Jenner, *The Tyranny of History.*

28. For example, Rawshi, "Economic and Social Foundations of Late Imperial Culture," 29–32; and Waston, "Rites or Beliefs."

29. Huang, "Why China Will Not Collapse."

30. See Hu, "Shengdiji ganbu yanzhong de dongxibu chaiju."

31. Zheng, "Power and Agenda."

32. For assessments of the 1994 taxation reform, see Wang, "China's 1994 Fiscal Reform"; and Hu, "Fenshuizhi: pingjia yu jianyi."

33. For discussions of the central banking system reform, see Bowles and White, *The Political Economy of China's Financial Reforms;* and Chen, *Zhongguo jinrong tizhi gaige.*

34. Interviews in the Development Research Center, the State Council, May 6, 1998.

35. Burns, *The Chinese Communist Party's Nomenklatura System;* and Burns, "Strengthening Central CCP Control of Leadership Selection."

36. From the author's database.

37. Zang, "The Fourteenth Central Committee of the CCP," 794.

38. Bo, *Chinese Provincial Leaders.*

39. For example, see Yan, *Lianbang Zhongguo gouxiang;* and Jin, *Lianbang zhi.*

40. For discussions, see Fitzgerald, "'Reports of My Death Have Been Greatly Exaggerated'"; and Waldron, "Warlordism Versus Federalism."

# ⊞ 14 ⊞

# Globalization, Legitimacy, and Post-Communism in China: A Nationalist Potential for Democracy, Prosperity, and Peace

## *Edward Friedman*

When considering the Fifteenth National Congress of the Chinese Communist Party in September 1997, what clues are offered on how new and powerful forces such as "globalization" or "postmodernism" interact with the difficult and painful transitions out of Leninist command economies to strengthen or weaken the likelihood, in China, of continuing high-speed growth and domestic tranquillity, and, in China's foreign policy, of regional peace? Do the combination of a weakened center and a heightened nationalism hold promise for a more democratic and peaceful future?

In tentatively sketching the different and contested futures that await this complex set of possibilities and processes, one can hope at least to clarify the major factors at work and the logic of the new age—that is, the reagents involved and the laws on how they mix. Much, however, remains necessarily contingent, from out-of-control international events to the domestic political strategies of both powerholders and challengers. Clarification is not prediction. Much that is crucial, however, can be clarified.

All ruling groups, whether their politics are democratic or authoritarian, must grapple with the imperatives of the new technologies that make for globalization. The world of information technology combines with the post–Bretton Woods trillions of dollars beyond the easy control of governments to foster an unexpected but inescapable logic of international finance. It is a volatile and perhaps a polarizing world. To deal successfully with financial globalization requires extraordinary discipline, openness, and flexibility. A politics premised on corrupt cronyism may place citizens and regime stability at risk.

In Beijing, ruling groups have looked to how Singapore dealt with this extraordinary world of finance without deepening the process of democratization. In general, ruling groups in China have tried to adapt to globalist

233

imperatives with minimal disruption to the system that privileges ruling groups. Consequently, despite the obvious weaknesses of South Korea's *chaebol* cronyism, decisionmakers in Beijing will not readily abandon the project of turning China's money-losing state-owned enterprises (SOEs) into world-class competitors à la Korea's Samsung. Powerful provincial leaders, who are well-represented in the party's Central Committee, insist that the state-subsidized firms in their regions not be abandoned as bankrupt but instead be turned into winners, as the United States supposedly did with Chrysler Motors. The Fifteenth Party Congress therefore continued Beijing's commitment to gradual and partial reform meant to conserve as much of the old order as possible. At the Fifteenth Party Congress, China's reformers were also conservatives.

Nonetheless, China must adapt in basic ways. As Michael Swaine shows in Chapter 7, if rulers in Beijing have the ambition of making China one of the few greatest powers on the planet—as they most certainly do—then they must conclude that they cannot allow the United States to extend its lead in the new high-tech generation of weaponry. In sum, whatever the will of supernationalistic powerholders in Zhongnanhai, there is a globalist technologic that is shaping the policy options open to China's seemingly—but misleadingly—all-powerful rulers. There is no gainsaying the impact of globalization on politics and policy.

## THE IMPETUS FOR CHANGE

An odd combination of arrogance and anxiety informs how China's powerholders have dealt with the challenges of postmodern globalization. A virtually natural arrogance arises from China's great economic achievement in the post-Mao era, the fastest economic growth over two decades, ever, anywhere on the planet. Such success could make any people arrogant. China's extraordinary achievement fosters a feeling that nothing can or should keep the twenty-first century from being China's century. The popular feeling is that it is about time that China again rise to the top of the heap.

Oddly, a similar feeling infused Japan in 1991, when it seemed that the strong yen was buying up the world and that Japanese travelers abroad could live like pashas (or like arrogant Americans of the 1960s?). In the early 1990s a slew of books were published in Japan about how the twenty-first century would be Japan's century, volumes with titles such as "The Asian Century" and "The Age of Japanization." Awash in self-adoration about being, gloriously, "the premier economic power of the world" in contrast, pitifully, to "American economic decline," the Japanese did not face up to their impending financial crisis.[1] Years of economic stagnation, political alienation, and societal fragmentation ensued. Similar stagnation, alienation, and fragmentation could not be absorbed so quietly among the much poorer, more impatient, and angrier Chinese. Consequently, how Beijing grapples with the remaining reform dilemmas imposed by the economic irrationalities of a Leninist command economy is a matter of both domestic and global moment. At issue are civil tranquillity and international peace, both life-and-death matters.

The question, then, is whether Beijing will face up to its explosive economic problems. The documents of the Fifteenth Party Congress suggested instead stalemate and more of the same. A core reason for Beijing's unwillingness truly to take on major changes is explored by Fred Teiwes in Chapter 5 of this book. Ruling groups in China are committed to unity and stability at almost any price. They have, since post-Mao reform began, pushed the most difficult issues—banking and SOE reform—to back burners, where they simmered and soon threatened to boil over, set afire, and burn down China's great progress to date.

## UNITY AND ORDER

The regime's priority of unity and stability, in fact, has legitimized it. Allowing economic dynamite to pile up was the inescapable cost of maintaining civil peace at any price. But if state revenues decline while the state takes on the burden of bad bank debt, if growth and foreign investment slow significantly while bankrupt state enterprises have their feeding tubes disconnected, then the authoritarian state may lose its ability to co-opt societal needs and demands. China will confront the classic dilemma of relative deprivation, as raised expectations are followed by real and serious declines that dash hopes and discredit those who raised them.

Three forms of regime legitimization are alive in China: nationalism, performance, and Hobbesianism, with all threatened by globalization. Nationalistic legitimization has received the most public attention, a "specter of a possible Chinese national chauvinism, a frightening mix of Confucian and Marxian anti-individualism, statism, irredentism, and xenophobia."[2] Through the Fifteenth Party Congress, Beijing had been promoting anti-Americanism to the Chinese people, although anti-Japanese nationalism, in large part actually aimed toward China's unpopular former rulers, was far more pervasive. Either way, global events from 1996 to 1998 sobered ruling groups and, at least momentarily, turned them against roiling up the rages of nationalism. In 1998 they tamped down antiforeign nationalism. That choice enhances the importance of other forms of legitimization. Nonetheless, even though there is no escape from pressing economic problems, the chauvinist discourse is so close to being hegemonic, and conservative political forces are so entrenched, that one should expect that, in the near future as in the recent past, optimism about a political turn in Beijing toward openness and reconciliation is likely to prove an illusion.

In short, globalization compels rulers of China's Leninist dictatorship into making choices they dislike. All over the Asia-Pacific region, nations responded negatively to the People's Republic of China's (PRC's) threatening military exercises in March 1996 just off Taiwan's two great port cities. China's neighbors then sought to woo and welcome the U.S. military. Beijing's military chauvinism turned out to be counterproductive for China's great power ambitions, however, and in 1997–1998, Beijing's rulers backed away from expansive chauvinism.

The self-destructive character of narrow nationalism reverberated to Beijing again during the 1997–1998 Asian financial crisis. Good relations with the international financial community, particularly the United States, suddenly seemed a prerequisite for continuous high Chinese growth. Thus, China's new goal became gaining a reputation as a respected and powerful player in this crucial arena. China's dignity has been sullied when international bodies such as the International Labour Organization bar China from leadership positions because it is a dictatorship. Whatever they might say, Chinese leaders are well aware that repressive practices and human rights violations detract from their country's international stature. China wants to be respected, and Chinese rulers seek the highest global standing. National dignity can even propel them toward democracy.

During the 1997–1998 financial crisis, leaders in Beijing worried about being out-competed by Japan, Taiwan, and the United States. In wooing wounded Asian neighbors, Beijing suspected the worst (i.e., anti-Beijing) motives, especially from Taiwan, in their efforts to bail out suffering Asian countries. Beijing's chauvinist invective made it seem, to some, the enemy of economic resurgence in places such as Indonesia, Thailand, and Malaysia, even while International Monetary Fund (IMF) discipline was popularly condemned as a U.S. plot.

In short, globalization presents rulers in Beijing with the Hobson's choice of acting responsibly or acting chauvinistically. It is not obvious how ruling groups will zig or zag given the difficult and dangerous international environment, since Beijing's leaders want the benefits of both strong nationalism and global economic participation. But in China's up-and-coming regions, indications are that local powerholders prefer responsibility and rapid growth over irresponsibility, provocative nativism, and expansive militarism. Incorporated regionalism and constitutional federalism, therefore, would indicate that China is moving in the direction of supporting regional peace. Thus, as with national dignity, mentioned above, and other factors to be sketched below, the imperatives of growth and performance legitimacy can propel China toward a democratic opening.

Regional powerholders tend to be the beneficiaries of a second kind of legitimacy in China, performance legitimacy. People tend to equate the center with self-serving nepotism and the locale with at least some potential for power in the hands of people who care about the material well-being of their own kind of people. Devolution and development can therefore sound synonymous. Thus, despite Beijing's many policies that have facilitated rapid wealth expansion, the central regime is not significantly the more legitimate for it.

And yet the most brutally corrupt levels of governance actually tend to be the local ones. Local tyrants can long go unrestrained and, regardless of their cruelty, stand unaccountable. Reports of riots supposedly caused by the center's neglect of pensioners or producers are in fact usually an eruption of outrage at local despots whom locals view as ripoff artists. There is, actually, all over China, an amazing level of tolerance toward screw-ups from the center because it is seen to shoulder awesomely difficult responsibilities. The demand for democracy, for accountable rulers who cannot arbitrarily mistreat citizens, is strongest at the local level, where the authoritarian state seems most inhuman. This suggests that an opening to democratization can be legitimate in China if the breakthrough is local and real, without delivering full, national democracy all at once.

In fact, the work committee reports presented to elders at Beidaihe in August 1997 in preparation for the Fifteenth Party Congress are said to have supported just such a real expansion of local-level democracy. Rumor has it, however, that elders quashed a democratic project of the next generation, at least temporarily. Should it become clear that popular elections can advance the goal of unity and order, then, I would suggest, a deepening of democratization can move higher on China's national political agenda in the not-too-distant future.

These popular preferences for unity and order that can be premised on gradual democratization also remind us that Beijing's basic legitimacy is neither nationalistic nor performance-based, but Hobbesian. The central government receives credit for delivering civil peace and civil order. To be sure, there actually is much violence and disorder in China. Often, the police are close to useless, and people are palpably afraid that order could break down into a war of all against all, as presaged by a spread of gangs, crime, and brutal revenge.

The Chinese fear the uncontrolled situation in Rwanda and Burundi. Consequently, all other alternatives to the current order can seem qualitatively worse than the evils now in power that deliver Hobbesian peace, a civil normality that allows people to take control of their own destiny and to plan, work, and save for a better future. This powerful Hobbesian legitimacy is often overlooked by analysts who discover a lack of performance legitimacy for Beijing and then note a panicky Beijing quest for nationalistic legitimacy. In the immediate post-Mao era, Beijing actually was solidly legitimate in a Hobbesian way. And Hobbesian legitimacy is a most powerful form of legitimacy.

But because central ruling groups benefit so much from Hobbesian legitimacy, they have not faced up to the need for thorough economic reforms that could end up turning huge numbers of workers into a massive and potentially volatile army of the unemployed. Not to act to end the remaining economic irrationalities of the command economy is to let more dynamite pile up. To act, however, is to risk a near-term explosion. As nations in Southeast Asia scapegoat residents of Chinese ancestry for economic turmoil, so may the Chinese scapegoat what they consider alien—which can even include rulers who cause great economic hardship or who are perceived to have betrayed the people or served foreign interests. Understandably, ruling groups feel caught on the horns of a painful dilemma. It is no wonder that political forces at the Fifteenth Party Congress were stalemated. The old Leninist system has left behind unbelievably difficult and pressing problems.

Indeed, I was in Beijing in August 1997 while leaders at Beidaihe prepared for the September Congress. In shuttling back and forth between people and institutions on differing sides of the issues, I sensed no new life-saving initiatives but only momentary victory for the policies of the status quo, taken as the Deng Xiaoping heritage: moderate economic reform, relative social openness, and political repression.[3]

In large part, the unforeseen forces of post-Communism are at work here. Expectations of an easy transition to a flourishing and popular market-oriented economy built from the residue of a Leninist command economy have been frustrated and deflected all around the world—so, too, in China. The unexpected legacies of the old system turned out to produce much that clogs and blocks a smooth transition. In trying to make the transition, leaders discover negative things about the Communist system that often previously were virtually invisible. It has been extraordinarily difficult to move toward a next stage, one beyond the trammels of the command economy. The old economic irrationalities linger and gum up the works, leaving each Leninist society to struggle with an unexpectedly difficult legacy, the harsh realities of post-Communism. No political analyst or economist, no matter whether an advocate of gradualism or shock therapy, has come up with policies that preclude the protracted and potentially destabilizing pains of this process.

This need to grapple with prolonged pain while remaining legitimate has made democratization a politically palatable option for some. Democracy facilitates a nationwide political dialogue, setting a national agenda that legitimizes a particular sharing of the pain as "fair." Democracy can soothe and co-opt potential troublemakers, increasing the likelihood that peace and stability will continue to mark the prolonged transition. The backlash against false optimism both at the national and regional levels when pains persist, therefore, cannot help but create the policy option of democratization as the better way to work through the drawn-out difficulties of economic change.

Indeed, it seems that since the Fifteenth Party Congress, a commitment to a "first stage of socialism" has rationalized a promotion of "the new democracy." A gradual opening in 1997–1998 could widen should the proponents of reform prove successful in purging the burdensome remnants of the old system. But this has never been easy anywhere. Premier Zhu Rongji has a tough road ahead. Therefore, if post-Communist reform produces more dislocation than expected or promised, one cannot write off altogether a resurgence of chauvinistic forces, who will scapegoat reformers as the alien. It is all too believable that only foreign forces could cause Chinese such pain. Such witch-hunting is a worldwide phenomenon in an age in which post-Communism is entangled with the new globalization. Post-Communist dilemmas readily unleash nasty political dynamics. Prospects for red-brown alliances flourish wherever command economy irrationalities are confronted, from India to Yugoslavia. Even democratization will not destroy this evil political genie now that it is out of the bottle.

In calling attention to the shaping power of the globalization combined with post-Communism, I do not mean to slight the importance of the internal particulars still being deciphered by Kremlinology, especially for political actors in China. To build a coalition capable of a successful transition requires knowing who one's friends are. In the opaque secrecy of the Leninist system, even players can make ill-conceived moves because of a lack of information. In the late 1960s and early 1970s in Canton, former Red Guard leaders were divided into two large factions. Both erroneously saw the struggle in Beijing after the 1968–1969 crushing of the Cultural Revolution's vigilante mass movements, the dispersal of rampaging young activists to the countryside, and the beginnings of restoring some economic rationality, as overwhelming proof of victories for capitalist roaders in the anti-Mao faction of red bureaucrats headed by Premier Zhou Enlai. The amateur Kremlinologists in Guangzhou could not imagine that the purported great leader of the anticapitalist crusade, Mao himself, in fact had chosen this reformist direction.[4] And those in the region, facing an opaque political system, could not imagine a proper political strategy. The transparent openness attendant to a democratic breakthrough might enhance the likelihood of forming and sustaining a broad, moderate coalition to guide China peacefully through the dangerous shoals and roiling waters that still lie ahead. Democracy is, and can come to seem to be, the friend of stability and normality.

There is no guarantee that China's rulers will succeed in overcoming the problems of post-Communism. If the reformers fail, financial globalization could disrupt growth and unleash a backlash that would greatly strengthen nativist, antireform forces. Among ruling groups in Beijing, options are shaped by a need for legitimacy and a desire to hold on to power in a global context that throws nations all over the planet hither and yon. Thus, it is all too easy to put off painful reforms. In 1997 Asian political leaders, happily aware that they sat on U.S.$700 billion of reserves and running seemingly protected national financial systems, did not worry much about the trillions of dollars that moved daily in global financial markets. Yet, it turned out that even currencies that were not freely convertible could be battered by global finance. No one at Beidaihe preparing for the Fifteenth Party Congress could imagine the financial turmoil that was about to engulf Asia. A desire for domestic gradualism can prove a weak reed from which to construct a strong new political-economic edifice during an international typhoon.

## NATIONALISM

It is much too easy, when unexpected and unfair pain spreads, to mobilize nativist sentiments by blaming alien financial forces for popular suffering and by placing them in the context of out-of-control globalization. Insightful analyses of Chinese nationalism by superb scholars such as Barry Sautman and John Fitzgerald further spotlight the rise of racist nationalism promoted in post-Mao China.[5] I have heard Chinese call this tendency "militarily expansionistic fascism," à la Japan in the 1930s. But using the word "fascism" is too much like name calling, too little like an analytical category.

The political passion at issue is much akin to the poisoned tendency that Michael Swaine labels "populist authoritarianism" in Chapter 7. Chinese who support such tendencies zero in on Taiwan's currency devaluation in 1997 and scapegoat Taiwan for the 1997–1998 Asian financial turmoil. In addition, the IMF-promoted conditions for bailouts are perceived as a U.S. plot to destroy the Asian statist agencies that are considered the source of Asia's rise, so that the United States can dominate the world. Awareness of the strength of such chauvinism even in such democratizing former state-leveraged economies as India and South Korea suggests that militaristic nationalism, as against a Chechnya or a Bosnia, remains potent in post-Communism. Likewise, it is powerful in China. Fitzgerald and Sautman are correct that some in Beijing have helped sow poisoned seeds of arrogant, hegemonic, racist nativism, which may wreak havoc for quite a while.

Once such germs and genies are in the political atmosphere, they cannot readily be squeezed back into the bottle anywhere in the world, including the United States and Japan. In general, Chinese are patriotic and proud about recent achievements. This development is natural and virtually inevitable. But post-Mao rulers have been infusing this ordinary national-ism with a racist content. Whereas Mao forbade the worship of the Yellow Emperor, post-Mao rulers promoted it. Whereas Mao thought the ancient rulers Yao, Shun, and Yu mythical, post-Mao rulers promoted belief in China as a pure people, one blood-vein of history going back at least to the Xia, a dynasty treated by most archeologists outside China as mythical. China's State Councilor Song Jian has run a well-funded effort to get archeologists to produce data to support the historicity of the Xia as part of a 5,000- or 6,000-year-old monist, racial Chinese continuity. It is this dan-gerously expansionist nasty racism that increasingly informs much of China's natural national pride. The reactionary race project may be doing far better in China than the similar project pushed by far-right racist coun-terparts in the United States or Japan.

Given the upsetting ills that post-Communist reform is virtually guar-anteed to deliver, there is much fertile soil on which to grow poisoned shoots of nativism that blame aliens for Chinese suffering. However much such scapegoating might strike some as paranoid fantasy, it would be wrong to underestimate the popular reception such anti-Americanism (as well as anti-Japanese and generally xenophobic sentiment) receives. This kind of nationalism certainly is no more merely a local, passing paranoid fantasy about foreign enemies out to get China than the nationalism of the populist left and the populist right in the United States, which imagine the IMF and globalization as an anti-American plot. There is rich loam in post-Communist China for nurturing an expansive red-brown alliance in an age of globalization, to be fertilized if and when Chinese people begin to feel the pinch of the needed reforms that the regime has for so long put off. The rise of a well-meaning Zhu Rongji to the premiership in the wake of the Fifteenth Party Congress could mean that most difficult reforms finally are about to be implemented in China. One can only hope that the Zhu era turns out very differently than the Weimar era in Germany.

Premier Zhu was given great credit by Asian elites for not devaluing China's currency in 1997–1998, for not carrying out a self interested act that could have intensified the economic crunch throughout Asia. Zhu and China are thereby seen as uniquely responsible. His policies enhance the likelihood that China will seem the unstoppable twenty-first-century Asian hegemon, whereas Japan, however unfairly, is perceived as paralyzed and leaderless, and the United States, however inaccurately, as unreliable and distant from Asia. Whatever the true value of these views of Japan and the United States, they are widespread in Asia. They further viewpoints help-ful to the nationalistic legitimacy of all-out reform in China and to the image of China as the responsible leader for all of Asia. At the same time, however, this popular legitimacy can serve the cause of a political opening toward democracy, a political system devolving more authority to the regions.

## MOVING AWAY FROM THE CENTER

Given the legitimacy (in Beijing) of muddling through post-Communism as a guarantor of Hobbesian social peace, why are federalist projects not on the immediate political agenda? That is, why are Chinese political leaders not more attracted to a Chinese version of the European Union? In looking for solutions to post-Communist problems in large, centralized institutions in Korea and authoritarian practices in Singapore, some of the better practices have been ignored.

Incantations of Deng Xiaoping Theory delay action on needed, market-oriented, decentralizing institutional reform, probably in part because federalism seems too identified with feudalism, warlordism, backwardness, and chaos. Yet failing to empower regions and restructure their links to the center may intensify the weight of cronyist corruption that could vitiate so much of the great achievement of post-Mao economic reform. Political inaction could strengthen localist identities and mistrust of the center so much that China might one day break apart. Restructuring the relation of center and region is a pressing matter all over the world. Once again, political democratization can hope to preserve civil tranquillity.

With globalization in the post–Bretton Woods era, political responsibility has tended to move to the regions because the old centers no longer can readily deliver growth with equity. Yet the center is vital to economic success. Only the center can negotiate and manage mutually beneficial international economic interchange. The task of the center in maintaining the currency, upgrading skills and infrastructure, and nurturing high technologies is ever more crucial. Globalization does not signify the end of the nation-state, as some pundits wrongly contend.

But everywhere—Quebec, Lombard, Scotland, Sao Paulo—regional politico-cultural imperatives also have to be satisfied. Chinese democrats, thinking and acting in a confederationist way, can legitimately attract even Taiwan. All over China, despite the reactionary center's promotion of narrow and insular race consciousness, regional identities are experienced as cross-border identities, remembering and imagining the greatness that was China and can again be China in terms of cross-border origins and the glories of international openness and historical exchanges. Such consciousness grows both in the hinterland and on the coast, in Xian and in Guangzhou. It is a reminder that a federalist or confederationist notion of Chineseness could better serve future Chinese greatness than would purist, centrist racism. The political choices confronting China are wide open and so crucial. The political contest in China is far more open than a superficial reading of the documents of the Fifteenth Party Congress as stagnant stalemate might suggest.

The point, then, is not that the extraordinary nationalist passions that have surged in China since 1992 will disappear, but that patriotic emotions can also be energized by identities that promise a peaceful and prosperous future in the Asia-Pacific region. A globalization that is not out of control and destructive, one that is managed in some larger mutual interest (a win-win game) would best serve the purposes of a Chinese political opening in this happier direction. But that transformed globalization requires far more innovation than the major powers seem capable of mustering. Without that transformation, domestic dynamite could continue to pile up in China and elsewhere.

Analysts must study China not just as Beijing but also with an eye toward central-local relations.[6] A major problem is brewing from the way rural-urban (that is, poor-rich) tensions interact with the growing ranks of the unemployed and pensioners. In Jilin province, for example, 30 percent of the urban work-force is said to be in difficulty. Will major cities, threatened by a need to fund a growing number of those no longer working because state enterprises are bankrupt, see an invasion of poor peasants as a plague? Will they view them as a threat to law and order, a threat to jobs for our own people, a threat to what is right and fair? How would a law-and-order military, which also historically identifies national liberation with the sacrifice of poor peasant martyrs, respond to such a conflict?

In other words, the probable answer to crafting a political path out of China's dilemmas is largely regional. That is, different regions will respond quite differently to the challenges ahead. A regional approach is worth trying to clarify how these forces might line up or join together, even though the likelihood is that much in regional tensions and alliances is necessarily hidden from view. Regionalism, after all, is the other side of globalization, not a separate and arbitrary topic. In the logic of post-modernity are tendencies that push power from the national center to the global level and also to the local level.

Numerous excellent analysts have been studying regional realities and region-center relations in China in recent years because the topics are so manifestly decisive for China's future. Arthur Waldron, for one, expects "lines of cleavage to be cultural and linguistic: the Mandarin-speaking north; the area around Shanghai; the Hong Kong–Guangzhou region; Taiwan and Fujian; and the deep-inland region of Sichuan and the southwest." He boldly predicts that "Hong Kong will become the effective capital of the south and Shanghai the capital of the center; Beijing will remain the capital of the north. The result, if all goes well, will be the 'federalism' that Chinese reformers have long advocated. If things go badly, there will be civil war."[7]

Although my crystal ball is no clearer than any other, I am suspicious about predictions of regional splits that do not focus on the tensions and angers that will appear in areas such as the rust-belt of China's northeast when state subsidies are withdrawn. One major divide occurs between those regions with money-losing SOEs that profit from the center's dole and money-earning, globally oriented regions whose profits subsidize the command economy losers in the state-subsidized region. The successes, the coastal regions, have far fewer redundant state employees to subsidize and are far more welcoming of an influx of poor migrants who are the hardest of workers and who would earn far less back home.

The rust-belt, money-losing, coal-mining Shanbei region, centered on cities such as Xian and Taiyuan, strikes me as most implosive, fearful of its own poor peasants fleeing to urban areas and adding to the hardship of redundant state enterprise workers. (The northeast lacks a miserably poor, densely populated countryside.) But the people of the angry suffering region could scapegoat the coast or the south as unfairly privileged, rather than seeing themselves as yesterday's privileged beneficiaries of economically irrational Mao-era policies.

Would the military be persuaded that Mao is to blame? Or would it interpret reform-era tensions and inescapable pains as the result of the reforms themselves, of a favoring of the regionally undeserving, of accepting alien ways? Regionalism and racism, in their accumulation of angers, can facilitate national corrosion and chaos. The outcome of the interplay of complex forces is not obvious. In the north China plain, especially the old base areas of the Huabei region, networks of advancement seem built on old military ties. Would downsizing, caused by a need to end the financial hemorrhage of post-Communism, plus abandoning the *chaebol* option for SOEs, be experienced as a spur to a backlash of populist authoritarianism, red-brown alliance, prestige diplomacy, fascism, or whatever one would call such an antireform thrust? No region wants to be a loser.

All-out reform confronts sensitive political forces. Sadly, persuasive answers to such big, future-oriented questions about how the regions will line up are not readily available in the scholarly literature. Some see a division among the coast, center, and far west. Others focus on different international ties, to northeastern Asia, Central Asia, Southeast Asia, and so on. The data are ambiguous and obscure. But in general, militaries that are deeply involved in productive enterprises are difficult to talk back into the barracks. Instead, entrepreneurs in each region try to offer regional militaries stakes in the regional economies. This is crucial, since the relationship among the economic regions can be full of mistrust, anger, and finger-pointing. A regional devolution of power that decreases the need for all parts to strike fair bargains on every issue can serve the cause of domestic tranquillity. Again, decentralization in a democratic direction cannot help but reappear high on a Chinese political agenda where Hobbesian legitimacy takes priority.

## CONCLUSION

As Lowell Dittmer explains in Chapter 3, election for the Central Committee already pays close attention to issues of regional representation.[8] Budget deals are already being struck with the provinces. Compelled to act on the imperatives of globalization and to transcend the pains of post-Communism, mere path dependency seems already to hold the promise of legalizing a grand bargain that could include an opening to democracy in which large amounts of power devolve to the regions, a development that need not compromise Taiwan's autonomy.

What is most amazing in the flux of today's globalized world is how rapidly the impossible becomes the inevitable. Before the Fifteenth Party Congress, chauvinistic nationalism in China had made democratization feel like treason. That is, democratization seemed the ideology of Taiwanese, imagined as separatists. Yet soon after the Fifteenth Party Congress, in the context of the Asian financial turmoil that made an unaccountable cronyist economy seem a major source of economic decline, almost instantaneously, accountability became a more popular issue, one that legitimates a freer media and makes corrupt leaders answerable to a tax-paying citizenry.[9]

In addition, is the good governance attendant on political accountability part of what it takes to woo and hold long-term foreign direct investment in this age of globalization? Can the social stability of safety nets, in the form of large amounts of tax funds for pensions, retraining, and unemployment, be raised and seem fair without making representatives of affected groups party to a transparent decisionmaking process? These questions lead analysts to speculate whether village elections and National People's Congress assertiveness are harbingers of some larger change in center-local relations.[10] This set of forces makes it possible that the logic of the economically successful regions, such as the south and the coast, will prevail in China. These rapidly rising regions, which fill the center's treasury, would insist on balancing budgets and ending subsidies as the only way to a fiscal responsibility that wins foreign direct investment. Such a tendency could infuse China's nationalism with a more open and peaceful promise.

It is wrong to think of Chinese nationalism as inherently a one-dimensional, chauvinistic, and unchanging essence. Globalization can facilitate a legitimate nationalism that delivers not only the economic goods but also tranquillity at home and abroad and that is in harmony with powerful regional identities. This is not a prediction. The dangers in the explosive mix of globalization, post-Communism, and a need for new legitimacy are obvious to all. But the potential negatives should not obscure from the view of policy analysts how a happier future is also possible.

Already the regions run their own international economic policies. It could soon seem that federalism is not a chaos-oriented policy of prolonging backwardness but a living reality and that federalist nationalist projects may have a way to hold people's allegiance and deliver a materially better standard of living. Again, this is not a prediction. Too much, as the sudden 1997–1998 Asian financial turmoil indicates, is contingent. Tocqueville long ago warned that it is only after the fact that revolution seems inevitable. It always comes as a surprise. We should not be surprised, however, that the apparent stalemate of the Fifteenth Party Congress, occurring in the context of unprecedented globalization, a potent Hobbesian legitimacy, and the painful dilemmas of a post-Communist devolution of power, also holds a happier possibility among its contested projects, a possibility of success for those regions whose political identity promises political reform for China and peace and prosperity for the region.

## NOTES

1. Field, *In the Realm of a Dying Emperor,* 245, 278.
2. Nathan, *China's Transition,* 230.
3. Su, "The Prospects for Democratization in China," 52–56.
4. Wang, "Guanyu Li Yizhe sichao," 17–19.
5. Sautman, "Myths of Descent," 75–95; Fitzgerald, *Awakening China.*
6. See Chung, "Studies of Central-Provincial Relations," 487–508.
7. Waldron, "The End of Communism," 46–47.
8. See also Miller, "Preparing for Change," 12.
9. "Evolution or Revolution?" *Far Eastern Economic Review,* February 5, 1998, 5.
10. Feinerman, "Give and Take," 16–23.

# Appendix:
# Fifteenth Party Congress
# Politburo Members

## Politburo Standing Committee Members (in rank order)

- Jiang Zemin (71): CCP general secretary; head of leading group on foreign affairs; chairman of the Central Military Commission; president of the PRC
- Li Peng (69): chairman of the NPC Standing Committee
- Zhu Rongji (69): premier of the State Council; head of the leading group on financial and economic work
- Li Ruihuan (63): chairman of the Chinese People's Political Consultative Conference
- Hu Jintao (55): member, Central Party Secretariat; in charge of organizational affairs; president of Central Party School
- Wei Jianxing (66): chairman of the Central Discipline Inspection Commission; member, Central Party Secretariat; in charge of security affairs
- Li Lanqing (65): vice premier of the State Council, in charge of foreign trade and investment

## Politburo Members (in alphabetical order):

- Chi Haotian (68): vice chairman of the Central Military Commission; minister of national defense
- Ding Guangen (68): member, Central Party Secretariat; head of the leading group on thought and propaganda work
- Huang Ju (59): party secretary of Shanghai
- Jia Qinglin (57): party secretary of Beijing
- Jiang Chunyun (67): vice premier of the State Council; head of the leading group on agriculture

- Li Changchun (53): party secretary of Guangdong Province
- Li Tieying (61): chairman of the Commission for Restructuring the Economy; head of the Chinese Academy of Social Sciences
- Luo Gan (62): member, Central Party Secretariat; deputy head of the Central Organization Commission; state councilor without portfolio
- Qian Qichen (69): vice premier of the State Council; deputy head of the leading group on foreign affairs
- Tian Jiyun (68): vice chairman of the National People's Congress Standing Committee
- Wen Jiabao (55): member, Central Party Secretariat; vice premier of State Council; general secretary, leading group on financial and economic work
- Wu Bangguo (56): vice premier of the State Council, deputy head of the leading group on financial and economic work; in charge of SOE reform
- Wu Guanzheng (59): party secretary of Shandong Province
- Xie Fei (65): (former) party secretary of Guangdong Province; currently without portfolio
- Zhang Wannian (69): vice chairman of the Central Military Commission; member, Central Party Secretariat

## Politburo Alternates

- Wu Yi (58): minister of Foreign Trade and Economic Relations; the only woman on the Politburo
- Zeng Qinghong (58): director of the Central Committee General Office; member, Central Party Secretariat

# Acronyms

| | |
|---|---|
| ABM | antiballistic missile |
| AEW | airborne early warning |
| APEC | Asia-Pacific Economic Cooperation |
| ARATS | Association for Relations Across the Taiwan Strait |
| ARF | ASEAN Regional Forum |
| ASEAN | Association of Southeast Asian Nations |
| BMD | ballistic-missile defense |
| CC | Central Committee |
| CCP | Chinese Communist Party |
| CDIC | Central Discipline Inspection Committee |
| CMC | Central Military Commission |
| DPP | Democratic Progressive Party |
| FALSG | Foreign Affairs Leading Small Group |
| GDP | gross domestic product |
| GNP | gross national product |
| ICBM | intercontinental ballistic missile |
| IMF | International Monetary Fund |
| KMT | Kuomintang |
| MIRV | multiple independent reentry vehicle |
| NPC | National People's Congress |
| PBSC | Politburo Standing Committee |
| PLA | People's Liberation Army |
| PLAAF | People's Liberation Army Air Force |
| PLAN | People's Liberation Army Navy |
| PRC | People's Republic of China |
| ROC | Republic of China |
| SAR | Special Autonomous Region |

| | |
|---|---|
| SEF | Straits Exchange Foundation |
| SOE | state-owned enterprise |
| TALSG | Taiwan Affairs Leading Small Group |
| TMD | theater missile defense |
| TRA | Taiwan Relations Act |

# Bibliography

Allen, Kenneth, Glenn Krumel, and Jonathan D. Pollack. *China's Air Force Enters the 21st Century.* Santa Monica, CA: RAND/Project Air Force, 1995.

Anonymous (Students of Beijing Shifan Daxue). "Xiagang zhigong zhuangkuang diaocha" (Inquiry on the situation of laid-off employees and workers). *Jingji yanjiu ziliao* (Peking), no. 8 (1997): 3–10.

"Army Paper on 'New Security Concept.'" *Beijing Jiefangjun Bao,* FBIS-CHI-98-015, January 5, 1998.

Arnett, Eric. "Military Technology: The Case of China." *SIPRI Yearbook 1995: Armaments, Disarmament and International Security.* Oxford: Oxford University Press, 1995.

Austin, Greg. *China's Ocean Frontier: International Law, Military Force and Economic Development.* Sydney: Allen and Unwin, 1998.

———. "The Strategic Implications of China's Public Order Crisis." *Survival* 37, no. 2 (1995): 7–23.

Axelrod, Robert. *The Evolution of Cooperation.* New York: Basic Books, 1984.

Bachman, David. "China in 1993: Dissolution, Frenzy, and/or Breakthrough?" *Asian Survey* 34, no. 1 (January 1994): 30–40.

———. "The Limits on Leadership in China." *Asian Survey* 32, no. 11 (November 1992): 1046–1062.

———. "Structure and Process in the Making of Chinese Foreign Policy." In Samuel S. Kim, ed., *China and the World.* 4th ed. Boulder, CO: Westview Press, 1998.

———. "Succession, Consolidation, and Transition in China's Future." *Journal of Northeast Asian Studies* 15, no. 1 (Spring 1996): 89–106.

———. "Succession Politics and China's Future." *Journal of International Affairs* 49, no. 2 (Winter 1996): 370–389.

Barme, Geremie R. *Shades of Mao: The Posthumous Cult of the Great Leader.* Armonk, NY: M. E. Sharpe, 1996.

Barry, Brian. *Sociologists, Economists and Democracy.* Chicago: University of Chicago Press, 1978.

Baum, Richard. *Burying Mao: Chinese Politics in the Age of Deng Xiaoping.* Princeton, NJ: Princeton University Press, 1994.

————. "China After Deng: Ten Scenarios in Search of Reality." *The China Quarterly*, no. 145 (March 1996): 153–175. *The China Quarterly*.

————. "The Fifteenth National Party Congress: Jiang Takes Command?" *The China Quarterly*, no. 153 (March 1998): 141–156.

Becker, Jasper. *Hungry Ghosts: China's Secret Famine*. London: John Murray, 1996.

Béja, Jean-Philippe, and Michel Bonnin. "La Chine ou la crise comme mode d'exercice du pouvoir" (China, or crisis as a mode of exercising power). In P. Kende, eds., *Le système communiste: Un monde en expansion*. Paris, Economica, 1982.

Bennett, Robert J., ed. *Decentralization, Local Governments, and Markets*. Oxford: Clarendon Press, 1990.

Bernstein, Richard, and Ross Munro. *The Coming Conflict with China*. New York: Alfred A. Knopf, 1997.

Bernstein, Thomas. "In Quest of Voice: China's Farmers and Prospects for Political Liberalization." Paper for the University Seminar on Modern China, Columbia University, February 10, 1993.

Bitzinger, Richard A., and Bates Gill. "Gearing Up for High-Tech Warfare? Chinese and Taiwanese Defense Modernization and Implications for Military Confrontation Across the Taiwan Strait, 1995–2005." Center for Strategic and Budgetary Assessments, Washington, DC, February 1996.

Bo, Zhiyue. *Chinese Provincial Leaders: Economic Performance and Political Mobility*. Ph.D. diss., Department of Political Science, University of Chicago, 1995.

Bowles, Paul, and Gordon White. *The Political Economy of China's Financial Reforms: Finance in Late Development*. Boulder, CO: Westview Press, 1993.

Breslin, Shaun Gerard. *China in the 1980s: Center-Province Relations in a Reforming Socialist State*. London: Macmillan, 1996.

Broadman, Harry. *Meeting the Challenge of Enterprise Reform*. Discussion paper no. 283. Washington, DC: World Bank, April 1995.

Brosseau, Maurice, eds. *China Review: 1996*. Hong Kong: Chinese University Press, 1997.

Burns, John, ed. *The Chinese Communist Party's Nomenklatura System*. Armonk, NY: M. E. Sharpe, 1989.

————. "Strengthening Central CCP Control of Leadership Selection: The 1990 Nomenklatura." *China Quarterly*, no. 138 (June 1994): 458–491.

Chan, Anita. "The Challenge to the Social Fabric." In David S. G. Goodman and Gerald Segal, eds., *China at Forty: Mid-Life Crisis?* Oxford: Clarendon Press, 1989.

————. "Revolution or Corporatism? Workers and Trade Unions in Post-Mao China." *Australian Journal of Chinese Affairs*, no. 29 (January 1993).

Chen, Yuan. *Zhongguo jinrong tizhi gaige* (Reform in China's financial system). Beijing: Zhongguo caizheng jingji chubanshe, 1994.

Cheng, J. Chester, ed. *The Politics of the Chinese Red Army: A Translation of the Bulletin of Activities of the People's Liberation Army*. Stanford: Hoover Institution Publications, 1966.

Cheung, Tai Ming. "China's Entrepreneurial Army." In C. Dennison Lane, ed., *Chinese Military Modernization*. Washington, DC: AEI Press, 1996.

————. "The Chinese Army's New Marching Orders: Winning on the Economic Battlefield." In Jorn Brommelhorster and John Frankenstein, eds., *Mixed Motives, Uncertain Outcomes: Defense Conversion in China*. Boulder, CO: Lynne Rienner, 1997.

*China Journal,* no. 34 (July 1995): 1–205.

"China: Roundup Comparing New Security Concepts." *Beijing China Radio International* (FBIS-CHI-98-001) (1 January 1998).

Chinese Banking Society. *Almanac of China's Banking and Finance 1986.* Beijing: China Financial Publishing House, 1996.

Chu, Yun-han. "The Political Economy of Taiwan's Mainland Policy." *Journal of Contemporary China* 15 (July 1997): 229–257.

———. *The Security Challenge for Taiwan in the Cold War Era.* East Asian Institute Report, Columbia University, February 1995.

Chung, Jae Ho. "The Expanding Space of Provincial Politics and Development: Thematic Suggestions for the Future Research Agenda." *Provincial China: Research, News and Analysis,* no. 4 (1997): 4–18.

———. "Studies of Central-Provincial Relations in the People's Republic of China: A Midterm Appraisal." *The China Quarterly,* no. 142 (June 1995): 487–508.

Commonwealth of Australia. *Asia's Global Powers: China-Japan Relations in the 21st Century.* Canberra: East Asia Analytical Unit, Department of Foreign Affairs and Trade, 1996.

Dittmer, Lowell, and Samuel Kim. "In Search of a Theory of National Identity." In Lowell Dittmer and Samuel Kim, eds., *China's Quest for National Identity.* Ithaca, NY: Cornell University Press, 1993.

Domenach, Jean-Luc. *The Origins of the Great Leap Forward: The Case of One Chinese Province.* Boulder, CO: Westview Press, 1995.

Donnithorne, Audrey. *China's Economic System.* New York: Praeger, 1967.

Dumbaugh, Kerry. *Taiwan: Texts of the Taiwan Relations Act and the US-China Communique.* Washington, DC: Library of Congress, March 18, 1996.

Fairbanks, Charles. "The Nature of the Beast." *The National Interest,* no. 31 (Spring 1993): 46–56.

Feinerman, James. "Chinese Participation in the International Legal Order: Rogue Elephant or Team Player?" *The China Quarterly,* no. 141 (March 1995): 186–210.

———. "The Give and Take of Central-Local Relations." *The China Business Review* (January–February 1998): 16–23.

Feng, Lanrui. "Unemployment in China: 21% by the Year 2000?" *China Perspectives,* no. 6 (July–August 1996): 9–17.

Fewsmith, Joseph. *Dilemmas of Reform in China: Political Conflict and Economic Debate.* Armonk, NY: M. E. Sharpe, 1994.

———. "Reaction, Resurgence, and Succession: Chinese Politics Since Tiananmen." In Roderick MacFarquhar, ed., *The Politics of China,* 2d ed.: *The Eras of Mao and Deng.* New York: Cambridge University Press, 1997.

Field, Norma. *In the Realm of a Dying Emperor.* New York: Random House, 1991.

Fitzgerald, John. *Awakening China.* Stanford: Stanford University Press, 1996.

———. "'Reports of My Death Have Been Greatly Exaggerated': The History of the Death of China." In David S. G. Goodman and Gerald Segal, eds., *China Deconstructs: Politics, Trade and Regionalism.* London: Routledge, 1994, 21–58.

Foreign Broadcast Information Service (FBIS). *China,* 26–48, Article 66, 26 January 1994.

Frankenstein, John, and Bates Gill. "Current and Future Challenges of Chinese Defense Industries: Organization, Acquisitions, and Modernization." Paper presented at the CAPS/CAPP Conference on "The PLA Towards 2000." Island Shangri-la Hotel, Hong Kong, July 13–15, 1995.

Garside, Roger. *Coming Alive: China After Mao.* London: Andre Deutsch, 1981.

Gellner, Ernest. *Encounters with Nationalism.* Oxford: Blackwell, 1994.

Gill, Bates, and Taeho Kim. "China's Arms Acquisitions from Abroad: A Quest for Superb and Secret Weapons." *SIPRI Research Report* no. 11. Oxford, England: Oxford University Press, 1995.

Gladney, Dru. "Ethnic Identity in China: The New Politics of Difference." In William Joseph, ed., *China Briefing, 1994.* Boulder, CO: Westview Press, 1995.

Godwin, Paul H. B. "Force Projection and China's Military Strategy." Paper prepared for the Sixth Annual Conference on the Chinese People's Liberation Army, Coolfont, West Virginia, June 1995.

———. "From Continent to Periphery: PLA Doctrine, Strategy and Capacities Towards 2000." *The China Quarterly,* no. 145 (March 1996): 464–487.

Goldstone, Jack A. "The Coming Chinese Collapse." *Foreign Policy,* no. 99 (Summer 1995).

Goodman, David S. G. *Deng Xiaoping and the Chinese Revolution: A Political Biography.* London: Routledge, 1994.

———. "In Search of China's New Middle Class: The Creation of Wealth and Diversity in Shanxi during the 1990s." *Asian Studies Review* (March 1998): 39–62. Based on seminar presentation, University of Sydney, October 27, 1997.

Goodman, David S. G., ed. *China's Provinces in Reform: Class, Community and Political Culture.* London and New York: Routledge, 1997.

Goodman, David S. G., and Gerald Segal, eds. *China Deconstructs: Politics, Trade and Regionalism.* London: Routledge, 1994.

Green, Donald P., and Ian Shapiro. *Pathologies of Rational Choice Theory.* New Haven, Conn.: Yale University Press, 1994.

Hamrin, Carol Lee, and Zhao Suisheng, eds. *Decision-making in Deng's China.* Armonk, NY: M. E. Sharpe, 1995.

Hao, Yufan. *Dilemma and Decision: An Organizational Perspective on American China Policy Making.* Berkeley: Institute of East Asian Studies, 1997.

Harding, Harry. "China's Cooperative Behavior." In Thomas Robinson and David Shambaugh, eds., *Chinese Foreign Policy: Theory and Practice.* Oxford: Clarendon Press, 1994.

———. *A Fragile Relationship.* Washington, DC: Brookings Institution, 1992.

Harris, Stuart. "China's Role in the WTO and APEC." In David S. G. Goodman and Gerald Segal, eds., *China Rising: Nationalism and Interdependence.* London: Routledge, 1997.

Hasegawa, Tsuyoshi. "The Connection Between Political and Economic Reform in Communist Regimes." In Gilbert Rozman, ed., *Dismantling Communism.* Woodrow Wilson Center Press and Johns Hopkins University Press, 1992.

Hawkins, William. "For All the Tea in China: The 'Commercial Temptation' in US Foreign Policy." *Strategic Review* 25, no. 4 (1997): 7–18.

He, Qinglian. *Xiandaihua de xianjing* (The trap of modernization). Peking: Jinri Zhongguo chubanshe, 1997.

Hirschman, Albert. "The Rise and Decline of Developing Economics." In Hirschman, *Essays in Trespassing: Economics to Politics and Beyond.* New York: Cambridge University Press, 1981.

Hu, Angang. "Fenshuizhi: pingjia yu jianyi" (The taxation-division system: assessment and recommendations). *Zhanlue yu guanli* (Strategy and management), no. 15 (1996): 1–9.

———. "Shengdiji ganbu yanzhong de dongxibu chaiju" (East-West disparities in the views of provincial and prefectural government officials). *Zhanlue yu guanli* (Strategy and management), no. 5 (1994): 88–90.

Huang, Yasheng. *Inflation and Investment Controls in China: The Political Economy of Central-Local Relations During the Reform Era*. New York: Cambridge University Press, 1996.

———. "Why China Will Not Collapse." *Foreign Policy,* no. 99 (Summer 1995): 58–59.

Jacobsen, Harold, and Michel Oksenberg. *China's Participation in the IMF, the World Bank and GATT: Towards a Global Economic Order*. Ann Arbor: University of Michigan Press, 1990.

Jenner, W. J. F. *The Tyranny of History: The Roots of China's Crisis*. London: Penguin Press, 1992.

Jia, Hao, and Lin Zhimin, eds. *Changing Central-Local Relations in China: Reform and State Capacity*. Boulder, CO.: Westview Press, 1994.

*Jiang Zemin's Report at the Fifteenth National Congress of the Communist Party of China*. Beijing: September 1997.

Jie, Chen, Yang Zhong, and Jan William Hillard. "The Level and Sources of Popular Support for China's Current Political Regime." *Communist and Post-Communist Studies* 30, no. 1 (1997): 45–64.

Jin, Ji. *Lianbang zhi: Zhongguo de zuijia chulu* (Federalism: China's best way). Hong Kong: Baixing wenhua shiye youxian gongsi, 1992.

Jin, Yi. "Dalu de dingshi zhadan: Gongchao" (A time-bomb on the mainland: The labor movement). *Dongxiang* (The trend), Hong Kong, no. 150 (February 1998): 28–31.

Joffe, Ellis. "The Chinese Army and the Economy: The Effect of Involvement." *Survival* (Summer 1995).

———. *The Military and China's New Politics: Trends and Counter-Trends*. CAPS Papers no. 19, Chinese Council of Advanced Policy Studies, Taipei, Taiwan, Republic of China, September 1997.

———. "Party-Army Relations in China: Retrospect and Prospect." *The China Quarterly,* no. 146 (June 1996): 299–314.

Johnston, Alastair Iain. "China's New 'Old Thinking.'" *International Security* 20, no. 3 (Winter 1995–1996).

———. "Prospects for Chinese Nuclear Force Modernization." *The China Quarterly,* no. 146 (June 1996): 548–595.

*Joint Publications Research Service, China* (JPRS-CAR-90-052), 16 July 1990.

Joseph, William, ed. *China Briefing*. Boulder, CO: Westview Press, 1994.

Kam, Yiu-yu. "Decision-making and Implementation of Policy Toward Hong Kong." In Carol Lee Hamrin and Zhao Suisheng, eds., *Decision-making in Deng's China*. Armonk, NY: M. E. Sharpe, 1995.

Katzenstein, Peter J. *Cultural Norms and National Security: Police and Military in Post War Japan*. Ithaca, NY: Cornell University Press, 1996.

Kelly, David. "Chinese Marxism Since Tiananmen: Between Evaporation and Dismemberment." In David S. G. Goodman and Gerald Segal, eds., *China in the Nineties: Crisis Management and Beyond*. Oxford: Clarendon Press, 1991.

Keohane, Robert. *After Hegemony: Cooperation and Discord in the World Political Economy*. Princeton, NJ: Princeton University Press, 1984.

———. "Reciprocity in International Relations." *International Organization* 40, no. 1 (Winter 1986): 1–27.

Kim, Samuel S., ed. *China and the World*. 4th ed. Boulder, CO: Westview Press, 1998.

———. "China's International Organisational Behavior." In Thomas Robinson and David Shambaugh, eds., *Chinese Foreign Policy: Theory and Practice*. Oxford: Clarendon Press, 1994.

Kontorovich, Vladimir. "The Economic Fallacy." *The National Interest*, no. 31 (Spring 1993): 35–45.

Lampton, David. "Chinese Politics: The Bargaining Treadmill." *Issues and Studies* 23, no. 3 (1987): 11–41.

———. "A Growing China in a Shrinking World: Beijing and the Global Order." In Ezra Vogel, ed., *Living with China: US-China Relations in the Twenty-first Century*. New York: W. W. Norton, 1997.

Lane, C. Dennison, ed. *Chinese Military Modernization*. Washington, DC: AEI Press, 1996.

Lardy, Nicholas R. *China's Unfinished Economic Revolution*. Washington, DC: Brookings Institution Press.

———. "The Chinese Economy Under Stress." In Roderick MacFarquhar and John K. Fairbank, eds., *The Cambridge History of China*, vol. 14: *The People's Republic, Part I: The Emergence of Revolutionary China 1949–1965*. Cambridge: Cambridge University Press, 1987.

Lee, Hong Yung. *From Revolutionary Cadres to Party Technocrats: The Changing Cadre System in Socialist China*. Berkeley: University of California Press, 1991.

Leung, Trini W. Y. "Worker Rebellions in the 90's: Getting Organised to Protect One's Rights." *China Perspectives*, no. 19 (September–October 1998): 6–21.

Lewis, John, Sergei Goncharov, and Xue Litai. *Uncertain Allies*. Stanford: Stanford University Press, 1993.

Lewis, John, and Xue Litai. *China Builds the Bomb*. Stanford: Stanford University Press, 1988.

———. *China's Strategic Seapower*. Stanford: Stanford University Press, 1994.

Li, Cheng, and Lynn White. "The Fifteenth Central Committee of the Chinese Communist Party: Full-Fledged Technocratic Leadership with Partial Control by Jiang Zemin." *Asian Survey* 38, no. 3 (March 1998): 231–264.

Lieberthal, Kenneth. *Governing China: From Revolution Through Reform*. New York: W. W. Norton, 1995.

Lieberthal, Kenneth, and David M. Lampton, eds. *Bureaucracy, Politics and Decision Making in Post-Mao China*. Berkeley: University Press of California, 1992.

Lieberthal, Kenneth, and Michel Oksenberg. *Policy Making in China: Leaders, Structures, and Processes*. Princeton, NJ: Princeton University Press, 1988.

Lilley, James. R. "The Fifteenth Party Congress: A Balancing Act." Unpublished paper; available at http://www.IntellectualCapital.com, September 25, 1997.

Liu, Drew. "The Current Power Struggle in the CCP." *China Strategic Review* 2, no. 4 (July–August 1997): 68–91.

Liu, Zehou, and Vera Schwarcz. "Six Generations of Modern Chinese Intellectuals." *Chinese Studies in History* 17, no. 2 (Winter 1983–1984).

Lyons, Thomas P. *Economic Integration and Planning in Maoist China*. New York: Columbia University Press, 1987.

Ma, Shu-yun. "Recent Changes in China's Pure Trade Theory." *China Quarterly*, no. 106 (June 1986): 291–305.

Maass, Arthur, ed. *Area and Power: A Theory of Local Government*. New York: Free Press, 1959.

MacFarquhar, Roderick, ed. *Sino-American Relations, 1949–71.* New York: Praeger, 1972.

*MAC News Briefing.* Mainland Affairs Council, no. 0042, September 22, 1997, 2.

Manion, Melanie. "The Electoral Connection in the Chinese Countryside." *American Political Science Review* 90, no. 4 (December 1996).

———. *Retirement of Revolutionaries in China: Public Policies, Social Norms, Private Interests.* Princeton, NJ: Princeton University Press, 1993.

March, James G., and Johan P. Olsen. "The New Institutionalism: Organizational Factors in Political Life." *The American Political Science Review* 78 (1984) 734–749.

Markwick, Roger. "What Kind of State Is the Russian State—If There Is One?" Presentation to the Conference of the Australasian Association for Communist and Post-Communist Studies, Sydney, November 15–16, 1997.

McKinnon, Ronald I. *The Order of Economic Liberalization: Financial Control in the Transition to a Market Economy.* 2d ed. Baltimore, MD: Johns Hopkins University Press, 1993.

Miles, James. *Legacy of Tiananmen: China in Disarray.* Ann Arbor: University of Michigan Press, 1996.

Miller, H. Lyman. "Preparing for Change with the Promises of Continuity." *The China Business Review* (January–February 1998), 12.

*Minzhujinbudang Zhongguo zhengce yantao hui, huiyi shouce* (DPP China Policy Forum, forum handbook). Taipei: DPP Central Party Department, February 1998.

Montinola, Gabriella, Qian Yingyi, and Barry R. Weingast. "Federalism, Chinese Style: The Political Basis for Economic Success in China." *World Politics* 48, no. 1 (1995): 50–81.

Mulvenon, James. "Appendix A: Chinese Unconventional and Conventional Capabilities and Doctrine." In Elizabeth Economy and Michel Oksenberg, eds., *China Joins the World.* New York: Council on Foreign Relations, 1999.

———. *Chinese Military Commerce and US National Security.* Santa Monica, CA: RAND, 1997.

———. *Professionalization of the Senior Chinese Officer Corps: Trends and Implications.* Santa Monica, CA: RAND, National Defense Research Institute, 1997.

Nathan, Andrew. *China's Transition.* New York: Columbia University Press, 1997.

———. "A Factionalism Model for CCP Politics." *China Quarterly,* no. 53 (March 1973): 34–66.

Nathan, Andrew, and Robert Ross. *The Great Wall and the Empty Fortress.* New York: W. W. Norton, 1997.

National Defense University. *Strategic Assessment.* Washington, DC: National Defense University, 1997.

National People's Congress, Standing Committee for Legislative Affairs, Work Committee. *Zhonghua renmin gongheguo falu fenlei zonglan, jingji fa* (Zhongshou) (A classified compendium of laws of the People's Republic of China, economic law). Vol. 2. Beijing: Legal Publishing House, 1994.

Naughton, Barry. *Growing Out of the Plan: Chinese Economic Reform, 1978–1993.* New York: Cambridge University Press, 1995.

Ning, Lu. *The Dynamics of Foreign Policy Decision-making in China.* Boulder, CO: Westview Press, 1997.

Norris, Robert, Andrew Burrows, and Richard Fieldhouse. *Nuclear Weapons Databook,* vol. 5: *British, French, and Chinese Nuclear Weapons.* Boulder, CO: Westview Press, 1994.

Oi, Jean. *State and Peasant in Contemporary China: The Political Economy of Village Government.* Berkeley: University of California Press, 1989.

Oksenberg, Michel. "Will China Democratize? Confronting a Classic Dilemma." *Journal of Democracy* 9, no. 1 (January 1998).

Orleans, Leo A. "Graduates of Chinese Universities: Adjusting the Totals." *China Quarterly,* no. 111 (September 1987).

Pei, Minxin. "Is China Democratizing?" *Foreign Affairs* 77, no. 1 (1998):68–82.

Perry, Elizabeth J. "Intellectuals and Tiananmen: Historical Perspective on an Aborted Revolution." In Daniel Chirot, ed., *The Crisis of Leninism and the Decline of the Left: The Revolutions of 1989.* Seattle: University of Washington Press, 1991.

―――. "Labor's Battle for Political Space: The Role of Worker Associations in Contemporary China." In Deborah Davis, ed., *Urban Spaces in Contemporary China.* New York: Woodrow Wilson Center Press and Cambridge University Press, 1995.

―――. "Shanghai's Strike Wave of 1957." In Timothy Cheek and Tony Saich, eds., *New Perspectives on State Socialism in China.* Armonk, NY: M. E. Sharpe, 1997.

Pye, Lucian. "China: Erratic State, Frustrated Society." *Foreign Affairs* 69, no. 4 (1990): 56–74.

―――. *The Dynamics of Chinese Politics.* Cambridge: Oelgeschlager, Gunn, and Hain, 1981.

Qiao, Jian. "1997–1998 nian: Zhongguo zhigong zhuangkuang baogao" (Years 1997–1998: Report on the situation of the *zhigong* in China). In Ru Xin, *1998 nian: Zhongguo shehui xingshi fenxi yu yuce* (1998: Analysis and prospects of the social situation in China). Peking: Shehui kexue wenxian chubanshe, 1998.

Rawshi, Evelyn, S. "Economic and Social Foundations of Late Imperial Culture." In David G. Johnson, Andrew Nathan, and Rawshi, eds., *Popular Culture in Late Imperial China.* Berkeley: University of California Press, 1985.

Rigby, T. H. "New Elites for Old in Russian Politics." Paper presented to the Conference of the Australasian Association for Communist and Post-Communist Studies, Sydney, November 15–16, 1997.

Ross, Robert. "Assessing the China Challenge." *Asian Security Series,* Henry L. Stimson Center, May 14, 1997.

―――. "Beijing as a Conservative Power." *Foreign Affairs* 76, no. 2 (1997): 33–44.

Rush, Myron. "Fortune and Fate." *The National Interest,* no. 31 (Spring 1993): 19–25.

―――. *Political Succession in the USSR.* New York: Columbia University Press, 1968.

Sautman, Barry. "Myths of Descent, Racial Nationalism and Ethnic Minorities in the People's Republic of China." In Frank Dikotter, ed., *The Construction of Racial Identities in China and Japan.* Honolulu: University of Hawaii Press, 1997.

Scalapino, Robert. "China's Multiple Identities in East Asia: China as a Regional Force." In Lowell Dittmer and Samuel Kim, eds, *China's Quest for National Identity.* Ithaca, NY: Cornell University Press, 1993.

Schram, Stuart R. "China After the 13th Congress." *The China Quarterly,* no. 114 (June 1988): 177–197.

Schroeder, Paul Edward. *Regional Power in China.* Ph.D. diss., Department of Political Science, Ohio State University, 1987.

Schwarcz, Vera. "Behind a Partially Open Door: Chinese Intellectuals in the Post-Mao Reform Process." *Pacific Affairs* 59, no. 4 (Winter 1986–1987): 577–604.

*Selected Works of Deng Xiaoping (1975–1982).* Beijing: Foreign Languages Press, 1983.

"Several Factors Affecting China's State Security." Trans. from the Chinese. In BBC Monitoring, *Summary of World Broadcasts,* Reading, UK, October 16, 1996, FE/2744 S2/1–13.

Shambaugh, David. "Building the Party-State in China, 1949–1965: Bringing the Soldier Back In." In Timothy Cheek and Tony Saich, eds., *New Perspectives on State Socialism in China.* Armonk, NY: M. E. Sharpe, 1997.

———. "China's Commander-In-Chief: Jiang Zemin and the PLA." In C. Dennison Lane, ed., *Chinese Military Modernization.* Washington, DC: AEI Press, 1996.

———. "China's Military in Transition: Politics, Professionalism, Procurement and Power Projection." *The China Quarterly,* no. 146 (June 1996).

———. "China's Military: Real or Paper Tiger?" *The Washington Quarterly* 19, no. 2 (Spring 1996).

———. "China's Post-Deng Military Leadership." Paper presented at the Seventh Conference on the PLA, Aspen Institute/Wye Woods Conference, Maryland, September 14–16, 1997.

———. "The Insecurity of Security: The PLA's Doctrine of Threat Perception Toward 2000." *Journal of Northeast Asian Studies* 13, no. 1 (Spring 1994).

———. "The Soldier and the State in China: The Political Work System in the People's Liberation Army." *The China Quarterly,* no. 127 (September 1991): 527–568.

Sheng, Lijun. "China Eyes Taiwan: Why Is a Breakthrough So Difficult?" *Journal of Strategic Studies* 21, no. 1 (March 1998): 65–78.

Shi, Haohai. *Central-Local Relations in the People's Republic of China.* Ph.D. diss., Department of Government and International Studies, University of South Carolina, 1993.

Shirk, Susan L. *The Political Logic of Economic Reform in China.* Berkeley: University of California Press, 1993.

Shue, Vivienne. *The Reach of the State: Sketches of the Chinese Body Politic.* Stanford: Stanford University Press, 1988.

Solinger, Dorothy. *China's Transients and the State: A Form of Civil Society?* Hong Kong: Chinese University Press, Institute of Asia-Pacific Studies, 1991.

Starr, John Bryan. "China in 1995: Mounting Problems, Waning Capacity." *Asian Survey* 36, no. 1 (January 1996): 13–24.

State Planning Commission, Ministry of Finance, and People's Construction Bank of China. "Interim Regulations Converting All State Budgetary Capital Construction Investment from Appropriations to Loans." In Chinese Banking Society, *Almanac of China's Banking and Finance 1986,* VI-79-VI-82.

State Statistical Bureau. *China Statistical Yearbook 1996.* Beijing: China Statistical Publishing House, 1996.

Steinfeld, Edward. *Forging Reform in China: The Fate of State-Owned Industry.* Cambridge: Cambridge University Press, 1998.

Su, Ning, and Lu Zhongyuan. "State-Owned Enterprises' Financial Problems and Their Remedies." *Caimao jingji* (Finance and trade economics), no. 8 (1994), republished in Joint Publications Research Service, *China Report,* August 11, 1994.

Su Shaozhi. "The Prospects for Democratization in China." *Harvard Asia-Pacific Review* (Summer 1998).

Sutter, Robert. *China Policy: Managing US-PRC-Taiwan Relations After President Lee's Visit to the US.* Washington, DC: Congressional Research Service, June 19, 1995.

———. *Executive-Legislative Consultations on China Policy, 1978–79.* Washington, DC: U.S. Government Printing Office, 1980.

Swaine, Michael D. "China." In Zalmay Khalilzad, ed., *Strategic Appraisal 1996.* Santa Monica, CA: RAND, 1996.

———. *China: Domestic Change and Foreign Policy.* Santa Monica, CA: RAND, MR-604-OSD, 1995.

———. "Chinese Military Modernization: Motives, Objectives, and Requirements." In *China's Economic Future: Challenges to U.S. Policy,* submitted to the Joint Economic Committee, 104th Congress of the United States, 2d session, August 1996, 320–338. Washington, DC: U.S. Government Printing Office, 1996.

———. "Chinese Political and Bureaucratic Calculations and Behavior Regarding Taiwan." Mimeo. Santa Monica, CA: RAND, 1996.

———. *The Role of the Chinese Military in National Security Policymaking.* Santa Monica: RAND, National Defense Research Institute, 1996.

Swaine, Michael D., and Ashley J. Tellis. *Interpreting China's Grand Strategy.* Santa Monica, CA: RAND (forthcoming).

Swaine, Michael D. and Alastair Iain Johnston. "China and Arms Control Institutions." In Elizabeth Economy and Michel Oksenberg, eds. *China Joins the World.* New York: Council on Foreign Relations, 1999.

Swidler, Ann. "Culture in Action: Symbols and Strategies." *American Sociological Review* 51, no. 2 (1986): 273–286.

Tang, Xiaozhou. In *Kaifang* (Opening) (Hong Kong) (March 1992): 16.

Teiwes, Frederick C., with Warren Sun. *China's Road to Disaster: Mao, Central Politicians, and Local Leaders in the Unfolding of the Great Leap Forward, 1955–1959.* Armonk, NY: M. E. Sharpe, 1998.

———. *Leadership, Legitimacy, and Conflict in China: From a Charismatic Mao to the Politics of Succession.* Armonk, NY: M. E. Sharpe, 1984.

———. "The Paradoxical Post-Mao Transition: From Obeying the Leader to 'Normal Politics.'" *The China Journal,* no. 34 (July 1995): 55–94.

———. *Politics and Purges in China: Rectification and the Decline of Party Norms 1950–1965.* 2d ed. Armonk, NY: M. E. Sharpe, 1993.

———. *Politics at Mao's Court: Gao Gang and Party Factionalism in the Early 1950s.* Armonk, NY: M. E. Sharpe, 1990.

———. "Restoration and Innovation." *The Australian Journal of Chinese Affairs,* no. 5 (January 1981): 167–177.

Teiwes, Frederick C., and Warren Sun. *The Tragedy of Lin Biao: Riding the Tiger During the Cultural Revolution, 1966–1971.* London: C. Hurst, 1996.

Tetlock, Philip. "Learning in US and Soviet Foreign Policy: In Search of an Elusive Concept." In George Breslauer and Philip Tetlock, eds., *Learning in US and Soviet Foreign Policy.* Boulder, CO: Westview Press, 1991.

Text of Joint Statement of China and ASEAN Countries, 1997. FBIS-CHI-97-350, December 16, 1997.

Tong, James, ed. "Death at the Gate of Heavenly Peace: The Democracy Movement in Beijing, April–June 1989 (I)." *Chinese Law and Government* 23, no. 1 (Spring 1990): 69–72.

Tsai, Wei. *Zhonggong duitai zhengce de juece zuzhi yu guocheng.* (The decision-making apparatus and process of the PRC's Taiwan policy) *Zhongguo dalu yanjiu (Journal of mainland China studies)* 40, no. 5 (May 1997).

Tsou, Tang. "Chinese Politics at the Top: Factionalism or Informal Politics? Balance-of-Power Politics or a Game to Win All?" *The China Journal*, no. 34 (1995): 95–156.

Tucker, Nancy Bernkopf. *Taiwan, Hong Kong, and the United States, 1945–1992.* New York: Twayne Publishers, 1994.

Unger, Jonathan, ed. *The Pro-Democracy Protests in China: Reports from the Provinces.* Sydney: Allen and Unwin, 1991.

———. "State and Peasant in Post-Revolution China." *Journal of Peasant Studies* 17, no. 1 (October 1989): 114–136.

USIS Asia-Pacific Wireless File, February 27, 1995.

U.S. Senate, 79th Congress, "Hearings Before the Subcommittee on Separation of Powers of the Committee of the Judiciary: Second Session on the Taiwan Communiqué and Separation of Powers." serial number J-97-B7.

Walder, Andrew G. *Communist Neo-Traditionalism: Work and Authority in Chinese Industry.* Berkeley: University of California Press, 1986.

———. "Does China Face an Unstable Future? On the Political Impact of Rapid Growth." Paper presented at the Conference on "China and World Affairs in 2010." Stanford University, April 25–26, 1996.

———. "When States Unravel: How China's Cadres Shaped Cultural Revolution Politics." Paper presented at the "State Capacity in East Asia" conference organized by the State and Society in East Asia Network, Copenhagen, September 27–29, 1996.

Waldron, Arthur. "The End of Communism." *Journal of Democracy* (January 1998).

———. "Warlordism Versus Federalism: The Revival of a Debate?" *China Quarterly*, no. 121 (March 1990): 116–128.

Wang, Shaoguang. "China's 1994 Fiscal Reform: An Initial Assessment." *Asian Survey* 37, no. 9 (September 1997): 801–817.

———. *Failure of Charisma: The Cultural Revolution in Wuhan.* Hong Kong: Oxford University Press, 1995.

Wang, Shaoguang, and Hu Angang. *Zhongguo guojia nengli baogao* (A study of China's state capacity). Hong Kong: Oxford University Press, 1994.

Wang, Xizhe. "Guanyu Li Yizhe sichao." *Zhongguo zhi chun*, no. 135 (December 1994).

Waston, James L. "Rites or Beliefs? The Construction of a Unified Culture in Late Imperial China." In Lowell Dittmer and Samuel S. Kim, eds., *China's Quest for National Identity.* Ithaca, NY: Cornell University Press, 1993.

Weber, Max. *The Theory of Social and Economic Organization.* Edited, with an introduction, by Talcott Parsons. New York: Free Press, 1964.

Wedeman, Andrew. "Corruption and Politics." In Maurice Brosseau, ed., *China Review: 1996.* Hong Kong: Chinese University Press, 1997.

White, Lynn, and Li Cheng. "The Fifteenth Central Committee of the Chinese Communist Party: Full-Fledged Technocratic Leadership with Partial Control by Jiang Zemin." *Asian Survey* 38, no. 3 (March 1998): 231–265.

Whiting, Allen S. "The PLA and China's Threat Perceptions." *The China Quarterly*, no. 146 (June 1996): 596–615.

*Who's Who in China: Current Leaders.* 2d ed. Beijing: Foreign Languages Press, 1994.

Wilhelm, Alfred. *China and Security in the Asian Pacific Region Through 2010.* Virginia: Center for Naval Analyses, CRM 95-226/March 1996.

Womack, Brantly. "Modernization and Democratic Reform in China." *Journal of Asian Studies* 43, no. 3 (May 1984): 417–439.

World Bank. *China GNP Per Capita.* Washington, DC: World Bank, 1994.
———. *China's Management of Enterprise Assets: The State as Shareholder.* Washington, DC: World Bank, June 1997.
———. *From Plan to Market.* New York and Oxford: Oxford University Press, 1996.
Wu, Guoguang, and Zheng Yongnian. *Lun zhongyang difang guanxi* (On central-local relations). Hong Kong: Oxford University Press, 1995.
Xia, Wenzi, "Qiao Shi xiatai neimu" (Behind the scenes of Qiao Shi's departure). *Kaifang* (Opening) (Hong Kong) (October 1997): 10–13.
Xie, Ying, and Hua Jingfen. "China: Worsening Social Order in Rural Areas." *Beijing Renmin Gongan Bao.* FBIS-CHI-97-279, August 12, 1997.
Xin, Xiangyang. *Daguo zhuhou: Zhongguo zhongyang yu difang guanxi zhijie* (Dukes in a great nation: Central-local relations in China). Beijing: Zhongguo shehui chubanshe, 1996.
Yahuda, Michael. "Political Generations in China." *China Quarterly,* no. 80 (December 1979).
Yan, Jiaqi. *Lianbang Zhongguo gouxiang* (The conception of a federal China). Taipei: Lianjing chuban shiye gongsi, 1992.
Yang, Dali. "Reform and Restructuring of Central-Local Relations." In David S. G. Goodman and Gerald Segal, eds. *China Deconstructs: Politics, Trade, and Regionalism.* London: Routledge, 1994, 59–98.
Yang, Kai-huang. "An Explanation and Evaluation of PRC's Taiwan Policy" (*Zhonggong duitai zhengce jieshi yu pinggu*). *Soochow Review of Political Science* (*Dongwu zhengzhi xuebao*) 7 (1997): 66–103.
Yang, Yiyong, et al. *Shiye chongjibo—Zhongguo zai jiuye baogao* (The shockwave of unemployment—A report on the development of re-employment in China). Beijing: Jinri Zhongguo chubanshe, 1997.
You, Ji. "China's Foreign Policy Toward Post-Cold War Asia and the Pacific." Paper delivered at an international conference on the challenge of Asia-Pacific collective security in the post–Cold War era, sponsored by the Institute for National Policy Research, April 11–14, 1995, Taipei.
———. "Jiang Zemin: In Quest of Post-Deng Supremacy." In Maurice Brosseau, Suzanne Pepper, and Tsang Shu-ki, eds., *China Review 1996.* Hong Kong: Chinese University Press, 1996.
———. "Zhao Ziyang and the Politics of Inflation." *The Australian Journal of Chinese Affairs,* no. 25 (July 1991): 69–91.
Yung, Christopher. *People's War at Sea: Chinese Naval Power in the Twenty-First Century.* Virginia: Center for Naval Analyses, CRM 95-214/March 1996.
Zang, Xiaowei. "The Fourteenth Central Committee of the CCP." *Asian Survey* 33, no. 8 (August 1993): 787–803.
Zheng, Joan. "China Reaches for a Homegrown Path Forward." *Global Data Watch.* New York: Morgan Guaranty Trust Company, July 24, 1998.
Zheng, Yongnian. *Institutional Change, Local Developmentalism, and Economic Growth: The Making of Semi-Federalism in Reform China.* Ph.D. diss., Department of Politics, Princeton University, 1995.
———. "Power and Agenda: Jiang Zemin's New Political Initiatives at China's Fifteenth Party Congress." *Issues and Studies* 33, no. 11 (November 1997): 35–57.
*Zhongguo jiaoyu nianjian, 1949–1981* (Chinese education yearbook, 1949–1981). Beijing: Zhongguo da baike quanshu chubanshe, 1994.

# The Contributors

**David Bachman** is chair of the China Studies Program and professor at the Henry M. Jackson School of the University of Washington. He is the author of *Chen Yun and the Chinese Political System* (1985) and *Bureaucracy, Economy, and Leadership in China* (1991) and is coeditor and cotranslator of *Yan Jiaqi and China's Struggle for Democracy* (1991). He has written extensively on Chinese domestic politics and foreign policy, and is now working on a book on the Chinese military-industrial complex under Mao.

**Richard Baum** is professor of political science at the University of California at Los Angeles. He is the author of *Burying Mao: Chinese Politics in the Age of Deng Xiaoping* (1996).

**Michel Bonnin** is senior lecturer at the Ecole des Hautes Etudes en Sciences Sociales, Paris. He has been the founder and director of the French Research Center on Contemporary China and of the magazine *China Perspectives,* both based in Hong Kong. His main research interest lies in the relationship between power and society in post-1949 China. He has written on the democracy movement, the campaign to send urban youth to the countryside, rural-urban migrations, and on employment questions. He has also written extensively on Hong Kong affairs.

**Yun-han Chu** is professor of political science at National Taiwan University and vice president of Chiang Ching-kuo Foundation for International Scholarly Exchange. He previously served as coordinator of the political science section of the National Science Council and as visiting associate professor at Columbia University. His publications include *Crafting Democracy* *in Taiwan* (1992), *Consolidating the Third Wave Democracies: Themes and Perspectives* (coedited with Larry Diamond, Marc Plattner, and Hung-mao Tien, 1997), *The Predicament of Modernization in East Asia* (coedited with Eric Wu, 1995), and *The Asian Regional Economy* (coedited with Hung-mao Tien, 1993).

**Lowell Dittmer** is professor of political science at the University of California at Berkeley and former chair of the China Center and the Group in Asian Studies. From 1997 to 1999, he was on leave while serving as director of the Beijing China Study Center of the University of California's Education Abroad Program. He is the author or coauthor of *Liu Shaoqi and the Chinese Cultural Revolution* (1974; pirated Chinese ed., 1989; 2nd rev. ed., 1998), *China's Continuous Revolution* (1986), *Sino-Soviet Normalization and Its International Implications* (1992), *China's Quest for National Identity* (1993), *China Under Reform* (1994), and numerous scholarly articles.

**Edward Friedman** is the Hawkins Chair Professor of Political Science at the University of Wisconsin, Madison. His three most recent books are *Chinese Village, Socialist State* (1991); *The Politics of Democratization* (1994), and *National Identity and Democratic Prospects in Socialist China* (1995).

**Stuart Harris** is professor in the Department of International Relations in the Research School of Pacific and Asian Studies of the Australian National University and convenor of the University's Northeast Asia Program. From 1984 to 1988, while on leave from the university, he was secretary (vice minister) of the Australian Department of Foreign Affairs and Trade.

**Ellis Joffe** is professor of Chinese studies and international relations at the Hebrew University of Jerusalem. He is the author of two books and many articles and book chapters on the Chinese military.

**Nicholas R. Lardy** is a senior fellow in the foreign policy studies program at the Brookings Institution. He is also the Frederick Frank Adjunct Professor of International Trade and Finance at the Yale University School of Management. Lardy has written and edited numerous articles and books on the Chinese economy. The result of his current project at Brookings, *China's Unfinished Economic Revolution,* was published in September 1998. Some of his other publications include "China and the Asian Contagion" in *Foreign Affairs* (July–August 1998); and *China in the World Economy* (1994). Lardy serves on the board of directors and executive committee of the National Committee on United States–China Relations and is a member of the editorial board of *The China Quarterly*.

**Kenneth Lieberthal** is professor of political science and William David-son Professor of Business Administration at the University of Michigan at Ann Arbor, where he has been on the faculty since 1983. He is the author of numerous books and articles about Chinese domestic and foreign policy.

**Michael D. Swaine** is research director of the Center for Asia-Pacific Policy at the RAND Corporation. His major publications include *The Chinese Future* (with Michel C. Oksenberg and Daniel Lynch, 1997), *The Role of the Chinese Military in National Security Policymaking* (1996), and *China: Domestic Change and Foreign Policy* (1995).

**Frederick C. Teiwes** holds a personal chair in Chinese politics at the University of Sydney. He is the author of various books on Chinese elite politics, including *Politics and Purges in China* (1979, 1993); *Leadership, Legitimacy, and Conflict in China* (1984); and *Politics at Mao's Court* (1990). In recent years he has collaborated with Warren Sun on a number of publications, including *The Politics of Agricultural Cooperativization* (1993); *The Tragedy of Lin Biao* (1996); and, most recently, *China's Road to Disaster: Mao, Central Politicians, and Local Leaders in the Unfolding of the Great Leap Forward* (1998).

**Hung-mao Tien** is president of the Institute for National Policy Research. He also serves as national policy adviser to President Lee Teng-hui, as a member of the National Unification Council, and as a trustee of the Foundation for International Cooperation on Development (Taiwan's overseas development assistance agency). In December 1996, he was named deputy co-convenor of the National Development Conference, which met to debate Taiwan's constitutional reform. Prior to his current appointments in Taipei, he was professor of political science at the University of Wisconsin. Among numerous other books, articles, and edited volumes, he has published *Consolidating the Third Wave Democracies: Themes and Perspectives* (ed., 1997); *Taiwan's Electoral Politics and Democratic Transition: Riding the Third Wave* (ed., 1995); *The Asian Regional Economy* (co-ed., 1993); *The Great Transition: Social and Political Change in the Republic of China* (1989); and *Government and Politics in Kuomintang China, 1927–37.*

**Zheng Yongnian** is a research fellow of the East Asian Institute at the National University of Singapore. He is the author of *Discovering Chinese Nationalism in China: Reform, Identity Change and International Relations* and other works. He is currently researching de facto federalism in reform China.

# Index

# About the Book

*China Under Jiang Zemin* represents the first major scholarly effort to analyze the evolution of China's new leadership, taking as its starting point the pivotal Fifteenth Congress of the Chinese Communist Party, held in September 1997.

Proceeding from a detailed portrait of the political landscape at the opening of the Jiang Zemin era, the authors provide rich detail of the various personalities and policy platforms that have been contending for control, as well as the successful strategies used by Jiang to consolidate his position. Subsequent chapters address the increasingly crucial role played by the People's Liberation Army in various policy domains, the all-important issues of economic reform and its consequences for social stability, and the implications of the leadership transition for China's interactions with the outside world, and especially with Taiwan. The concluding section of the book analyzes the evolving pattern of center-local relations and explores the forces that may hold the seeds of a genuine political reform.

**Hung-mao Tien** is president and chairman of the board of the Institute for National Policy Research in Taiwan. **Yun-han Chu** is vice president of Chiang Ching-kuo Foundation for International Scholarly Exchange and professor of political science at National Taiwan University.